How to Become a Deadly Chess Tactician

David LeMoir

Illustrations by Ken LeMoir

First published in the UK by Gambit Publications Ltd 2002
Reprinted 2002

A copy of the British Library Cataloguing in Publication data is available from the British Library.

ISBN 1 901983 59 5

DISTRIBUTION:
Worldwide (except USA): Central Books Ltd, 99 Wallis Rd, London E9 5LN.
Tel +44 (0)20 8986 4854 Fax +44 (0)20 8533 5821. E-mail: orders@Centralbooks.com
USA: BHB International, Inc., 302 West North 2nd Street, Seneca, SC 29678, USA.

For all other enquiries (including a full list of all Gambit Chess titles) please contact the publishers, Gambit Publications Ltd, P.O. Box 32640, London W14 0JN.
E-mail: info@gambitbooks.com
Or visit the GAMBIT web site at http://www.gambitbooks.com

Edited by Graham Burgess
Typeset by John Nunn
Printed in Great Britain by The Cromwell Press, Trowbridge, Wilts.

10 9 8 7 6 5 4 3 2

Gambit Publications Ltd
Managing Director: GM Murray Chandler
Chess Director: GM John Nunn
Editorial Director: FM Graham Burgess
German Editor: WFM Petra Nunn

Contents

Part Three: Calculation

Symbols

+	check
++	double check
#	checkmate
!!	brilliant move
!	good move
!?	interesting move
?!	dubious move
?	bad move
??	blunder
Ch	championship
1-0	the game ends in a win for White
$\frac{1}{2}$-$\frac{1}{2}$	the game ends in a draw
0-1	the game ends in a win for Black
(D)	see next diagram

Acknowledgements

This is my second chess book, and once again I would like to thank my father, Ken, for some great illustrations featuring his new creation Hissing Sid, the wily but dangerous cobra. Thanks, too, to Owen Hindle for explaining the realities of nineteenth century chess to me, and to the Gambit team, Graham Burgess, Murray Chandler and John Nunn, who continue to make the birth of a book a remarkably painless experience.

Without the patience and encouragement of my wife, Sue, I would probably not have started this book, let alone finished it, and I would particularly like to thank her for not asking what happened to all the jobs around the garden that I promised to do nine months ago.

Introduction

Three Steps to Becoming a Deadly Chess Tactician

Most of us love to play through games that contain sacrifices and combinations. They have the power to lift our hearts, amaze us and inspire us. But when it comes down to playing our next chess game, it's back to grinding out an advantage, scrambling for a draw or suffering miserably as our opponent crawls all over us. No wonder that many players believe that successful sacrificial play is mainly the preserve of masters and grandmasters.

Occasionally we play a little sacrifice, or concoct a simple combination. For weeks afterwards we are talking about or demonstrating our little masterpiece, apologizing that it wasn't very deep or spectacular, and keeping it away from the club champion for fear that he will – as he always does – prove it to be unsound. We nervously hope that our audience admires our effort as much as we treasure it. The achievement of an occasional fragment of chess art is what keeps many people playing the game.

Better tactics mean better results, and we do our best to train ourselves in the tactical arts. We are expected to learn and absorb a host of combinational patterns, but we never seem to create the positions in which they can be played. All that learning turns out to be a waste of effort.

We should not despair. I would lay a large bet that all of us often create positions in which sacrifices and combinations are possible, but we are not looking for them, so we don't see them. We could probably create even more such positions if we could anticipate the sacrificial possibilities in advance.

It seems to me that three factors hold us back from sacrificing more often than we do.

Firstly, something deep within us resists taking risks, so our eyes and minds are closed to the deliberate loss of material. If our opponent makes a threat, we act to prevent it. It's a reflex action. We don't consider letting him carry out his threat, even though it may lead to disaster for him.

Similarly, we don't look at moves that actively lose material for us. We have a rigid table of piece values in our head. Like pennies and pounds, marks and pfennigs, dimes, nickels and quarters, everything has its value in our mind. A pawn is a pawn. If we lose one, our opponent will win the king and pawn endgame. If we exchange our rook for his bishop, we are the equivalent of two pawns behind. There are so many situations in which those values simply don't apply, but we are afraid to make that judgement. We aren't *motivated* to sacrifice.

Secondly, we tend only to recognize sacrificial and combinational opportunities that are clearly visible. It is easy to see sacrifices that are self-evidently forcing, namely those made with captures or checks. Looking through chess books and magazines, the sacrifices which attract most praise (and exclamation marks) are generally those where no capture is made and the king is not put in check. They are difficult to foresee, for both players. When a player unearths such a sacrifice, the chances are that his opponent hasn't foreseen it. The shock alone can force him into error and end the game early. We don't see these sacrificial possibilities because we cannot *imagine* them.

Thirdly, if we are confronted by a sacrificial opportunity, we lack the confidence to play it. We fear that we will be unable to anticipate the moves that both sides will make, to visualize the positions that will arise and to judge them correctly. In short, we lack confidence in our ability to *calculate*.

In this book, we will try to make progress on all three factors.

In Part One we will work on *motivation*, by looking into the minds of some of the great sacrificers. We will see what motivates them to sacrifice, and seek inspiration from their example. We will seek to understand what makes us materialistic and try to adjust our own attitude to risk and the idea of deliberately losing material.

In Part Two we will feed the *imagination* with a host of examples of sacrifices that would normally be difficult to visualize. By confronting, understanding and practising what we have previously been missing, we will feed our imagination and intuition so that we should be able to recognize possibilities over the board that were previously hidden from us.

Throughout the book, we will practise our *calculation* skills, and in Part Three we will also learn about how to improve them. Through numerous graded exercises, the reader can progress from recognizing and calculating relatively simple sacrifices and combinations to many which are tougher than he or she would have thought possible to handle.

In short, our aim is to take the current raw material and work to become Deadly Chess Tacticians.

The Deadly Tactician Database
During the preparation of this book, I searched my fairly extensive library of chess books, magazines, CD-ROM databases and my own

scorebooks for examples of the hard-to-foresee types of sacrifice. My search yielded more than 900 positions. To keep the material fresh, I tried to avoid too many famous examples, and on the occasions when I have felt obliged to use them I have either dealt with them briefly or tried to help my readers to see them in a new way.

I have avoided duplicating examples from John Emms's recent book *The Most Amazing Chess Moves of All Time*. For a move to amaze us, it will normally be very hard to foresee, and I was not surprised when I found that the great majority of the sacrificial games in Emms's book would qualify for inclusion in mine. I have included just one of Emms's examples, Bogoljubow-Alekhine, Hastings 1922, for reasons that will become clear when we reach it.

The Most Amazing Chess Moves of All Time has a 'find the combination' format, so one advantage of my approach, besides helping to give my readers good value for their money, is that I can recommend Emms's book as further practice to follow on from the exercises and tests in my book.

I have included more than twenty examples from my own games. The ideas behind my sacrifices are less complex than in an average grandmaster game, so using my own games helps me to demonstrate and explain sacrificial ideas clearly, and they also make relatively easy exercises. Finally, some of them are pretty good and are worth an airing in public.

The Exercises

At the end of each topic, there are some exercises for you to try, and in Part Three there is a series of tests containing 36 further exercises.

There are three levels of exercises from Level 1 (least difficult) to Level 3 (most difficult). Few of the exercises are exactly easy, as we are concentrating our attention on sacrifices that are inherently difficult to discover.

In each position, at least you know that the possibility of a sacrifice exists – the players themselves were not armed with prior knowledge.

Most sections end with one example on each level, but the shorter sections have only one or two examples, normally at the lower levels.

With only three levels, there is naturally a great variation in difficulty within each level. I have aimed Level 1 at players who know something about tactics but have little confidence in their tactical ability. At this level I have generally included guidance notes under each position to help less experienced readers towards the solution. More experienced players can try solving the exercises without looking at the hints.

Very roughly, Level 1 positions (with the hints) should be solvable by players rated from 1200 to 1600 Elo (approximately 75 to 125 BCF), Level 2 positions by those rated 1600 to 2000 Elo (125 to 175 BCF) and Level 3 positions by higher rated players.

My advice is to try the Level 1 exercises first, trying to calculate the solution without moving the pieces. If you cannot work it out that way, then start to move the pieces. When you have found the solutions, move on to the higher level exercises. It is quite likely that you will need to move the pieces to solve many of the Level 2 and 3 exercises. The more you learn as you go through the book, the more positions you should eventually be able to solve in your head.

Each solution is set out in a way that should help you to learn more about the sacrifice(s) involved, even if you have not been able to solve it. I hope that my readers may be able to advance from one level to the next if they repeat the exercises a few times over a few months. If you are rated 1400 Elo (100 BCF) and you can eventually complete many of the Level 2 exercises, then your opponents should watch out!

Part One: Motivation

1 The Old Romantics

To burrow into the psyche of the Deadly Tactician we need to go back into history, starting with the golden age before Morphy and Steinitz, when men were men and (so we are told) their only object in playing chess was to win as beautifully as possible.

The crowning glory of the era was Adolf Anderssen, a teacher from Breslau in Germany. The public was stunned by the sheer beauty of his published games, two of which were so astonishing that one was dubbed 'Immortal' and the other 'Evergreen'.

Both games have remained justly famous until the present day, so it is rare to find a chess-player who is not familiar with them. Nonetheless, let us look at them briefly.

The diagram on the following page is from the Immortal Game. Anderssen targets the black queen, and is willing to leave his bishop *en prise* in order to gain the time to go after it.

11 ♖g1! cxb5 12 h4 ♛g6 13 h5 ♛g5 14 ♛f3

The threat is the lethal 15 ♗xf4, so Black must either give back the piece or retreat the

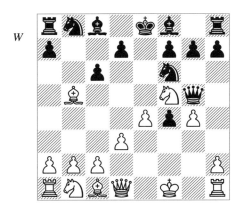

Anderssen – Kieseritzky
London 1851

knight to its starting square. He chooses the latter.

14...♞g8 15 ♗xf4 ♕f6

Black has only his queen in play. Meanwhile, Anderssen can develop his knight to c3, with the intention of playing it to d5 with gain of time.

16 ♞c3 ♗c5

It is quite likely that Anderssen's keen analytical vision saw this possibility when he played 11 ♖g1, and that the double rook sacrifice that follows figured in his thoughts even then.

17 ♞d5 ♕xb2 18 ♗d6 ♗xg1 19 e5 ♕xa1+ 20 ♚e2

Apparently, this is the crucial position for assessing Anderssen's idea.

20...♞a6

There are many other ways for Black to play, and all of them have since been proven to fail. The move played by Kieseritzky looks very reasonable – he covers c7 so that 21 ♞xg7+ ♚d8 22 ♗c7+ is no longer mate, and it is hard to see how Anderssen's deficit of two rooks and one bishop can be justified.

Anderssen proves that it can, however, and in a way that makes the game truly immortal.

He will throw in his queen as well.

21 ♞xg7+ ♚d8 22 ♕f6+!! ♞xf6 23 ♗e7# (1-0)

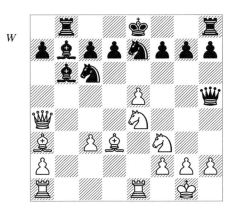

Anderssen – Dufresne
Berlin 1852

This is the Evergreen Game. Anderssen starts with a piece sacrifice to open up the e-file.

17 ♞f6+ gxf6 18 exf6 ♖g8!

Unfortunately, the sacrifice has also opened the g-file for Black and that, combined with the bishop on the long diagonal and the queen on h5, could spell trouble for White on f3 and g2. Anderssen must hurry to finish the game or risk being mated himself. That is just the recipe for abject failure... or dramatic beauty.

19 ♖ad1!

Anderssen leaves the knight *en prise* because he has seen a magnificent mating finish. Understandably not seeing what is to come, Dufresne eats a hearty meal.

19...♕xf3? *(D)*

Anderssen, already two pieces behind, now throws in a rook and his queen to force a beautiful two-bishop mate. Every move must be a check as Black threatens his own immediate mate.

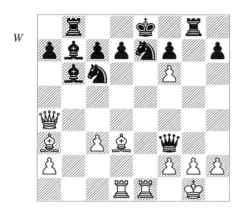

W

**20 ℤxe7+! ♘xe7 21 ♕xd7+!! ♔xd7 22
♗f5++ ♔e8 23 ♗d7+ ♔f8 24 ♗xe7# (1-0)**

Over the following century and a half,
these two games were scrutinized by many
analytical talents (latterly with the help of
computers), and were found to be less than
perfect.

In the Kieseritzky game, most of the moves
in the opening were deemed to be weak. We
can accept that. We are well aware that modern opening play is far more sophisticated
than it was way back then. However, even the
later play seems to have been a catalogue of
errors.

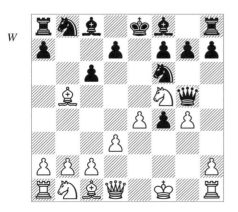

W

From **11 ℤg1** in the original diagram, Kieseritzky could have prevented the whole idea
of 12 h4 and 13 h5, pursuing of the queen, by
declining the bishop offer with 11...h5!?. After 12 h4 ♕g6, the queen is perfectly safe, and
White's king should soon feel the draught
caused by the bold advance of his g- and h-
pawns.

After **11...cxb5 12 h4 ♕g6 13 h5 ♕g5 14
♕f3 ♘g8 15 ♗xf4 ♕f6 16 ♘c3 ♗c5** Anderssen could have won without recourse to further sacrifices by 17 d4!, when 17...♗xd4 18
♘d5 wins back the piece, and a bishop retreat
leaves Black without counterplay and facing
the wrath of the well-developed white pieces.

Instead, Anderssen played the move that he
had probably originally envisaged, **17 ♘d5**,
and after **17...♕xb2** the spectacular **18 ♗d6**.
The analysts found that there were three ways
to win the game and this was not one of
them! 18 d4, 18 ♗e3 and 18 ℤe1 have all
been shown to win, whereas the move played
should have led to at least a draw for Black after 18...♕xa1+ 19 ♔e2 ♕b2!, which gains a
tempo for the defence. One typical line runs
20 ♔d2 ♗xg1 21 e5 ♗a6 22 ♘c7+ ♔d8 23
♕xa8 ♗b6 24 ♕xb8+ ♗c8 25 ♘d5 ♗a5+ 26
♔e3 ♕xc2 27 ♕xa7, when Black can take
perpetual check if he can find nothing better.

Black captured the rooks another way, by
18...♗xg1 and now Anderssen cut off the
queen's path back to the defence with **19 e5!!
♕xa1+ 20 ♔e2**, after which no good defence
has been found to the mating threats. The
moves 20...f6, 20...♗b7 and 20...♗a6 have all
been analysed, but they all tend to lose prosai-
cally. Luckily for Anderssen, and for the
chess world, Kieseritzky tried the more direct
defensive try **20...♘a6**, and was mated after
21 ♘xg7+ ♔d8 22 ♕f6+!! ♘xf6 23 ♗e7#.

In the position where we joined the Dufresne game, White's advantage is so large
that he should be able to win without risky
sacrifices.

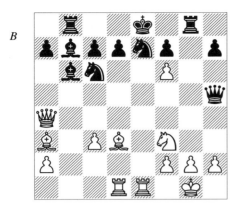

This is the position a couple of moves later, after **19 ♖ad1**. It has been shown that, instead of **19...♕xf3?!**, 19...♖g4 would have avoided Anderssen's brilliant mating combination and left the size of White's advantage somewhat unclear.

It's all good exercise for the analysts, but in the end it doesn't really matter. The games would not have become famous if they had been more accurate. More importantly, we should understand that *the games had no real competitive importance*.

In those far-off days, there were few tournaments and matches. Players like Anderssen would sit down with their playing partners and rattle off a number of games at one sitting. The result of any single game was not important. If a beautiful game resulted from the session, then the winner could try to get it published. A player would gain great fame if many of his best wins found their way into print.

Anderssen loved chess and snatched any opportunity to play. With his great combinative gifts, he tried to create beautiful games whenever he could. When formal tournaments and matches began to take place, however, winning became more important than beauty. Anderssen proved he was the strongest player in the world by winning important

formal matches and tournaments, including the first great tournament of London 1851, but he did so without recourse to the risks that he took in the great mass of his offhand games. Most of these formal games were surprisingly dry. In them, he combined only when really necessary, or when the win was already assured.

Possibly his best combinative display in formal chess was a game from the match that he narrowly lost to Steinitz in 1866.

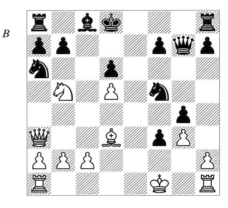

Steinitz – Anderssen
Match (game 8), London 1866

Steinitz won the match by confidently out-combining his illustrious opponent. In this game, he has failed to find a way through Anderssen's defences despite spending a knight and a pawn in the attempt. Now, however, Anderssen appears to allow him a glimmer of hope.

20...♘c5 21 ♗xf5

Steinitz removes the defender of the d-pawn, no doubt hoping for something like 21...♗xf5 22 ♘xd6 ♗xc2 23 ♕xc5 ♕xb2 24 ♘xf7+! ♔e8 25 ♖e1+ ♔xf7 26 ♕e7+, when he achieves perpetual check. Anderssen shuns the recapture of the bishop and goes over to a deadly counterattack.

21...♕h6!

The intention is 22...♕d2 against just about anything.

22 ♗d3 ♖e8 23 h4 ♕d2 24 ♖g1 ♖e2! 0-1

White must give up his queen (25 ♕a5+) to avoid immediate mate.

I think you will agree that this – the best that I can find from his formal games – was a surprisingly pedestrian combination for a player of Anderssen's reputation. It is in Anderssen's informal games that we must look for examples of his combinative sparkle, and we must accept that the informality of the proceedings would cause imperfections to creep into both attack and defence.

Kasparov made a notable comment on the sacrifice 17 ♘f6+ in the Dufresne game: "In accordance with his own romantic style and *public demand* Anderssen played 17 ♘f6+?!!" (my italics – DLM). Anderssen was not so foolish as to play to the gallery in tournament games and formal matches, but he could afford to give free rein to his imagination the rest of the time. If a sacrifice failed, the game would be lost to the public forever. If it succeeded, someone (even the loser) would seek to publish it. It was a case of "Heads I win, tails you lose".

One player in particular seemed to bring out the best in Anderssen. Rosanes lost two beautiful games which are well known but worth reflecting upon.

In the first (*see next diagram*), Anderssen has blithely given up two pawns in the opening for development and open lines. He determinedly avoids regaining material and rapidly builds up for the winning combination.

11...♘xe4 12 dxe4 ♗f5

12...♕d4 regains a pawn, but after 13 0-0-0 ♖xe4 14 ♗c3 ♕e3+ 15 ♕xe3 ♗xe3+ 16 ♗d2, White is comfortable. The move played tempts White to spend time weakening his position in order to avoid possible disaster on the e-file.

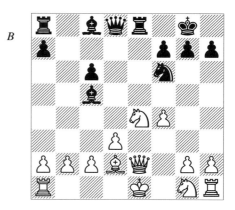

Rosanes – Anderssen
Breslau 1862

13 e5

The f5-bishop is now pointing menacingly towards the white king's only feasible short-term home – the queenside.

13...♕b6!

The combination takes shape. By threatening both the b-pawn and the g1-knight, Anderssen forces White's hand.

14 0-0-0 ♗d4!

Now a diagonal will be opened into the heart of the king's defences.

15 c3 ♖ab8 16 b3 ♖ed8?!

This quiet preparatory move prepares a beautiful queen sacrifice. The piece cannot be captured because 17 cxd4 ♕xd4 threatens 18...♕a1#. Unfortunately, Anderssen's search for beauty allows White a fighting chance which he would have been denied by the more accurate 16...♕a5!, winning by force. The prettiest variation is 17 ♔b2 ♗c5 18 b4 ♖xb4+! 19 cxb4 ♗d4+ 20 ♔b3 ♗e6+ 21 ♔c2 ♕xa2+ and Black forces mate within a few moves.

After the text-move, White has a spare move, so he seeks to force the bishop to move from d4.

17 ♘f3

17 g4 would be more constructive, but he has not foreseen the lovely queen sacrifice that follows.

17...♕xb3!

It's all so simple and straightforward, but it would all be to no avail without the 19th move, a sting in the tail which Anderssen has already foreseen.

18 axb3 ♖xb3 19 ♗e1 ♗e3+! 0-1

By uncovering the rook's line from d8 with gain of time, Anderssen ensures that 20...♖b1 will be mate.

The e3-square also plays a key role in the second game against Rosanes.

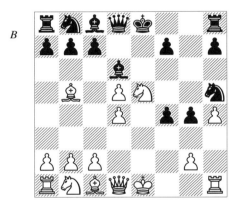

Rosanes – Anderssen
Breslau 1863

9...c6!

Anderssen will jettison a whole rook to get his pieces out quickly.

10 dxc6 bxc6 11 ♘xc6 ♘xc6 12 ♗xc6+ ♔f8! 13 ♗xa8 ♘g3 14 ♖h2

White sees no reason not to pocket all of the loot. Kasparov suggests that he could be a little less greedy by continuing 14 ♔f2 ♘xh1+ 15 ♕xh1 g3+ 16 ♔e1 ♕e7+ 17 ♔d1 ♗g4+ 18 ♗f3 ♗xf3+ 19 gxf3 ♖g8 20 ♕g2 ♕xh4 21 ♔e2 ♕h2 22 ♔f1 h5, but believes

that the h-pawn will be a decisive trump for Black.

14...♗f5 15 ♗d5 ♔g7 16 ♘c3

The good news is that this move covers e2 against the threat of 16...♖e8+ 17 ♔f2 ♖e2+. The bad news is that it leaves the d-pawn difficult to defend.

16...♖e8+ 17 ♔f2 ♕b6 *(D)*

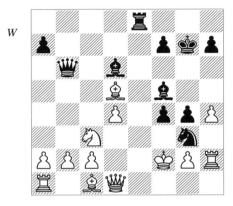

Anderssen probably realized long ago that the imminent ...♗e5! will leave the d-pawn defenceless, and that the white king cannot survive a bishop check on d4. Rosanes does all he can to stop it.

18 ♘a4 ♕a6 19 ♘c3

Allowing a repetition, if Black wants it, because defending the knight by 19 c4 runs into the queen sacrifice 19...♕xa4!!, when 20 ♕xa4 allows mate in three: 20...♖e2+ 21 ♔g1 ♗e1+ 22 ♔f2 ♖f1#. Anderssen is not interested in the draw. His concept of combining attacks along the e-file and the a7-g1 diagonal continues with a stunning move that changes the direction of his dark-squared bishop's influence.

19...♗e5!! 20 a4? *(D)*

It is mate in short order after 20 dxe5? ♕b6+ 21 ♔e1 ♕g1+ 22 ♔d2 ♕e3#. The retreat 20 ♔g1, although better, allows Black to return to his original plan with 20...♕b6 21

♖h1 ♗xd4+ 22 ♔h2 ♕f6! when the advanced h-pawn will prove White's undoing.

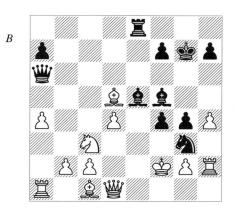

B

White is trying to prepare the defence of his d-pawn by ♘b5, but Black's plan doesn't require his queen as long as he can check on the a7-g1 diagonal with his bishop at a time when only one piece can interpose on e3, so...

20...♕f1+!! 21 ♕xf1 ♗xd4+ 22 ♗e3 ♖xe3! 23 ♔g1 ♖e1# (0-1)

Anderssen had a reputation as a tactical opportunist, an impression that his own words reinforced. According to Reuben Fine, when Anderssen was trounced by Morphy in their 1858 match, he complained "He who plays with Morphy must abandon all hope of *catching him in a trap*, no matter how cunningly laid..." (my italics – DLM).

The four games above show that, in a way, he believed in planning, not in the accepted positional sense, but in a tactical sense. In these games at least, he seemed to have a tactical path laid out well ahead.

This was not necessarily a good thing. The Kieseritzky game showed that when the game becomes complex, even a player with Anderssen's great calculating powers can overlook the weaknesses in his own ideas. In the fourth game of the Morphy-Anderssen match,

Anderssen tried to create a position in which he could attack Black's castled king with ♕h7+, supported by a bishop on b1. By the time the queen reached h7, there was no mate, only a check. Morphy had sidestepped the worst effects of the queen invasion and was able to exploit the central pawn that he had pocketed in the process. Over-reliance on long calculation rather than intuition can be both wasteful and unreliable.

On the other hand, we should not forget that it was largely this obsession with tactical ideas that made many of Anderssen's games great. Here are some exercises to see if you can spot some sacrifices and combinations that he played.

There are guidance notes to the exercises in the Introduction on page 8.

Exercise 1

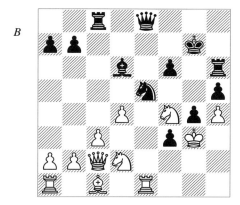

B

Level 1

Anderssen (Black, to play) has sacrificed a piece to reach this position. He concludes with a spectacular sacrifice that cuts off the king's retreat and forces mate in a few moves.

Exercise 2

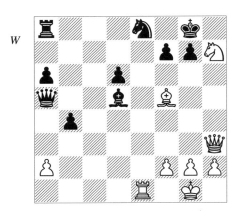

W

Exercise 3

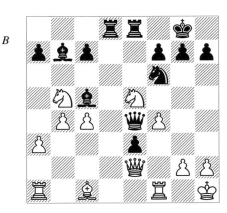

B

Level 2

If White (Anderssen) moves his knight to g5, to threaten mate in two moves by ♕h7+ and ♕h8#, then Black can defend comfortably by ...♘f6. He must be subtler than that. Two exact moves are required to start with, after which you should look for the quickest way to checkmate.

Level 3

Black has the better game. There are two sacrificial continuations that enable him to gain a decisive advantage. The way he chose eventually led to back-rank mate.

The solutions start on page 211.

2 The Birth of Dynamism

During Anderssen's chess career, two great figures arrived on the scene and transformed the way people played chess. First, the American Paul Morphy brought an understanding of positional play, especially as it related to open positions. Morphy was a dazzling tactical player against weak opponents, but he based his play on his positional understanding and generally won his serious games without recourse to sacrifices. A little later, the Austrian Wilhelm Steinitz did the same for closed positions.

The number of tournaments increased, which meant that there was more money to be made and more prestige to be gained and lost.

Chess professionals espoused the new positional methods, as they took much of the risk out of winning chess games. At tournament and match-play level, brilliant sacrificial attacks became rare and play became increasingly dour.

Players didn't lack the ability to play to the gallery, they simply lacked the incentive. In the old days, reputations were built on the ability to play brilliant informal games. Now they were built on the ability to win more often than lose. In the real world, that meant avoiding defeat. Purveyors of brilliance in tournament and match chess, such as Jacques Mieses and Henry Blackburne, dwindled in number. Luckily for the chess public, many top masters still played informal games, often against players far inferior to themselves, and many brilliant games resulted.

Take Carl Schlechter. Around the beginning of the twentieth century, he was feared as a dour positional player who was very hard to beat. Yet he was capable of flights of fancy such as the celebrated combination in the following game.

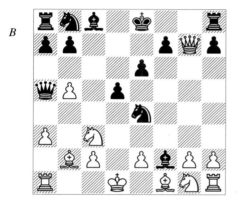

Fleissig – Schlechter
Vienna 1893

It could almost be Anderssen giving up two rooks by...

10...d4! 11 ♕xh8+ ♔e7 12 ♕xc8 dxc3 13 ♗c1 ♘d7! 14 ♕xa8

Now the brilliant finish is:

14...♕xb5 15 ♗f4 ♕d5+ 16 ♔c1 ♗e3+!! 17 ♗xe3 ♘f2!! 0-1

White is mated: 18 ♗xf2 (or 18 ♔b1 ♕b5+ 19 ♔a2 ♕b2#) 18...♕d2+ 19 ♔b1 ♕d1+ 20 ♔a2 ♕xc2#.

The game is similar to a great Anderssen sacrificial attack in another way, too. The final attack is not quite sound, as White can decline the rook by 14 ♕xb7. A typical variation is 14...♖d8 15 ♗f4 ♔f8 16 ♔c1 ♗c5 17 ♕a6 ♕xa6 18 bxa6 ♘f2 19 ♘h3 ♘xh1 20 g3,

and the complications result in a small advantage for White.

Early in the twentieth century, two bright stars emerged onto the increasingly dimly lit chess stage. The first, Rudolf Spielmann, maintained a love of sacrificing throughout his career and wrote the first definitive manual on sacrificial play, whose English title was *The Art of Sacrifice in Chess*. The second, Alexander Alekhine, sacrificed his way to fame and then added a mighty positional edge to become the first truly dynamic player, and one of the great world champions.

Rudolf Spielmann believed in the power of sacrifices. His book reverberates with that belief:

- "We honour Capablanca, but our hearts beat faster at the mention of the name of Morphy."
- Upon reaching a point in his analysis of his great game against Rubinstein, where he would have two pawns and an attack for a sacrificed bishop, with a draw an easy option, he wrote "He who would not boldly undertake to win such a position ... will never go far in the domain of the sacrifice."
- He believed strongly in the role of intuition, rather than exhaustive calculation, in assessing whether to play a sacrifice: "...intuitive play, unfortunately, is not rated very highly." "How difficult it is at times to see correctly a few moves ahead with their variations, and how often has such a useless waste of energy led to nervous exhaustion..." "The expert chess-player must be good at analysis, but he must not overdo it." "Faith in the position is required, and faith in oneself."
- His view on the psychological effects of a sacrifice was well ahead of its time: "A game of chess is not a mathematical problem, but a contest full of life, and in a contest, the attacker, in practice, always has the advantage." He repeated time and again

how hard it is to defend, to solve negative problems over the board.

Spielmann sacrificed because he loved attacking, and he believed (with plenty of supporting evidence) that sacrifices win games. As a sacrificer, he could be bettered – at least by Alekhine as we shall see – but let us briefly look at two of his games to see his sacrifices in action.

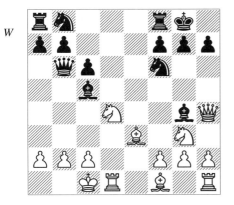

Spielmann – Tartakower
Munich 1909

Spielmann was not afraid to sacrifice against anybody if the opportunity arose. As a result, he beat top players like Bogoljubow, Rubinstein and, here, Tartakower in brilliant style. In this position, Black probably felt relaxed and confident as easy equality looks likely after 13 ♗e2, 13 ♖d2 or 13 f3.

13 ♗d3!

A shock. White leaves his rook to be consumed by the bishop. Meanwhile he points another piece at Black's king and gives his knights easy access to f5.

13...♗xd1 14 ♖xd1 ♘bd7 15 ♘gf5 ♘e5?

Black's defence is not easy, as an eventual ♘xg7 will be hard to meet.

15...♔h8 is better, when Spielmann said that White can continue his build-up with 16

g4 g6 17 g5 ♘g8 18 ♖g1 intending ♖g3-h3. To my mind, it is even worth considering 16 ♘xg7!? ♔xg7 17 ♗f5!, when it is quite difficult for Black to organize his defence.

Spielmann's faith in his initial sacrifice is justified – the defender encounters unexpected problems, and finds that he cannot cope.

16 ♘xg7! ♕d8

16...♔xg7 loses to 17 ♘f5+ ♔g8 18 ♕xf6.

17 ♘gf5 ♘g6 18 ♕h6 ♘e8 19 ♘f3 ♗xe3+ 20 fxe3 ♕f6 21 ♘g5 ♕h8 22 ♘e7+! 1-0

The black knight on g6 is blocking the bishop's line to h7. Now it is forced to move and after 22...♘xe7 Black is mated by 23 ♗xh7+ ♕xh7 24 ♕xh7#.

Spielmann played many beautiful combinations, but few were more difficult than the next example.

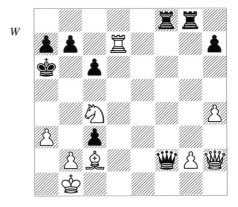

Spielmann – Mieses
Regensburg 1910

We are in the middle of a king-hunt – the black king has been hounded from e8 to a6 – but it appears that White has run out of steam. Black threatens ...♕f1+ winning the knight, and if White plays a defensive move the black queen will have time to join the defence of its king.

32 ♕c7!!

Spielmann lets his knight go, and is even willing to do so with check. He probably saw this idea several moves ago.

32...♕f1+ 33 ♔a2! ♕xc4+ 34 b3 ♕b5 35 a4 ♕b6 36 ♗d3+ ♔a5 37 ♕e5+ c5 38 ♖xb7!!

In view of Black's counter-threats, this sting in the tail had to be seen by the time he played 32 ♕c7.

38...♖xg2+ 39 ♔a3 ♖g4 40 ♖xb6 1-0

After 40...axb6 41 ♕c7 ♖a8 42 ♕c6 White threatens mates on both b5 and a8.

From his earliest years, Alekhine loved to attack. His games overflowed with sacrifices big and small.

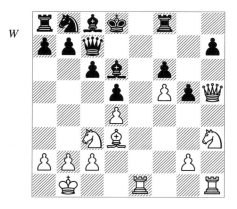

Alekhine – Rubtsov
Spring Tournament, Moscow 1908

Black is a pawn ahead, but he is well behind in his development and his king has already been disturbed. Alekhine pounces without hesitation.

18 ♘xg5!? fxg5 19 ♕xg5+ ♗e7 20 ♕g7 ♗b4

20...♗xf5 loses to 21 ♗xf5 ♖xf5 22 ♖xh7, because 22...♗d6 allows 23 ♖h8+, mating. Instead of the move played, 20...♕d6 gives chances of a successful defence, although after

21 ♖xh7 White's connected passed pawns will require careful attention.

21 f6! ♖f7 (D)

Black cannot swap queens as 21...♕xg7 22 fxg7 ♖g8 23 ♖xh7 ♔d7 24 ♗g6 followed by 25 ♗f7 costs Black a rook. The apparently safe text-move meets a drastic refutation.

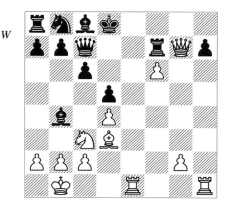

22 ♖xh7!!

It is even worth sacrificing his queen to create a monster passed pawn on g7.

22...♖xg7 23 fxg7 ♕g3 24 ♖f1 ♗d7

24...♗e6 doesn't help, in view of 25 ♖f8+ ♔c7 26 g8♕+ promoting with discovered check. Black must give up his queen for the pawn.

25 ♖h8+ ♔c7 26 g8♕ ♕xg8 27 ♖xg8 b6 28 g4 ♗e6 29 ♖h8 ♗xg4 30 ♖f7+ 1-0

In time, Alekhine developed his skills in all facets of the game. He often finished off his masterpieces with attractive sacrificial combinations, but aggressive positional play became the basis of his game. However, he was willing to sacrifice, particularly pawns, to grab the initiative and pursue his positional ends, and this made him probably the first truly dynamic player – interchanging material and other elements in the main phases of the chess battle.

Despite the restraint that he forced upon his bolder chess urges, he retained a love of the grand sacrifice. He indulged himself fully in exhibition games and simultaneous displays – even those played without sight of the board. Any player with his eyes open would treasure the exquisite little combination that he played in his famous blindfold game against Feldt.

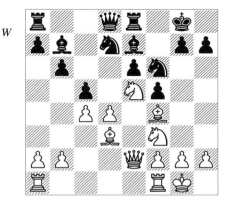

Alekhine – Feldt
Blindfold, Tarnopol 1920

15 ♘f7!! ♔xf7 16 ♕xe6+! ♔g6
Or: 16...♔xe6 17 ♘g5#; 16...♔f8 17 ♘g5 with mate to follow.
17 g4! ♗e4 18 ♘h4# (1-0)

Réti made an interesting observation about Alekhine's combinational style. He noted that with most players the surprise comes with the initial sacrifice, but with Alekhine the surprise often comes at the end of the combination.

Alekhine was so keen to play brilliant chess that he would look beyond the early moves of a combination, and perhaps its apparent failure, to see a hidden idea beyond. This is similar to Anderssen, who often played sacrifices with a view to further sacrificial possibilities

that lay beyond. In Alekhine's case, however, the later idea was often a quiet move, without sacrifices, and that made it all the more difficult to foresee.

Was Réti right? Let's start with the example that he gave in *Modern Ideas in Chess*.

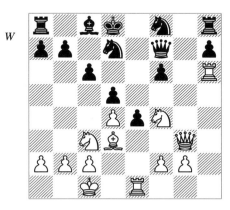

Alekhine – Fahrni
Mannheim 1914

Alekhine breaks open the central files.
18 ♗xe4! dxe4 19 ♘xe4 ♖g8
The black queen must stay on the second rank to guard against the invasion of the white queen. For example, after 19...♕xa2 20 ♘xf6 ♘xf6 21 ♕g7 ♕a1+ 22 ♔d2 ♕a5+ 23 c3 ♘6d7 24 ♕e7+ ♔c7 25 ♕d6+ ♔d8 26 ♖he6! mate is not far off. Now the white queen is attacked, and finding the right square for its retreat is crucial.
20 ♕a3!
Réti draws attention to this surprising move at the end of the combination. The intention is 21 ♘d6 ♕g7 22 ♘e8! ♕f7 (not 22...♕xh6 23 ♕e7#) 23 ♕d6 when the threat of 24 ♕c7# would force Black to give up his queen.
20...♕g7
20...♕e7 threatens the exchange of queens at the same time as pinning the knight along the e-file. In reply, Alekhine gives simply 21

♕a5+ b6 22 ♕c3! "and wins". The queen manoeuvre protects the e1-rook and attacks the newly weakened c-pawn so that White wins after 22...♗b7 23 ♘xf6 ♕xf6 24 ♖xf6 ♘xf6 25 ♕b4 and a queen invasion, and has a mighty attack after 22...♕g7 23 ♘d6! ♘b8 24 ♖e8+ ♔d7 25 ♘f5 ♕g4 26 ♕e3.

21 ♘d6 ♘b6 22 ♘e8!

Now it's all over. There is nothing to be done about the invasion by the white queen.

22...♕f7 23 ♕d6+ ♕d7 24 ♕xf6+ 1-0

Next we see one of Alekhine's simplest combinations, and yet thanks to the final point it is one of his most startling.

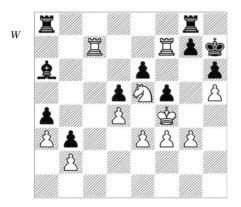

Alekhine – Yates
London 1922

First the knight comes round to f6, so that the g-pawn cannot be defended without losing the exchange.

35 ♘d7! ♔h8 36 ♘f6! ♖gf8

Not, of course, 36...gxf6 37 ♖h7#. After the text-move, however, White can apparently make no progress. The long-prepared final blow is beautiful indeed.

37 ♖xg7!! ♖xf6 38 ♔e5! 1-0

The rook is stranded as 38...♖(either)f8 allows mate in two moves by the white rooks.

Finally, here is one of Alekhine's later games, which shows that the knack of foreseeing surprising quiet points never left him.

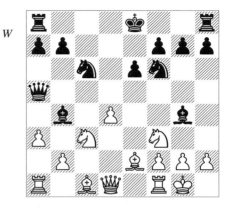

Alekhine – Podgorny
Prague 1943

The position looks innocent enough, but Alekhine probably looked a long way ahead when deciding whether to play his next move.

11 d5! exd5

After 11...♘xd5 12 ♘xd5 exd5 13 axb4! ♕xa1 14 ♕b3 ♗xf3 15 ♗g5! ♕xf1+ 16 ♗xf1 ♗e4 17 f3 ♗f5 18 ♕xd5 White's dominant queen gives him an advantage.

12 axb4 ♕xa1 13 ♘d2! ♗xe2 14 ♕xe2+ ♘e7

At the outset Alekhine had to foresee 14...♔f8 15 ♘b3 ♕a6 16 b5 ♕b6 17 ♘a4 ♘d4!, and now 18 ♕d1!! is the first really surprising quiet move. Black's knight is lost, and White has good chances against the king stuck in the centre. Kasparov, in *Mega Database 2001*, apparently had great fun analysing this position, coming up with 18...♘f3+ 19 ♕xf3 ♕xb5 20 ♘ac5 b6 *(D)*.

Kasparov's analysis continues 21 ♗h6!! ♔g8 (not 21...gxh6 22 ♕xf6 ♖g8 23 ♘e6+ ♔e8 24 ♘c7+) 22 ♘d4! ♕xc5 23 ♘f5 ♕c7 (23...g6 loses to 24 ♕c3! ♕xc3 25 ♘e7#) 24

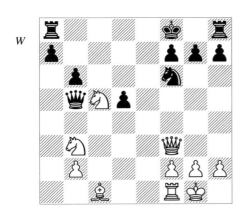

♗xg7 ♕e5 25 ♗h6 (threatening 26 ♕g3+ ♕xg3 27 ♘e7#) 25...♖e8 26 ♕h3! followed by 27 f4 and mate on the g-file. It is Kasparov's opinion that Alekhine must have foreseen 18 ♕d1, and its main variations, or he would not have played 11 d5 in the first place.

15 ♖e1 0-0 16 ♘b3!

This is the final surprising move that Alekhine needed to foresee when he played 11 d5. Naturally not 16 ♕xe7??, which loses to 16...♖fe8.

16...♕a6 17 ♕xa6 bxa6 18 ♖xe7 (D)

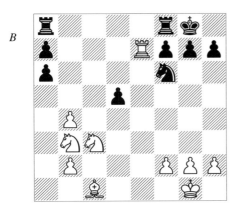

White has all the positional aces in this ending and Alekhine won comfortably.

18...♖ab8 19 b5! axb5 20 ♖xa7 b4 21 ♘e2 ♖fc8 22 f3 ♖a8 23 ♖xa8 ♖xa8 24 ♔f2 ♘d7 25 ♘f4 ♘b6 26 ♔e3 ♖c8 27 ♔d3 g5 28 ♘h5 1-0

Clearly, Réti was right. What is less clear is whether Alekhine found moves like 18 ♕d1 (in the notes) and 16 ♘b3 (in the game) in his analysis at the start of the combination, or whether his intuition told him to go ahead with his sacrifices and the quiet moves arose because his intuition was correct. It is a revealing comment on Kasparov that he believed it was all analysis. I suspect that he himself has a strong preference for using analysis rather than intuition, but more about him later.

Now it's your turn. Alekhine enjoyed the opportunity to exercise his sacrificial muscles in simultaneous exhibitions. Here are three examples of combinations with his classic surprising finishes.

Exercise 4

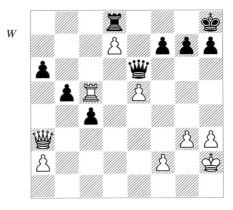

Level 1

White, to play, will promote his pawn. Look out for a big surprise on the second move. The fact that the black king is on h8, and not g8, is very significant. The solution is only three moves long.

Exercise 5

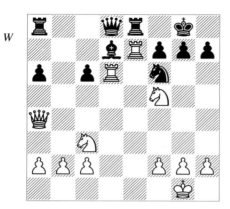

Level 2

Alekhine played **20 ♘e4**, despite the reply **20...♖xe7**. First question: what follow-up had Alekhine prepared, and what mating finish did he have in mind?

After Alekhine's follow-up, Black found a defence that, after a few moves, left him threatening both mate and two other pieces. Against that, Alekhine had prepared a simple but surprising move that held everything and left him a clear pawn up with a winning endgame. Second question: what was it?

Exercise 6

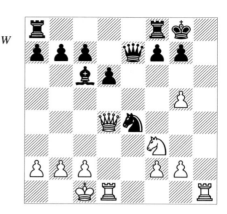

Level 3

Alekhine (White) had already sacrificed a piece, and now played **14 ♖h5**. Black's best defence is 14...♕e8, but he instead played **14...♕e6**. Two questions: how does White then finish the game, and what should he play against another feasible defence, 14...f6?

The solutions start on page 212.

3 The New Romantics

In the middle of the 1950s, along came Mikhail Tal, a man who needs no introduction. He was something of a throwback to bygone days, the New Romantic of the chessboard.

Tal's love of sacrificing was so strong that he felt compelled to make a habit of it. I once decided to count how often he sacrificed, so I took Thomas's book *Complete Games of Mikhail Tal 1960-66* and counted up the games and sacrifices that he played from the first event after he won the World Championship in 1960 to Reykjavik 1964, the tournament before the Amsterdam Interzonal. I discounted the 1962 Candidates tournament

at Curaçao on the grounds that Tal was very ill at the time.

The results? The book gives 231 competitive games, of which 96 featured at least one Tal sacrifice. That's over 40%. Many of the sacrifices were in combinations that finished off games, but plenty were played to grab the initiative or open up attacks. Some were unsound, fewer failed. We must ask the question: why could Tal find the excuse to play sacrifices in nearly half of his games when few other players, let alone grandmasters playing in the top flight, could manage it in a small fraction of their games? It was said by Reuben Fine that Alekhine "... would almost literally shake combinations out of his sleeve", but even in his young days his efforts could not compare with Tal's prolific output of sacrifices.

The comparison with Alekhine is worth taking further. As Alekhine progressed, he refined his positional play in order to cope with the leading players of his day. He still played sacrifices, but more and more they formed the keystones of combinations that merely completed the work that his fine positional play had started. The first objective was to create a winning position; sacrifices could finish the job.

By contrast, throughout his life Tal would play sacrifices in any phase of the game. Sometimes they were played simply because he wanted an interesting game. No game says more about the man than the following effort against Barcza.

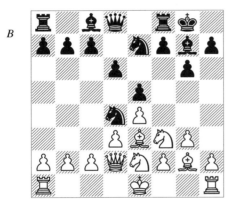

Barcza – Tal
Tallinn 1971

Barcza has clumsily left himself open to an easy shot that wins material.

9...♗h3! 10 ♘fxd4

Nothing helps. 10 0-0 ♘xf3+ 11 ♗xf3 ♗xf1 is probably best, hoping to survive the exchange behind. The text-move loses a piece;

Barcza was possibly hoping that Tal would allow his bishop to be trapped.

10...♗xg2 11 ♖g1 exd4 12 ♘xd4 c5 13 ♘b5 ♗f3 14 g4 d5!?

Black could come out a whole piece ahead and release the bishop by playing 14...♕d7 and, after White saves his attacked knight, 15...♗xg4. But Tal is not interested in that. He has seen a fascinating idea, and is happy to give up his material advantage – and more – to bring it about.

15 ♗xc5 ♖c8 16 ♗a3 dxe4 17 dxe4 ♕b6!

Bang goes the extra piece. White is handed an exchange advantage instead.

18 ♗xe7 ♕xb5! 19 ♗xf8 ♕xb2 20 ♗xg7 ♔xg7 21 ♖c1 *(D)*

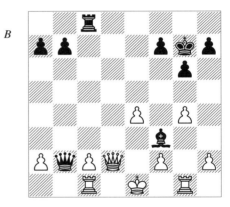

21...♖d8!! 22 ♕e3

22 ♕xd8 ♕xc1+ is mate next move.

22...♕xc2!! 23 ♔f1

Or 23 ♖xc2 ♖d1#.

23...♖d1+ 0-1

After 24 ♖xd1 ♕xd1+ 25 ♕e1 ♕d3+, it is mate next move.

Tal's success as a sacrificer resulted from both his personality and his mental faculties. He loved a fight. He had great intuition, a rich imagination and a love of beauty. He was able to calculate at great speed and visualize future positions with remarkable clarity. He had an uncanny judgement of the effects of strange material imbalances. He had a great sense of humour, one effect of which was to help him to see paradoxical ideas.

A short section on the greatest sacrificer of all time can scarcely do full justice to all of his characteristics, but we can hope to see some of them in action and allow ourselves to be inspired by them.

Tal sacrificed with many possible ends in mind. My favourite combination of his merely resulted in a favourable endgame. Here it is.

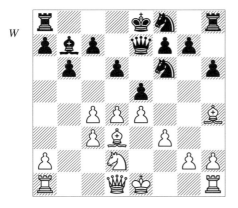

Tal – Hecht
Olympiad, Varna 1962

First, Tal opens the centre.
13 c5 dxc5 14 dxe5 ♕xe5 15 ♕a4+ c6 16 0-0 ♘g6 17 ♘c4 ♕e6 18 e5! b5

Black has been allowed to attack a bishop, knight and queen simultaneously...
19 exf6!!
...and Tal declines to save his queen.
19...bxa4?!
The calm 19...0-0! is the critical test of Tal's idea.
20 fxg7!
He even allows Black to save his own queen if he wishes, but 20...♕d5 21 ♗xg6 ♖g8 22

♖fe1+ ♔d7 23 ♖e7+ ♔c8 24 ♗f5+! ♕xf5 25 ♘d6+ wins for White.

As we shall see later in the book, the pawn's dash from the fourth to the seventh rank (in this case from e4 to g7) in consecutive moves – with heavy material sacrifices on the way – was to become a Tal trademark.
20...♖g8 21 ♗f5!!
With his h4-bishop still *en prise*, Tal puts both of his other minor pieces at his opponent's disposal.
21...♘xh4
In fact, it is only the h4-bishop that can be captured, as 21...♕xf5 is met by 22 ♘d6+, regaining all but a pawn and keeping White on the attack, while 21...♕xc4 loses beautifully in its main variation: 22 ♖fe1+ ♕e6 23 ♖xe6+! fxe6 24 ♗xg6+ ♔d7 25 ♖d1+ ♔c7 (or 25...♔c8 26 ♗f6) 26 ♗g3+ ♔b6 (or 26...♔c8 27 ♗f7!) 27 ♖b1+ ♔a6 28 ♗d3+ ♔a5 29 ♗c7#.
22 ♗xe6 ♗a6 23 ♘d6+ ♔e7
Tal still has two pieces *en prise*, but he knows what he is doing.
24 ♗c4! ♖xg7 25 g3 ♖xd6 26 ♗xa6
The dust has cleared. What has Tal achieved with his grandiose combination? A better ending, and not necessarily a winning one, either. Black is still a pawn ahead, but White has the better minor piece and far better pawns.
26...♘f5?
A typical problem for the defender, who over-relaxes once the barrage is over. 26...♖b8, and if 27 ♖ab1 then 27...♖b6!, would give him good chances of saving the game. Now Tal takes control of the b-file and eventually wins the ending.

It is typical of the man that he was willing to undertake such mundane (and delicate) duties after firing the big guns, and also typical that he would play such endgames so much better than his shell-shocked opponents.
27 ♖ab1 f6 28 ♖fd1+ ♔e7 29 ♖e1+ ♔d6 30 ♔f2 c4 31 g4 ♘e7 32 ♖b7 ♖ag8 33 ♗xc4 ♘d5 34 ♗xd5 cxd5 35 ♖b4 ♖c8 36 ♖xa4

♖xc3 37 ♖a6+ ♔c5 38 ♖xf6 h5 39 h3 hxg4
40 hxg4 ♖h7 41 g5 ♖h5 42 ♖f5 ♖c2+ 43
♔g3 ♔c4 44 ♖ee5 d4 45 g6 ♖h1 46 ♖c5+
♔d3 47 ♖xc2 ♔xc2 48 ♔f4 ♖g1 49 ♖g5 1-0

Tal was an expert ambusher. His opponent
would think he had seen a big hole in Tal's
plans, and aim straight for it, only to find that
Tal had discovered a twist that grabs advantage from the jaws of defeat. The following
game against Nikitin is a dramatic case.

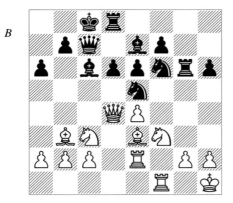

Nikitin – Tal
USSR Ch, Tbilisi 1959

Tal's attack is focused on the g2-square,
where the lines of the rooks on the g-file and of
the c6-bishop intersect. Nikitin is well aware
of this, having apparently foreseen that Tal
would leave his queen *en prise* and prepared a
wicked response.

20...♖dg8! 21 ♕a7 ♘xe4! 22 ♗b6

The bishop move attacks the queen and
discovers an attack on the e4-knight. Tal must
leave his queen to be taken and continue with
his assault on g2.

22...♘xc3! 23 ♗xc7 ♘xe2 24 ♗b6

The bishop must save itself and let the rook
capture on g2. 24 ♖f2 is no good, as 24...♔xc7
25 ♖xe2 ♗xf3! cracks open the g-file, winning

bags of material after 26 gxf3 ♘xf3 with the
mate threat at g1. This is no problem to Nikitin, as he believes that Tal has miscalculated.

24...♖xg2 25 ♗a4! *(D)*

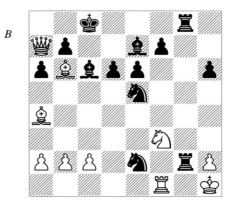

A brilliant idea. The c6-bishop can neither
move nor stay still, because 25...♗xf3 allows
26 ♕a8#, 25...♗xa4 leaves the b-pawn unguarded so that White can play 26 ♕a8+ ♔d7
27 ♕xb7+ mating, and leaving the bishop
where it is allows the same mating sequence
since the c6-bishop will be pinned once the
black king reaches d7.

It is not clear whether Tal foresaw this idea
when he started his combination, but I suspect that he did. As in his game against Hecht,
he is able to simplify down to a superior endgame with a nice forcing sequence.

25...♖g1+! 26 ♗xg1 ♖xg1+ 27 ♕xg1

27 ♖xg1 ♗xf3+ 28 ♖g2 ♘f4 is even better
for Black.

**27...♗xf3+ 28 ♖xf3 ♘xg1 29 ♖c3+ ♔d8
30 ♔xg1**

Tal has two pawns for the exchange, and
his compact central pawn-mass gives him a
pleasant advantage. His endgame play is too
good for Nikitin, and his pawns prepare for
touchdown.

**30...d5 31 ♖g3 ♗g5 32 b4 b5 33 ♗b3 f5
34 c3 ♔e7 35 a4 f4 36 ♖h3 ♘c4 37 axb5**

axb5 38 ♔f2 ♔d6 39 ♔e2 e5 40 ♗xc4 bxc4 41 ♖h5 e4 42 h4 f3+ 43 ♔d1 ♗f4 44 ♖f5 0-1

One of Tal's specialities was to put his opponent to sleep quietly. He would play a combination, and his opponent would think he had all of his bases covered. Then Tal would play an unforeseen move, probably a quiet one, and his opponent would suddenly realize that the game was up. In this way he was similar to Alekhine. They could both thank not only their extraordinary combinative vision, which enabled them to see so far in advance, but also their uncanny intuition, which told them that it was worth analysing along the routes that led to these strange debacles for their opponents.

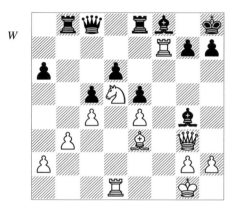

Tal – Rantanen
Tallinn 1979

The f7-rook is actively placed, but Tal's other rook is under attack. As many of his opponents discovered, attacking a Tal piece is no guarantee that he will move it.

24 ♘f6!! gxf6

Capturing the rook loses prettily: 24...♗xd1 25 ♕h4 h6 (or 25...h5 26 ♕g5!) 26 ♕xh6+! gxh6 27 ♖h7#.

25 ♕h4 ♗g7 26 ♗h6! ♗xd1

Rantanen presumably believed that Tal had overestimated the strength of the attack, so he removed the rook. The best defence is 26...♖g8, but then White wins by 27 ♖xd6, which threatens to kill the black king through overexposure starting with 28 ♗xg7+ ♖xg7 29 ♖xg7 ♔xg7 30 ♕xf6+ ♔g8 31 ♕g5+ ♔h8 32 ♕xe5+ ♔g8 and, now that the e-pawn is out of the way, finishing with 33 ♕g5+ ♔h8 34 ♕f6+ ♔g8 35 ♖d5, when the imminent rook check on g5 will be fatal. Black can meet this threat by 27...♖b7, but the weakening of the back rank allows White to simplify to a winning queen and pawn ending with 28 ♗xg7+ ♖xg7 29 ♖xb7 ♕xb7 30 ♖d8+ ♖g8 31 ♖xg8+ ♔xg8 32 ♕xg4+.

27 ♗xg7+ ♔g8

Now Rantanen was probably convinced that the attack was at an end. 28 ♕xf6 loses to 28...♖b7, while the attempt at perpetual check by 28 ♖xf6 (intending to meet 28...♔xg7 by 29 ♕h6+ ♔g8 30 ♖g6+!, drawing) fails to 28...♕g4. We can imagine his surprise when Tal calmly moved his bishop into the corner, leaving two of his three remaining pieces *en prise*.

28 ♗h8!!

Here comes that helpless feeling. Mate is threatened on h7 (whether or not he captures the bishop), while capturing the rook allows mate in two.

28...♔xf7 29 ♕xf6+ ♔g8 30 ♕g7# (1-0)

Tal was feared for his combinative play, but he was even more feared for his intuitive sacrifices. Some would later be proved to be unsound, but nearly always Tal would thread his way through the complications better than his opponent and emerge the winner. He differed from Alekhine, who preferred to sacrifice from a position of strength and was particularly careful when it came to playing against the strongest grandmasters. Tal feared no one, so anyone could find himself on the receiving end of one of his intuitive sacrifices.

In the British chess magazines of the mid-1960s there was a serious shortage of truly exciting games. I remember well the impact on the chess press of Tal's play in his 1965 world championship candidates matches against Portisch and Larsen. He won both matches by playing intuitive, risky sacrifices. These two leading grandmasters each suffered twice.

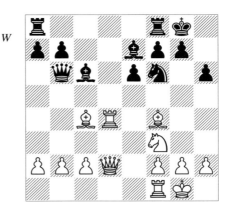

Tal – Portisch
Candidates match (game 4), Bled 1965

15 ♗xh6! ♘e4

The black king is blasted into oblivion after both 15...gxh6 16 ♕xh6 ♗xf3 17 ♕g5+ and 15...♗xf3 16 ♗xg7!.

16 ♕f4 gxh6

Now 17 ♕xh6 ♖ad8! should allow Black to hold the game, but Tal is not finished.

17 ♖xe4! ♗xe4 18 ♕xe4

White has a pawn for the exchange and the makings of a strong kingside attack.

As Spielmann pointed out, it is far easier to attack than to defend, and Tal soon ran out the winner.

18...♖ad8 19 b3 ♗c5 20 ♕f4 ♔g7 21 ♕e5+ f6 22 ♕g3+ ♔h7 23 ♖e1 ♖g8 24 ♕h4 ♖d6 25 ♔f1 f5 26 h3 ♖g6 27 g4! ♖d7 28 ♖xe6! ♖d1+ 29 ♔g2 ♖xe6 30 ♗xe6 fxg4 31 ♕xg4 ♖d8 32 ♘e5 1-0

In the diagram on the next page, Larsen was struck by a bolt from a clear blue sky.

16 ♘b5! cxb5 17 ♕xb5+ ♔d8 18 c4 ♕xe5

Larsen is so shocked that he decides to return the piece rather than face the consequences of 18...♘b6 19 ♕a5 or 18...♘f4 19 ♖d1+ (or 19 ♕a5+ b6 20 ♕d2+ winning back the piece) 19...♔c7 20 ♖d7+!.

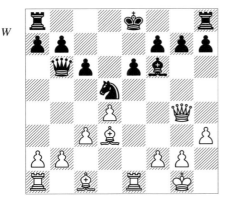

Tal – Portisch
Candidates match (game 2), Bled 1965

15 c4!?

One of those naïve-looking moves that Tal often played. It looks all wrong because after Black's reply both White's bishop and his d-pawn are attacked.

15...♘b4 16 ♖xe6+!

The point. The knight has been dragged away from the defence, and this sacrifice strands the king in the centre.

16...fxe6 17 ♕xe6+ ♔f8 18 ♗f4 ♖d8 19 c5 ♘xd3 20 cxb6 ♘xf4 21 ♕g4 ♘d5 22 bxa7

The position is completely unclear, but Portisch cannot cope with the changed situation. Best now is 22...g6, using the king to safeguard the kingside.

22...♔e7 23 b4 ♖a8 24 ♖e1+ ♔d6 25 b5 ♖xa7 26 ♖e6+ ♔c7 27 ♖xf6! 1-0

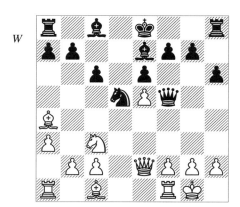

Tal – Larsen
Candidates match (game 6), Bled 1965

After the text-move, Black emerges a pawn ahead, but the exposure of his queen allows White to develop his pieces with gain of time and build up a powerful attack against the centralized enemy king.

19 cxd5 ♗d6 20 g3 ♕xd5 21 ♕e2 ♔e7 22 ♖d1 ♕a5 23 ♕g4 ♕f5 24 ♕c4 ♕c5 25 ♕d3 ♕d5 26 ♕c3 ♗e5 27 ♕e1 ♕c5 28 ♗d2 ♔f6 29 ♖ac1 ♕b6 30 ♗e3 ♕a6 31 ♕b4 b5 32 ♗xb5 ♕b7 33 f4 ♗b8 34 ♗c6 1-0

Tal was bold enough to play the riskiest sacrifice of them all in the winner-takes-all final game of the Larsen match (*see following diagram*).

16 ♘d5!?

Another shock for Larsen, as the move appears to lack the normal points of ♘d5 sacrifices in the Sicilian.

16...exd5 17 exd5 f5?

White has considerable firepower aimed at the black king's position, but 17...g6 was later shown to be sufficient to defend. Instead, Larsen voluntarily exposes his king's defences.

Tal went on to win prettily.

18 ♖de1 ♖f7 19 h4 ♗b7 20 ♗xf5 ♖xf5 21 ♖xe7 ♘e5 22 ♕e4 ♕f8 23 fxe5 ♖f4 24 ♕e3

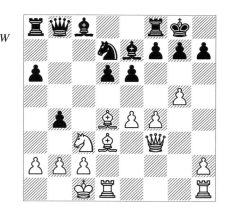

Tal – Larsen
Candidates match (game 10), Bled 1965

♖f3 25 ♕e2 ♕xe7 26 ♕xf3 dxe5 27 ♖e1 ♖d8 28 ♖xe5 ♕d6 29 ♕f4 ♖f8 30 ♕e4 b3 31 axb3 ♖f1+ 32 ♔d2 ♕b4+ 33 c3 ♕d6 34 ♗c5! ♕xc5 35 ♖e8+ ♖f8 36 ♕e6+ ♔h8 37 ♕f7! 1-0

Tal was a master of the apparently naïve move that looks like a blunder but hides a deep idea, as our final example demonstrates.

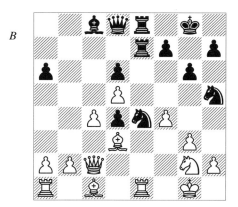

Thorbergsson – Tal
Reykjavik 1964

20...♞g5! 21 ♖xe7 ♞h3+

This doesn't seem to be a very clever idea, as the knight is apparently stuck at h3, and a sacrifice at f4 looks unlikely.

22 ♔f1 ♖xe7 23 ♗d2 ♞f6 24 ♞h4 ♞g4 25 ♞f3 ♖e3!

This move is not too surprising. The rook is untouchable for now (26 ♗xe3 ♞xe3+ wins the queen), but note how the white pieces protecting f4 have either been diverted or blocked.

26 ♔g2 ♛e7!

The knight is taboo (27 ♔xh3 ♖xd3! 28 ♛xd3 ♞f2+) and a sacrifice on f4 is in the air.

27 ♖e1 ♞xf4+! 28 gxf4 ♖xe1 29 ♞xe1 ♛h4 30 ♗c1

The only way to prevent mate without losing the queen is to return the piece.

30...♛xe1 31 h3 ♞h6 32 f5 ♞xf5 33 ♗f4 ♞h4+ 34 ♔h2 ♞f3+ 35 ♔g2

Tal now found a lovely finish, but that will have to wait for Exercise 8 below.

Since that is a Level 2 exercise, you should first do Exercise 7.

Exercise 7

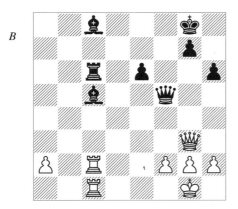

B

Level 1

Tal played the apparently silly **26...♗b7**. Surely now after 27 ♛b8+, the bishop must return to c8? Or must it...?

Exercise 8

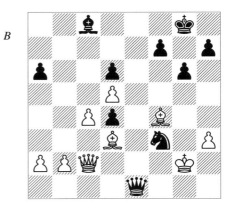

B

Level 2

See the preceding play in Thorbergsson-Tal above. Here Tal plays a sacrifice, then follows it with a quiet move leaving White helpless. What are these two moves?

Exercise 9

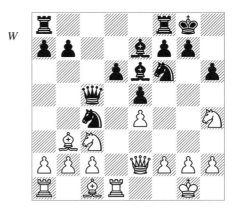

W

Level 3

Tal (White) played a move letting Beliavsky win material in return for a strong attack. What was it, and why was it good?

The solutions are on page 213.

4 The Dynamic Romantics

In Tal's time, both Spassky and Fischer played some striking sacrificial games but, as with Alekhine, their sacrifices tended to be attractive polishing agents for their excellent positional chess. Fischer, in particular, rarely sacrificed against the top players.

From a sacrificial point of view, Petrosian was an interesting character. He received a very bad press, often deservedly, for his over-cautious approach. However, his tactical vision was hard to fault – after all, very few players managed to land a sacrificial blow against him because he was so good at spotting danger from afar. When roused, he could play sacrifices, as he demonstrated in two

fine games in his first match against Spassky in 1966.

Later on, Karpov was likewise criticized for his dry play, but he too could sacrifice. He made a particular speciality of the exchange sacrifice, as we shall see later.

Through the 1970s, several younger players emerged, including Britons Tony Miles and John Nunn, who seemed increasingly willing to sacrifice. Their approach was dynamic, often sacrificing for positional compensation, to grab the initiative or to open attacks or, indeed, to stem the opponent's attacks.

Into this world came Garry Kasparov, whose sacrificial talent is the equal of Tal and

Alekhine's, and who has acted as an example to a generation of players who are capable of producing the most wonderfully dynamic sacrificial chess.

Early in 1980, at the European Team Championship at Skara, the English team made its big breakthrough into the top ranks of international chess. Quietly playing along on bottom board for the eight-man Soviet team was 16-year-old Garry. He scored 5½ out of 6 and I was not alone in thinking that he should be considered as a future world champion.

Within months, he had truly set the chess world alight. His short game against Marjanović at the 1980 Malta Olympiad saw a pattern emerge that was to become familiar to us. A pawn sacrifice in the opening gave him a strong initiative. Further sacrifices – this time of another pawn followed by a rook (which was declined) – announced the commencement of the attack on his opponent's king. A final sacrifice or two completed the demolition.

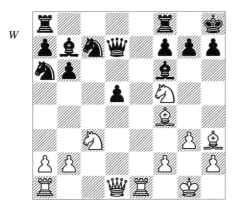

Kasparov – Marjanović
Olympiad, Malta 1980

We join the game as the attack is about to break. Notice how quickly Kasparov is able to bring his pieces to attacking squares.

17 ♘e4!
Exploiting the pin on the d-pawn, Kasparov sacrifices his b-pawn to bring this knight to g5.

17...♗xb2 18 ♘g5! ♛c6
Capturing the rook is fatal, as it allows the white queen to join the attack with decisive effect: 18...♗xa1 19 ♛h5 h6 20 ♘xh6! g6 21 ♘hxf7++ ♚g7 22 ♛h7+ ♚f6 23 ♘e4+! ♚e7 (or 23...dxe4 24 ♗g5#) 24 ♘e5+ and White mates.

19 ♘e7 ♛f6 20 ♘xh7!
A simple blow, as now 20...♚xh7 loses at once to 21 ♛h5+ winning the queen. Now that the king's position is breached, Kasparov's pieces rapidly finish the job.

20...♛d4 21 ♛h5 g6 22 ♛h4 ♗xa1 23 ♘f6+ 1-0
Black resigned, facing 23...♚g7 24 ♛h6+ ♚xf6 25 ♗g5#.

Throughout the following two decades, Kasparov regularly dismantled the world's top players in this fashion. He was not afraid to sacrifice in his world championship matches either, as Anand found out to his cost in his 1995 tilt at the PCA world title.

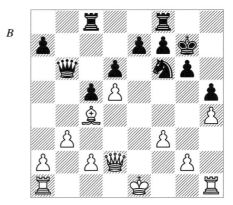

Anand – Kasparov
PCA World Ch (game 13), New York 1995

In situations such as this, White usually tries to build up pressure on the e7-pawn, which is backward on a half-open file. Kasparov sidesteps the anticipated pressure by sacrificing the e-pawn to open lines in the centre.

18...e5! 19 dxe6?

White would do better to decline the pawn and castle on the queenside, but with his natural play thwarted he would have few active prospects.

19...d5! 20 ♗e2

Not 20 ♗xd5, which loses a piece after 20...♖fd8 21 c4 fxe6.

20...c4!

Kasparov could still recapture the e-pawn, but he prefers to let it go in order to keep the e-file open. Instead, he busies himself with preventing White from castling.

21 c3?

Kasparov pointed out that White could keep lines closed more effectively by 21 ♖d1 c3 22 ♕d4.

21...♖ce8!

White is not going to castle on the queenside now, so Kasparov keeps both of his rooks on the kingside.

22 bxc4

Grabbing some material and hoping to survive the onslaught. 22 exf7 could lead to a pretty mating finish: 22...♖xf7 23 ♖f1 (23 ♔d1 is better, but White's position is hopeless after 23...♖fe7 24 ♖e1 d4! 25 cxd4 ♘d5) 23...♖fe7 24 ♖f2 ♖xe2+! 25 ♖xe2 ♕g1#.

22...♖xe6 23 ♔f1 ♖fe8 24 ♗d3 dxc4 25 ♗xc4

The black pieces are ready to finish the job, and Kasparov finds a lovely way to do it.

25...♘e4! 0-1

Unconcerned by the attack on his rook, Kasparov places his knight *en prise*. Anand resigned since although there are three ways to save his queen while preventing 26...♘g3#, they all lose:

a) 26 ♕e1 ♖d6! 27 fxe4 ♖f6+ 28 ♔e2 ♖xe4+ costs White his queen.

b) After 26 ♕d4+ ♕xd4 27 cxd4, the fork 27...♘d2+ wins the bishop.

c) 26 fxe4 ♖f6+ 27 ♔e1 ♖xe4+ 28 ♗e2 (28 ♔d1 ♖xc4 also wins for Black) 28...♕f2+ 29 ♔d1 ♖xe2 30 ♕xe2 ♖d6+ and White loses his queen.

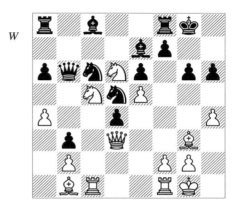

W

Kasparov – Piket
Tilburg 1997

Way back in the opening, Kasparov sacrificed a pawn for an initiative which has grown to threatening proportions.

First, note that Black has a threat here, namely 25...♘xe5!. For instance, if White pursues his attack with 25 h5, then Black can defend with 25...♘xe5! 26 ♗xe5 ♗xd6 27 ♗xd6 ♕xd6 28 hxg6 ♘f4 29 ♕e4 ♕b8!.

For that idea to work, Black must have his knight on c6 and his queen covering d6. Kasparov plays a pawn sacrifice that removes the threat by forcing either the queen or knight to move away.

25 a5! ♕xa5

If 25...♘xa5 then White can play 26 h5! with devastating effect since 26...♘b4, knocking the white queen away from covering the g6-square, allows 27 ♕xd4, which the knight had been preventing when it was on c6.

If White tries 26 h5 now, then 26...♘db4 is an awkward reply. Now is the time for the big breakthrough sacrifice.

26 ♘xf7! ♖xf7 27 ♕xg6+ ♔f8

Since the queen has been diverted to a5, the c6-knight is unprotected, so 27...♖g7 loses back the piece to 28 ♕e8+ ♗f8 29 ♕xc6.

28 ♘xe6+ ♗xe6 29 ♖xc6!

With the added participation of the rook, Kasparov's attack is overwhelming.

29...♗d7 30 ♕xh6+ 1-0

Once again, the speed of White's attack is striking. It is all over because 30...♖g7 31 ♖g6 wins the pinned rook, while 30...♔g8 31 ♖g6+ and 30...♔e8 31 e6 ♗xc6 32 exf7+ ♔d7 (or 32...♔xf7 33 ♕g6+ ♔f8 34 ♕xc6) 33 ♗f5+ ♔d8 34 ♕h8+ lead to mate.

Kasparov is able to turn his initiative into victory with such speed largely thanks to the depth and thoroughness of his analysis, fuelled by a fertile imagination. His thoroughness enables him to find quick wins where others might not even bother to seek one.

Consider the position in the next diagram. Kasparov has an obvious positional advantage, but can he exploit the weakness of the black kingside? I remember seeing the position at a training session for juniors. Even though everyone knew that there was a combination here, no one could even see a feasible sacrifice for White, let alone a quick win.

26 h6!!

The obvious starting point, and, arguably, not worthy of exclamation marks. But without it, the combination doesn't work, and already we can see some nice points.

26...♕e5

It was possible for the juniors to work out that 26...♖g8 allows 27 ♖d8! threatening 27 ♕g7#. Since 27...♕g6 loses the e7-knight, the only reasonable defence is 27...♘g6, when 28 ♘d5! threatens 29 ♖xg8+ ♔xg8 30 ♕d8+ ♘f8 31 ♘f6+, so Black must start to give up material with 28...♖xd5 or 28...f6.

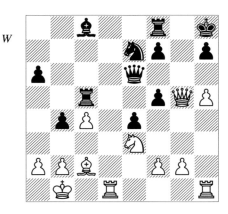

Kasparov – Lautier
Olympiad, Moscow 1994

Lautier's reply is the move that put everyone off. It covers g7 and threatens 27...♖g8. So what does Kasparov have in mind?

27 ♖h5!!

Can you see the point? Let me explain.

With both white and black queen and rook lined up on the fifth rank, Kasparov is threatening 28 ♘g4!, exploiting an unexpected pin on the f-pawn and knocking the queen off the diagonal that covers the g7-square. There are three defensive tries:

a) 27...♘g6 blocks the white queen's path to the g7-square, but then 28 ♖d8! threatens both 29 ♘g4 and 29 ♖xf8+ ♘xf8 30 ♕d8 ♔g8 31 ♖g5+ (the other point of bringing the rook to the fifth rank). Black's only defence is 28...♔g8, but then 29 ♘g4! fxg4 30 ♖xf8+ ♔xf8 31 ♕d8+ wins the c5-rook, since the queen must interpose.

b) 27...♘c6 is a clever defence that protects the queen on e5, but 28 ♘g4! still works, as after 28...fxg4, 29 ♕g7+ ♕xg7 30 hxg7+ ♔xg7 31 ♖xc5 again exploits the exposed position of the rook.

c) 27...♖g8, which Lautier played, and which seems to solve all of his problems.

27...♖g8 28 ♘g4!! 1-0

It comes anyway! Lautier resigned because he loses material in the attempt to avoid mate:

a) 28...fxg4 loses simply after 29 ♕xe5+ ♖xe5 30 ♖xe5.

b) 28...♕e6 loses control over g7, so 29 ♖d8! ♘g6 (or 29...♕g6 30 ♕xe7 fxg4 31 ♖xg8+ with mate to follow) 30 ♖xg8+ ♔xg8 31 ♕d8+ ♘f8 32 ♖g5+ wins the queen and then mates.

c) 28...♖xg5 seems to win a rook since 29 ♘xe5 can be met by 29...♖xh5, but it highlights a beautiful point of Kasparov's combination: White continues with 30 ♖d8+ ♘g8 31 ♘xf7#! If Black tries to get away with only the loss of the exchange by 29...♖xe5, then 30 ♖xg5 threatens mate by ♖d8+ and 30...♘c6 doesn't help because 31 ♗a4! is lethal.

The exercises feature two more of Kasparov's sudden finishes and a longer one.

Exercise 10

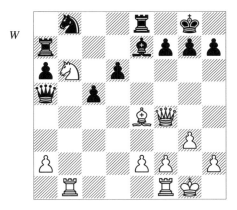

W

Level 1

Kasparov (White) is his customary pawn behind, but his opponent resigned after three moves. Kasparov's next move wins material thanks to the possibility of a mate threat on his second move.

Exercise 11

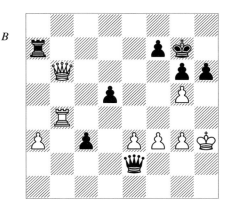

B

Level 2

Black (to play) has a passed c-pawn and an active queen. White threatens both 48 ♕xa7 and 48 ♕f6+ ♔h7 49 gxh6 ♔xh6 50 ♖h4#. However, Black has a pretty win. What is it?

Exercise 12

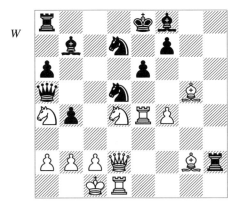

W

Level 3

White plays a typical Sicilian sacrifice, but the real surprise is his third move. Black's king and queen both come under attack.

The solutions start on page 213.

5 The Deadly Tactician's Make-Up

It will be clear from our study of some of the major tacticians in chess history that a great tactician needs highly advanced skills: tactical vision, imagination, intuition and calculating ability. Although we may not aspire to the phenomenal level of skills that our heroes have displayed, in this book we aim to develop our skills in each of these areas.

We shall develop vision, imagination and intuition, skills that are strongly linked, through study of sacrifices throughout the book, and in particular through building an understanding of hard-to-see sacrificial types in Part Two. The exercises and tests should help in improving calculating skills, and Part

Three also includes some useful advice on the subject.

The crucial element that we need to add is Motivation: the great tacticians *want* to sacrifice. They believe in the power of the sacrifice to win games, but most of all they are deeply fascinated with chess beauty. To become Deadly Tacticians, we need to believe in sacrifices too, and to love the chess beauty that they can help create.

I would go so far as to say that the great tacticians have a compulsion to create beauty. Tal often found, to his cost, that he endangered well-earned advantages in the pursuit of beauty. Alekhine and, especially, Kasparov have demonstrated greater restraint, but they have not entirely been immune and there is one episode from Alekhine's games that demonstrates how strong this 'beauty compulsion' can be.

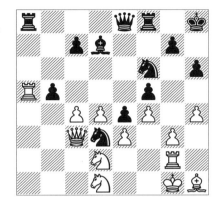

B

Bogoljubow – Alekhine
Hastings 1922

Alekhine fires the starting pistol on one of the most famous pawn-dashes in history.
29...b4! 30 ♖xa8 bxc3
This is given several exclamation marks by most authorities, including Kasparov. For sheer beauty, there is every justification.

Yet 30...♕xa8 wins more quickly and certainly. After 31 ♕b3 (or 31 ♕c2 ♘e1, winning the exchange) 31...♕a1 32 ♕b1 ♖a8, Black wins one of the knights stranded on the back rank. His work is over.

In *My Best Games of Chess 1908-1923* Alekhine states about 30...bxc3 "As will be seen, this continuation is much stronger than 30...♕xa8 31 ♕b3 ♗a4 32 ♕b1, after which White could still defend himself". The decisive 31...♕a1 (which threatens 32...♗a4) is really not that difficult to find. We are forced to the conclusion that the beauty of the pawn-dash, and the possibility of some neat play afterwards, blinded Alekhine to the extent that

he didn't look beyond it, either during play or when annotating the game.

In case you have not seen the rest of this magnificent game, here it is: **31 ♖xe8 c2! 32 ♖xf8+ ♔h7 33 ♘f2 c1♕+ 34 ♘f1 ♘e1! 35 ♖h2 ♕xc4 36 ♖b8 ♗b5 37 ♖xb5 ♕xb5 38 g4 ♘f3+ 39 ♗xf3 exf3 40 gxf5 ♕e2! 41 d5 ♔g8 42 h5 ♔h7 43 e4 ♘xe4 44 ♘xe4 ♕xe4 45 d6 cxd6 46 f6 gxf6 47 ♖d2 ♕e2 48 ♖xe2 fxe2 49 ♔f2 exf1♕+ 50 ♔xf1 ♔g7 51 ♔f2 ♔f7 52 ♔e3 ♔e6 53 ♔e4 d5+ 0-1**.

The Reflex Action

Another important element of motivation is the determination to avoid reflex actions. When our opponent attacks one of our pieces, we instinctively move it or defend it. When he threatens any action, we feel compelled to prevent it.

It is important to understand what our opponent is trying to do, but we don't always have to stop him. The reflex that obliges us to avoid material loss is very difficult to conquer. A recent personal example confirms the dangers of the materialist reflex action.

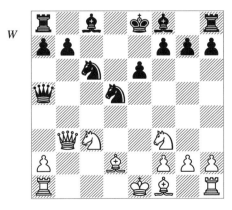

W

LeMoir – K. Richardson
Norfolk vs Surrey 2001

My two-pawn gambit has gone badly wrong, and Black is developing far too comfortably.

As anyone who has read my book *How to Be Lucky in Chess* will know, the natural (but not necessarily correct) thing for a player to do when he is a pawn or two ahead is to aim to bring the endgame closer by exchanging queens. In this position, Black can do that by moving his queen to a3 or b4. I was so sure that this was coming that I concentrated my attention on what I could do to gain from it.

After 11...♕a3 (say), I am free to capture the d5-knight with my own knight. Black takes my queen, and I can play a 'spite check' with the knight before recapturing the queen. As I analysed, I realized that this process drags the black king over to the queenside. I can take advantage of its absence from the kingside, and set up a potential ambush.

11 ♗b5

This is an important move: the bishop will capture on c6, which gives the f3-knight access to e5. It also threatens to regain a pawn by 12 ♘xd5, and so acts to confirm Black in the wisdom of his natural intentions.

11...♕a3?

As expected.

12 ♘xd5! ♕xb3 13 ♗xc6+ bxc6 14 ♘c7+ ♔d7 15 axb3 ♔xc7

The king has been dragged far away to a broken queenside, leaving f7 vulnerable to the white knight.

16 ♘e5 f6?

Here it is, the reflex action. Without stopping to analyse what White is trying to do, Black moves the attacked pawn.

16...♗e7, resisting the reflex, is the only way to give himself winning chances. After 17 ♘xf7 ♖f8 18 ♘e5 ♗f6 19 ♗c3, White has some compensation for his pawn thanks to the broken black pawns, but it's probably not enough.

17 ♗a5+

This forces the reply, as 17...♔d6 loses a rook to 18 ♘f7+.

17...♔b7 18 ♘f7 ♖g8 19 ♘d8+

This is the position that I foresaw before 11 ♗b5. Surely Black must play 19...♔b8, allowing perpetual check by 20 ♘xc6+, etc.?

19...♔a6?!

A reckless decision. Black allows his king to be forced up the board, and I begin to dream of mate.

20 ♗c7+ ♔b5 21 ♖a5+ ♔b4 22 ♘xc6+?

Another reflex action, and this time it is me who is guilty. When our play has forced a win of material, especially with check, it is natural to take it. Keres once said that when he found a good move, he would keep analysing in order to find a better one. I should have done that here.

22 ♔d2! is the move, squeezing the black king for room. After 22...♗d7 (not 22...♔xb3 23 ♖b1+ ♔c4 24 ♖a4+ ♔d5 25 ♔c3!, mating) 23 ♔c2! threatening 24 ♖ha1 and 25 ♖1a4#, Black is hard pressed to avoid defeat.

22...♔c3!

22...♔xb3 is disastrous in view of 23 ♔d2 e5 24 ♖b1+ ♔c4 25 ♖c1+ ♔b3 26 ♖c3+ ♔b2 27 ♖b5+ ♔a2 28 ♖c2+ ♔a3 29 ♔c3. Instead, the black king moves into the space that should have been occupied by the white king, and uses the white b-pawn as shelter.

Having missed my chance, I soon agreed a draw.

23 ♔e2 ♗b7 24 ♖c1+ ♔b2 25 ♔d2!? ♗xc6 26 ♖c2+ ♔b1 27 ♖c1+ ♔b2 28 ♖c2+ ♔b1 ½-½

6 Material Matters

Deadly Tacticians know that material has its uses: for instance to give up in return for something more useful. We must instil in ourselves a healthy disrespect for material things. That should help us to seek sacrificial opportunities and to avoid damaging reflex actions.

Deadly Tacticians know that pawns are there to be sacrificed. Although we should always seek a return on our investment, it is nonetheless true that even being a pawn down for nothing is not necessarily fatal.

Deadly Tacticians know that a minor piece can often be better than a rook, especially if an extra pawn is thrown in. They also appreciate

that a queen can be overpowered by an apparently inferior force.

We are accustomed to seeing minor pieces being given away, but we are about to see some examples of pawn, exchange and queen sacrifices. The examples are all 'real' sacrifices, the description given by Spielmann to sacrifices that are impossible for the players to analyse out to a definite conclusion. The sacrificer has to judge, guess or hope that his sacrifice will succeed.

The examples illustrate just some of the ways in which such sacrifices can be used. The examples demonstrate that pawns can profitably be dispensed with, rooks can struggle against minor pieces, and that queens are not always all-powerful. In short, material isn't everything.

The Expendable Pawn

I am excluding standard gambits from this discussion, but some pawn sacrifices are played so early in the game that they are practically gambits.

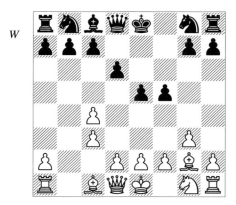

Hodgson – Psakhis
Metz 1994

6 c5!?

This move may have been prepared at home, since the diagram position had been reached before. Hodgson has in mind a follow-up sacrifice that blows a big hole in the centre through which the two white bishops can fire into the heart of the black position.

6...dxc5 7 ♗a3 ♕d6

A later game Lang-Ploehn, Bavaria 1998 saw the improvement 7...♘a6, and although White eventually won, it was somewhat unconvincing.

8 d4!? exd4 9 cxd4 ♕xd4

The second pawn sacrifice has blasted the position open for the white bishops. Psakhis

was soon in trouble, and Hodgson won as follows:

10 ♕c1! ♕f6 11 ♘h3 ♘d7 12 0-0 ♘e7 13 ♗b2 ♕f7 14 e4 0-0 15 ♘g5 ♕g6 16 exf5 ♖xf5 17 ♖e1 ♘d5 18 h4 ♘7b6 19 ♕xc5 c6 20 ♗e4 h6 21 ♘f3 ♘a4 22 ♕c2 ♘xb2 23 ♘d4 ♘e7 24 ♕xb2 ♕f7 25 ♘xf5 ♘xf5 26 ♗c2 c5 27 ♕b5 ♗e6 28 ♕xc5 ♖c8 29 ♕xc8+ ♗xc8 1-0

Most pawn sacrifices come later than move six. In the opening, they tend to be aimed at gaining time for development and open lines for the pieces. This one by Tal is typical, and rapidly results in a deadly attack.

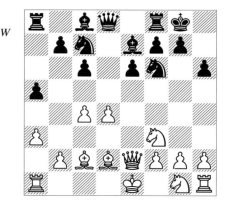

Tal – Speelman
Interzonal tournament, Subotica 1987

14 ♘e5! ♕xd4 15 ♗c3 ♕d8 16 ♘gf3

By sacrificing his d-pawn, White has obtained a big lead in development, which enables him to mount a very quick assault on the black king.

16...♘ce8 17 g4 b5 18 g5! hxg5 19 ♘xg5 ♖a6 20 ♕f3 b4 21 ♕h3! g6

Mate follows the capture of the bishop: 21...bxc3 22 ♗h7+ ♔h8 23 ♘exf7+ ♖xf7 24 ♘xf7#.

22 ♗xg6! bxc3

This time capturing the other bishop is instantly fatal: 22...fxg6 23 ♘xg6 ♔g7 24 ♕h7#. Tal now crashes through.

23 ♘exf7 ♕d2+ 24 ♔f1 ♖xf7 25 ♗xf7+ ♔g7 26 ♖g1 ♕xg5 27 ♖xg5+ ♔xf7 28 bxc3 e5 1-0

It occasionally happens that a pawn sacrifice can transform an awkward position by freeing important lines and squares. Witness the transformation that Judit Polgar achieved as a result of an apparently simple pawn sacrifice in the next position.

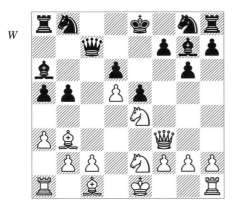

J. Polgar – Shirov
Donner Memorial, Amsterdam 1995

The game is still in the opening phase. Black is slightly behind in development, but his position appears solid while White's pieces are not particularly active. That all changes with a little pawn sacrifice.

12 c4! bxc4 13 ♗a4+

The pawn sacrifice releases the bishop, which helps the other white pieces to become more active.

13...♘d7 14 ♘2c3 ♔e7?

This allows a very nice breakthrough sacrifice of a knight. However, it is hard to find a move that is entirely without its problems:

a) 14...f5 15 ♘g5 eyes the e6-square.

b) 14...♘e7 allows invasion by 15 ♘f6+ ♗xf6 16 ♕xf6.

c) After 14...h6!? 15 ♘b5 ♗xb5 16 ♗xb5 f5 17 ♘d2 ♘gf6 18 ♗c6 White regains the pawn with an active position.

d) The best move may be 14...♖b8, as it prevents ♘b5 and takes the rook away from the white queen's diagonal.

15 ♘xd6! ♕xd6

After 15...♔xd6?, 16 ♘e4+ nudges Black's king out for a final short walk: 16...♔xd5 (16...♔e7 loses the queen after 17 d6+) 17 ♕xf7+ ♔xe4 18 ♗c2+ ♔d4 19 ♗e3#.

16 ♘e4 ♕xd5

16...♕b6 17 d6+ ♔f8 18 ♘g5 costs Black the a8-rook.

17 ♗g5+ ♘df6 18 ♖d1 ♕b7 19 ♖d7+ ♕xd7 20 ♗xd7 h6?

Black collapses, but White has a clear advantage after 20...♗b7 21 ♗a4.

21 ♕d1! 1-0

21...hxg5 leads to a nice mating sequence: 22 ♕d6+ ♔d8 23 ♗b5+ ♔c8 24 ♕c6+ ♔b8 25 ♕b6+ ♗b7 (or 25...♔c8 26 ♘d6#) 26 ♘d6 ♖a7 27 ♕d8+ ♗c8 28 ♕xc8#.

Pawn sacrifices often have positional motives. They can be used to weaken pawns or squares in the opposing camp, to eliminate important defensive pieces, to grab a strategically important line, and so on. The pawn sacrifice played by Nimzowitsch in the next example (*see diagram on following page*) led to an almost complete paralysis of Ståhlberg's position and the creation of a passed pawn that the defender simply could not blockade for long.

Ståhlberg is being pressed back, but his last move was 26 ♘e2-g1, intending to continue 27 ♘f3 followed by 28 ♘e5. Nimzowitsch's reply cuts out that possibility.

26...f4! 27 exf4 ♖e4 28 g3 ♕b5

Now the knight cannot emerge at f3 without allowing ...♖e2, and if White plays 29

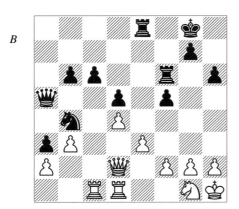

Ståhlberg – Nimzowitsch
Match (game 1), Gothenburg 1934

♖e1, the knight will jump into d3 – 29...♘d3 – and Black can open an attack on the white king after 30 ♖xe4 dxe4 31 ♖c3 g5!?. Ståhlberg avoids that possibility by covering the d3-square before challenging on the e-file, but he gives Nimzowitsch time to create a decisive trump – a passed d-pawn.

29 ♖c3 c5! 30 dxc5 bxc5 31 ♖dc1 ♖c6 32 ♖e3 ♖ce6 33 ♖xe4

33 ♖ec3 fails to achieve a repetition since 33...♖d4! unexpectedly traps the white queen. Challenging on the e-file with 33 ♖ce1 also allows 33...♖d4!, with the result that the white a-pawn cannot be saved:

a) 34 ♕xd4 cxd4 35 ♖xe6 ♘xa2 followed by the capture of the b-pawn and the advance of the black a-pawn.

b) 34 ♕e2 ♖xe2 35 ♖1xe2 ♖xe3 36 fxe3 (or 36 ♖xe3 ♖d2) 36...♖d1 followed by ...♖a1.

33...♖xe4 34 f3 ♖e8 35 ♖e1 ♖xe1 36 ♕xe1 ♕d7 37 ♕c1 d4!

The passed pawn advances, and there is nothing White can do to stop it.

38 ♘e2

Against 38 ♕xc5, Black can continue pushing the d-pawn with 38...d3 39 ♕xb4 d2.

38...♕b5

Possibly influenced by time-trouble, Nimzowitsch invites a repetition of position.

Black could play the decisive 38...d3 39 ♘c3 d2 40 ♕d1 ♘xa2! (40...♕d3 also wins, but less prettily) 41 ♘xa2 (or 41 ♘b1 ♘c3! 42 ♘xc3 ♕d4 followed by ...a2) 41...♕d4, when White is helpless against the dual threats of 42...♕f2 and 42...♕b2.

39 ♕e1

After 39 ♕d2, Black can exchange queens with 39...♕d3! 40 ♕xd3 ♘xd3 as 41 ♔g2 ♘b4 42 ♘c1 d3 wins the knight for Black. Instead, White could play 39 ♘g1, but 39...♕d7 would repeat position in readiness for 40 ♘e2 d3, as in the previous note.

39...♕d3 40 ♘c1 ♕xf3+ 41 ♔g1 ♔f7 42 ♕f2 ♕e4 43 ♕f1 d3 44 ♕d1 ♕e3+ 45 ♔g2 d2 0-1

After 46 ♘e2 ♘d3 there is no defence to ...♘b2, forcing the pawn home.

A pawn can be a small price to pay for an open file leading to the opponent's castled king, as Kramnik will now demonstrate.

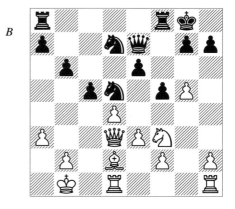

Gelfand – Kramnik
European Clubs Cup, Berlin 1996

18...b5! 19 ♕xb5 ♖ab8 20 ♕a5 ♖b3 21 ♔a2 ♖fb8 22 ♖b1 e5! 23 ♖hc1

The black queen cannot be kept out of the attack. After 23 dxe5 ♞xe5 24 ♞xe5 ♛xe5 25 ♝c3 ♞xc3+ 26 bxc3 ♛e4! 27 ♜bc1 ♜b2+ 28 ♚a1 ♛c4, mate is forced.

23...♛e6! 24 ♚a1 exd4 25 ♜xc5 ♞xc5 26 ♛xc5

Gelfand's ingenious exchange sacrifice has generated the awkward threat of 27 ♞xd4, forking queen and rook, a threat which Kramnik gloriously ignores.

26...♞c3! 27 ♞xd4 ♜xb2!! 28 ♜xb2 ♛a2+!! 0-1

It's a lovely mate after 29 ♜xa2 ♜b1#.

Pawn sacrifices are often played to prevent castling. Here is a very clever manoeuvre by Hodgson.

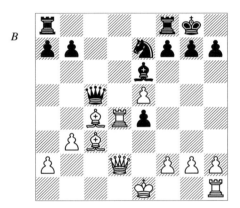

Schmittdiel – Hodgson
Bad Wörishofen 1994

White is threatening to capture the weak black e-pawn, and Hodgson doesn't want to be driven back onto the defensive. His next move is designed to keep the initiative at the cost of a pawn, but there is also a hidden idea behind it.

18...♞f5! 19 ♜xe4 ♜fd8 20 ♛b2

After 20 ♛c2 ♜ac8, White cannot castle yet because after 21 0-0?, 21...b5 22 ♝xe6

fxe6 23 ♜c1 ♛xc3! wins a piece thanks to back-rank mate.

20...♛c6! 21 f3

Retreating the rook loses the g-pawn, while 21 ♛c2 ♜ac8 renews the threat of 22...b5. However, this pawn move opens a diagonal that White would definitely prefer to keep closed.

21...♛c5!

That's it! The white king cannot castle and soon comes within the reach of the black pieces.

22 ♚e2 ♝d5 23 ♝xd5 ♛xd5 24 ♜c1 ♜ac8 25 ♝e1 ♛b5+ 26 ♚f2 ♛b6+ 27 ♚e2 ♛h6 28 ♜xc8 ♜xc8 29 h4 ♛a6+ 30 ♚f2 ♛b6+ 31 ♚e2 ♛g1! 32 ♝f2 ♛xg2 33 ♜g4 ♛h2 34 ♚d3 h5 35 ♜g5 ♛f4 36 ♛e2 ♛c1 37 ♚e4 g6 38 ♛d3 ♜e8 39 ♛c4 ♞d6+ 0-1

As in the opening, pawn sacrifices in the middlegame can serve to gain time for the development of an attack. In the next example, Larry Christiansen mysteriously offers a pawn that will take White a little time to capture. By the time the pawn is in the box, Black is ready for a nasty long-term sacrifice that seriously exposes his opponent's king.

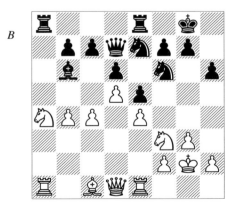

Hector – Christiansen
Reykjavik 1998

17...≜d4!? 18 ♘xd4 exd4 19 b5 ♘g6 20 f3 ♘e5 21 ♕xd4 ♘xf3!?

Here it is.

22 ♔xf3 ♕h3!

This quiet move strands the white king in the centre. The king will just manage to survive, but the passed pawn that Black gains in the process leads to a winning endgame.

23 ≜b2 ♖e7 24 ♘c3 ♖ae8 25 ♕g1 ♘g4 26 ♔e2 ♘xh2 27 ♔d3

Natural moves also bring problems. For instance, 27 ♔d1 ♘f3 28 ♕f1 ♕g4! 29 ♕e2 ♕xg3 30 ♖f1 ♘d4 31 ♕d2 ♖xe4! is a quick win for Black.

27...f5!?

Black shuns the chance to regain an exchange. He prefers to increase the pressure on the white position, which eventually cracks under the strain.

28 ♕f2 ♘g4 29 ♕g1 f4 30 ♔c2 fxg3 31 ♕h1 ♘h2 32 ♖e3 ♖f8 33 ♖g1 ♖f1! 34 ♖xf1 ♕xf1 35 ♕xf1 ♘xf1 36 ♖f3 g2 37 ♘e2 ♖xe4 38 ♘g1 ♖xc4+ 39 ♔d3 ♖c5 40 ♖f2 ♖xd5+ 41 ≜d4 c5 42 bxc6 bxc6 43 ♖xg2 c5 44 ♖xg7+ ♔f8 45 ♘e2 ♖xd4+ 46 ♘xd4 ♔xg7

...and Black won the knight and pawn ending.

The pawn sacrifice played by Capablanca in the following game is very odd (*see next diagram*). It appears that the position is heading for a draw. Rooks are likely to be exchanged and the pawn-structure is symmetrical. As far as I can tell, Capablanca's sacrifice simply aims at avoiding an early draw. In the end, his courage and patience are rewarded.

15...≜a3!? 16 ♘xe5 ≜xb2 17 ♕xb2 ♘xe5 18 ♕xe5 ♕a3

Black exerts some pressure on the dark squares. White will not be able to occupy the c-file, so Black can keep at least one pair of rooks on the board.

19 ♘e3 ♘g4 20 ♘xg4 ≜xg4 21 h3 ≜e6 22 ♖e2 ♖fd8 23 ♕b2 ♕c5 24 ♖d2 ♖xd2 25 ♕xd2 b6 26 ♖d1 g6 27 ♕e2 a5

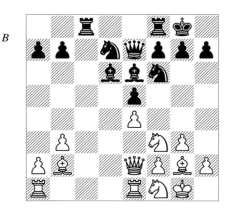

Kevitz – Capablanca
New York 1931

Another point begins to emerge. Black will attack the queenside pawns, tying down the white pieces.

28 ♔h2 b5 29 f4 a4 30 bxa4 bxa4 31 ♖d2 a3

White still has a healthy extra pawn. If he exchanges queens by 32 ♕f2 ♕xf2 33 ♖xf2 there is a draw by repetition after 33...♖b8 (threatening 34...♖b2) 34 ♖f3 ♖a8 35 ♖f2, etc. Kevitz presumably wants to win, and decides upon a kingside pawn advance. He soon regrets it.

32 g4? g5! 33 ♕f2?!

He finds that 33 f5 ♕e5+ 34 ♔h1 (not 34 ♔g1 ♖c1+ 35 ♖d1 ♕d4+, winning the pinned rook) 34...♖c1+ 35 ♖d1 ♕a1! 36 ♖xc1 ♕xc1+ 37 ♔h2 ≜c4! 38 ♕f2 ♕f4+! leaves him helpless to stop the black a-pawn. The calm 33 ♕f3 is safe for White, but Kevitz panics. The queen exchange line is no longer the same as in the last note, as Black can use the threat of an exchange of rooks to force the win of the a-pawn.

33...♕xf2 34 ♖xf2 gxf4 35 ♖f3

35 ♖xf4 loses to 35...≜xa2.

35...♖a8 36 ♖f2 f3! 37 ≜f1

37 ≜xf3 ♖b8 38 ♔g3 ♖b2 wins for Black.

37...♖b8 38 ♖xf3?

There is a better defence in 38 ♗d3!, with the point 38...♖b2 39 ♖xb2 axb2 40 ♗b1.

38...♖b2+ 39 ♔g3 ♖xa2 40 ♖c3 ♖a1 0-1

If you like a bit of mystery in your sacrifices, try this one by Jovanka Houska.

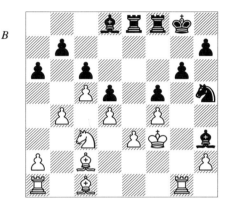

B

Sashikiran – J. Houska
British Ch, Scarborough 1999

There is an Elo rating gap of nearly 300 points in White's favour, but Houska rocks her Indian adversary with a stunning pawn sacrifice.

27...h6!!

"Here, have a pawn with check." Houska's idea is to get her rooks to the g-file before White can complete his development. If the pawn is declined, Black is able to follow up with ...g5, putting the white king in some danger.

28 ♖xg6+ ♔h7 29 ♖g1 ♖g8 30 ♗d2 ♔h8 31 ♘e2?

White can draw by 31 ♖xg8+ ♖xg8 32 ♗e1 ♗g4+ 33 ♔f2 ♗h3 34 ♔f3 ♗g4+, etc. In attempting to win, Sashikiran overlooks a trick.

31...♗g4+ 32 ♔f2 ♗h4+ 33 ♖g3

After the intended 33 ♘g3, 33...♘xf4! wins back the pawn with a better position, since accepting the knight offer by 34 exf4 ♖e2+ 35 ♔f1 ♖xd2 36 ♗d1 ♗h3+ 37 ♔e1 ♖xh2 costs White at least a piece.

33...♗xe2 34 ♔xe2 ♗xg3 35 hxg3 ♘xg3+

...and Black won with her extra exchange and passed h-pawn.

We should not shy away from playing pawn sacrifices. Even if a pawn sacrifice fails, there is no need to panic. It is very hard to win with an extra pawn unless it is possible to exchange into a simple endgame. It often happens that the player with the extra pawn starts to play very badly through laziness, over-confidence or confusion.

To get you into the habit of thinking about pawn sacrifices and the kinds of compensation that they can offer, here are a few exercises.

Exercise 13

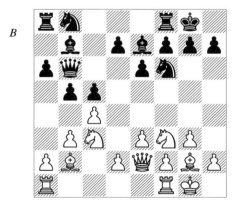

B

Level 1

Black plays a pawn sacrifice to gain control of the centre, which he is later able to exploit to build a big attack. What is it?

Exercise 14

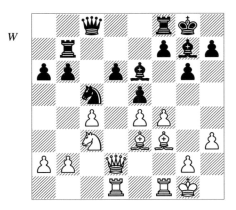

Level 2

What pawn sacrifice does White play here, and why? Think carefully about the reason for the sacrifice; for instance, what is White's intended follow-up move?

Exercise 15

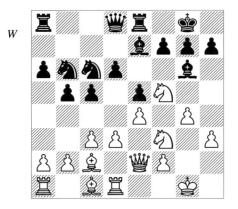

Level 3

White plays a long-term pawn sacrifice. In itself, it is not hard to see, but what are some of the ideas for following it up?

The solutions start on page 214.

The Out-Gunned Rook

The table of material values says that a minor piece is worth approximately three pawns, while a rook is worth five. As a result, we tend to flinch when our rook is attacked by a minor piece, and we shy away from exposing it to danger, keeping it tucked away on the first two ranks until we reach the endgame and the comparative safety of a half-empty board.

We are well aware that exchange sacrifices are possible. Many a famous old master's game features the opponent searching for rooks in the corner, allowing the master's pieces time and space to administer a quick and brilliant mate. Positional exchange sacrifices were not unknown either. Didn't Staunton once gum up St Amant's position by placing his rook on the fifth rank where a bishop could capture it, and gain a big space advantage when his pawn recaptured? Oh yes, and Botvinnik, Petrosian and Karpov have played a few successful exchange sacrifices. But it is never possible in our games, is it?

Well, look at the examples below, and ask yourself whether that is true.

Botvinnik's sacrifice against Liublinsky (*see diagram on following page*) is similar in effect to Staunton's, and shows how a rook can be completely starved of room if there are no open files.

25...♖d4!

Black throws his rook into the hole at d4.

26 ♘e2 ♗c8 27 ♘xd4 cxd4

Commentators have suggested that White would do better to capture with the bishop so that the knight can take up the good blockading square at d3. On the other hand, White probably feared that he would pay for having no dark-squared bishop.

As the game goes, White is no better off, as he can only sit and watch the black pawns and pieces overrunning his kingside.

28 ♗f2 c5 29 ♖f1 f5 30 ♗g3 ♗d7 31 ♖ad1 f4 32 ♗f2 g5 33 g4 fxg3 34 ♗xg3 ♗h3 35

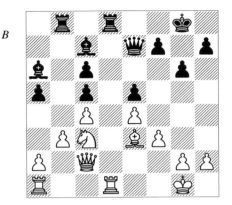

Liublinsky – Botvinnik
Moscow Ch 1943

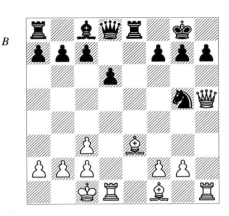

Kupreichik – Yusupov
USSR Ch, Vilnius 1980/1

♖f2 h5 36 ♖fd2 h4 37 ♗f2 ♖f8 38 ♖d3 ♖f4 39 ♔h1 ♔h7 40 ♖g1

Even the g-file brings no joy for the rooks, as there is no square beyond the first rank that is safe. Black is able to prise open the neighbouring f-file, where the white rooks have little influence, to force his way in.

40...♗d8 41 ♕e2 ♕f7 42 ♕d1 ♕h5 43 ♗e3 ♕xf3+ 44 ♕xf3 ♖xf3 45 ♗xg5 ♖xd3 46 ♗xd8 ♖e3 47 ♗b6 ♖xe4 48 ♗xc5 ♖e2 49 ♖d1 ♗g4 50 h3 ♗xh3 51 b4 ♗f5 52 ♗d6 d3 53 bxa5 h3 0-1

The principle of depriving the rooks of open lines is followed in most positional exchange sacrifices. In the following diagram, Yusupov even avoided picking up a second pawn for the exchange in order to keep lines closed.

Black's most obvious defence to White's kingside threats is 14...h6, but White can play 15 ♗d4 ♘e6 16 ♗xg7! ♘xg7 17 ♕xh6 f5 18 ♖d3 ♔f7 19 ♖g3 with a strong attack. Yusupov's solution is to sacrifice his rook for the bishop before it can do any damage.

14...♖xe3! 15 fxe3 ♕e7 16 ♗c4 h6!?

Yusupov plays it positionally. Rather than capture the pawn, opening another line for the

white rooks, he prepares to batten down the white e- and g-pawns, demonstrating that his knight is in no way inferior to a rook. In the end, Kupreichik is frustrated into giving back the exchange, but Black is able to simplify to a winning rook and pawn endgame.

17 ♖he1 ♗e6 18 ♕h4 ♖e8 19 ♕d4 a6 20 ♗d5 c5 21 ♕d3 ♗xd5 22 ♕xd5 ♘e4 23 ♖f1 ♕c7 24 ♖f5 g6 25 ♖f4 ♖e5 26 ♕d3 ♕e7 27 a4 ♕e6 28 ♔b1 h5 29 c4 g5 30 ♖f3 h4 31 ♕b3 ♕d7 32 ♕b6 ♔g7 33 ♖d3 f6 34 ♖f1 ♖e7 35 ♖fd1 ♕g4!? 36 ♖xd6 ♘xd6 37 ♕xd6 ♖f7 38 ♖d2 ♕xc4 39 b3 ♕c3 40 ♖d3 ♕e5 41 ♕d8 ♕c7 42 ♕d5 ♕c6 43 ♔c1 ♕xd5 44 ♖xd5 g4 45 ♔d2 ♔g6 46 ♔e2 ♖h7 47 ♔f2 ♖h5 48 e4 ♖e5 49 ♔e3 h3 50 gxh3 gxh3 51 ♔f2 ♖g5 52 ♖d3 h2 53 ♖d1 ♖g1 0-1

It isn't imperative to have a lot of fixed pawns to keep the rooks quiet. In the following diagram, the potential mobility of the sacrificer's own pawns does the job.

28 ♖xd4! cxd4 29 ♕xd4

Whilst it is not fixed, Black's d-pawn isn't going anywhere, and he must be on the lookout for the e5 thrust. Meanwhile, his a-pawn is weak and there are no open files for his rooks.

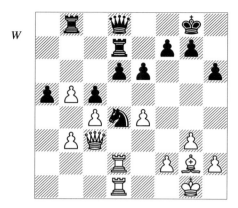

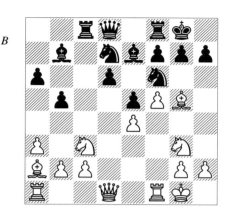

Bogoljubow – Nimzowitsch
Berlin 1927

Ermenkov – Portisch
European Team Ch, Skara 1980

Stuck for a plan, Nimzowitsch becomes frustrated, lets the a-pawn go, and allows the white pawns to run riot.

29...♖bb7 30 ♖a1 ♕c7 31 ♗f1 ♕c5 32 ♕e3 ♔f8 33 ♖xa5 ♖a7 34 b4 ♕xe3 35 fxe3 e5 36 ♗h3 ♖e7 37 b6 ♖ab7 38 c5 ♖e8 39 ♖a6 1-0

39...♖eb8 loses a rook to 40 c6 ♖xb6 41 c7.

So, exchange sacrifices can work by limiting the activity of the opponent's rooks. The other side of the coin is sacrifices that activate minor pieces and create weaknesses that the minor pieces can exploit. A typical example is the ...♖xc3 sacrifice in the Sicilian. In the Dragon Sicilian, if White has castled queenside, the sacrifice transforms the white king's neat three-pawn cover into an untidy collection of isolated and doubled isolated pawns, and the king often comes under heavy attack as a result.

It occurs less often in other Sicilian formations, but I recall it happening three times in the same tournament – the European Team Championship in Skara, 1980. One game by Portisch showed how Black can create chances on both sides of the board.

14...♖xc3! 15 bxc3 ♘xe4 16 ♘xe4 ♗xe4 17 ♗xe7 ♕xe7

A Sicilian player's dream: one pawn for the exchange, the white c-pawns are doubled and the f-pawn is vulnerable, and Black's centre pawns are potentially mobile. The black bishop is powerful, too, and if White now tries to eliminate it by 18 ♗d5, then after 18...♘f6! 19 ♗xe4 ♘xe4 the front c-pawn will disappear. Instead, White tries to eliminate some queenside pawns.

18 c4 ♖c8! 19 ♕e2 ♘f6! 20 ♖ac1 h5!

After a ...♖xc3 sacrifice, it is normally White whose queenside pawns are threatened. Here it is Black, and he chooses to sacrifice a pawn rather than waste time defending them. He uses the time gained to whip up a sudden and very strong kingside attack.

21 cxb5 axb5 22 ♕xb5 ♕a7+ 23 ♔h1 h4 24 ♕b3 ♘g4 25 h3 ♘e3 26 ♖g1 ♘xf5 27 ♔h2 d5 28 c4 ♖b8 29 ♕c3 ♕f2! 30 ♕xe5 ♖b2 31 cxd5 ♕xg2+! 32 ♖xg2 ♖xg2+ 33 ♔h1 ♘g3+ 0-1

Another ...♖xc3 sacrifice from the same event deserves our attention, although this time White's response allows Black to turn it into a brilliant short-term combination rather than a long-term sacrifice.

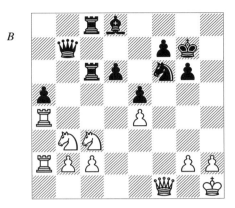

Lechtynsky – Marjanović
European Team Ch, Skara 1980

26...♖xc3! 27 bxc3 ♘xe4 28 ♕f3

After 28 ♖a1 ♖xc3, Black has excellent long-term compensation for the exchange in two pawns and a potential kingside attack starting with ...♗b6. Now, however, he is able to land a couple of huge blows based on White's weak back rank. The knight and the queen will both be sacrificed.

28...♖xc3! 29 ♕xe4 ♕xb3!!

The point is 30 cxb3 ♖c1+, mating. Now Black has two pawns for the exchange, but it is his deadly kingside attack that wins the game.

30 g3 ♕b1+ 31 ♔g2 ♗b6 32 ♕e2 ♕g1+ 33 ♔h3 ♖e3 34 ♕g2 ♕d1 35 ♖h4 ♖e2 0-1

Similar exchange sacrifices can be made on other squares. Sacrifices against knights at f6 often result in doubled f-pawns for Black in front of his king. Another popular pawn-doubling sacrifice occurs against kingside fianchetto structures where Black has pawns on e7, f7, g6 and h7, and a bishop on e6. If the e-file is open, an exchange sacrifice on e6 can

be very effective, as the doubled e-pawns restrict Black's position and are easy targets for the white pieces.

On the subject of fianchetto structures, another typical theme for exchange sacrifices is to enhance (for its owner) or eliminate (for the opponent) a fianchettoed bishop.

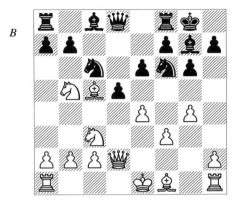

Kochiev – Miles
World Junior Ch, Manila 1974

Kochiev has spent valuable time manoeuvring his bishop to c5. Miles decides to let the threatened rook go, partly because his fianchettoed bishop becomes very powerful when its opposite number disappears, but also because the time gained allows him to go straight onto the attack.

11...a6! 12 ♗xf8 ♔xf8 13 exd5 exd5 14 ♘a3 b5 15 ♘d1 b4 16 ♘b1 ♗xg4! 17 ♗g2!

Capturing the bishop allows the black pieces to run riot: 17 fxg4 ♘e4 18 ♕e3 ♕h4+ 19 ♔e2 ♘d4+ 20 ♔d3 ♘c5+ 21 ♔d2 and now 21...♗h6 demonstrates the monstrous power of the dark-squared bishop.

17...♕e7+ 18 ♕e3 ♘e4! 19 fxe4

In *Informator*, Marjanović gives the variation 19 c3 ♕h4+ 20 ♔f1 ♖e8 21 fxg4 d4 as an improvement over the game. After 22 ♕e2 dxc3, I'll give just a couple of lines that show

how powerful the bishop becomes as the position opens up:

a) 23 ♗xe4 cxb2 24 ♘xb2 ♗xb2! 25 ♕xb2 ♖xe4 26 ♕f2 ♕h3+ 27 ♕g2 ♕d3+ and Black mates in a few moves.

b) 23 bxc3 ♘xc3 24 ♕f2 ♕xg4 25 ♕c5+ ♔g8 26 ♘bxc3 bxc3 27 ♗xc6 (or 27 ♕xc6 ♕e2+ 28 ♔g1 ♗d4+, mating) 27...♕e2+ 28 ♔g1 ♖e5 29 ♕xe5 ♗xe5 and the queen, bishop and c-pawn will polish the game off quickly.

Black is also doing well after 19 fxg4 ♗d4 20 ♕h6+ ♔g8, as 21 ♘e3 (to avoid the discovered check) allows the simple 21...♘f6, regaining the piece with a strong attack.

After the move played, Black picks up a pawn at once and soon forces material gains by making his d-pawn passed.

19...♗xd1 20 ♘d2 ♗xc2 21 ♖c1 d4 22 ♕h3 d3 23 0-0 ♔g8 24 e5 ♖d8 25 e6 fxe6 26 ♖ce1 ♘d4 27 ♔h1 ♘f5 28 ♖e4 ♕g5 29 ♘f3 ♕h6 30 ♖h4 ♕e3 31 ♖xb4 d2 32 ♘xd2 ♕xh3 33 ♗xh3 ♖xd2

...and White lasted 13 more moves before resigning.

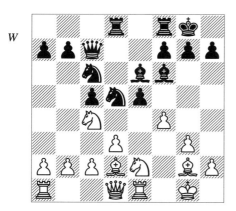

Conquest – Nunn
Lloyds Bank Masters, London 1993

Conquest tries to grab space with his next move, but Nunn prefers to offer the exchange to remove the fianchettoed white bishop and leave his own light-squared bishop unopposed.

13 f5 ♗xf5! 14 ♗xd5 ♖xd5 15 ♘e3 ♕d7 16 ♘xd5 ♕xd5 17 ♘c3 ♕d7 18 ♗e3 ♘d4 19 ♗xd4 ♕xd4+

Now Black has two unopposed bishops, and the white king cannot expect to survive the coming attack.

20 ♔g2 ♗d7 21 ♕e2 ♗c6+ 22 ♔f1 ♕d7 23 ♔g1 e4! 24 dxe4 ♗d4+ 25 ♔g2 f5 26 ♖f1 ♖e8 27 ♖ae1 b5 28 ♕h5 g6 29 ♕g5 b4 30 ♘d1 ♗xe4+ 31 ♔h3 ♔g7 32 c3 ♗f6 33 ♕c1 f4+ 34 g4 ♕d3+ 0-1

Exchange sacrifices can be distinctly more complex than those that we have seen so far. The sacrificer can look for compensation in the initiative, an attack, open lines, a strong pawn-centre and a myriad of other factors. Here are two dynamic examples.

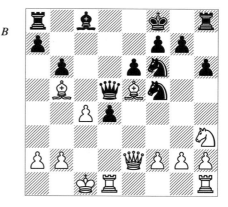

Shirov – Ivanchuk
Linares 1998

Black is a pawn ahead, but he cannot castle, and his queen is being knocked about. Ivanchuk decides to give up the exchange in order to exploit the trumps in his position.

18...♕c5! 19 ♕f3 ♕xe5! 20 ♕xa8 ♕c7 21 ♕c6?! ♕b8!

Black has a useful passed pawn and his minor pieces are better placed than White's. Ivanchuk retains queens in order to convert these advantages into an attack on the white king.

22 ♕f3 ♗b7 23 ♕a3+?! ♔g8 24 f3 g5! 25 ♗a4 e5 26 ♖he1 ♔g7 27 ♗c2 ♘h4 28 ♖d2 ♖c8 29 ♔b1 ♖xc4 30 ♘g1 ♖c5 31 g3 ♖a5 32 ♕d3 ♘g6 33 ♗b3 ♕d6 34 ♖c2 e4!

With two pawns and well-placed pieces, Black's advantage is clear. The final attack is brilliantly played by Ivanchuk.

35 ♕c4 ♘e5 36 ♕c7 ♕b4! 37 ♖d1 ♗d5! 38 ♗xd5 ♖xd5 39 fxe4 ♘xe4 40 a3 ♕b5 41 ♔a2 d3 42 ♖cc1 d2 43 ♖c2 ♘d3 44 ♖cxd2 ♖c5 45 ♕d8 ♕c4+ 46 b3 ♘c3+ 47 ♔a1 ♖a5 0-1

If either queen or knight is captured, White will be mated.

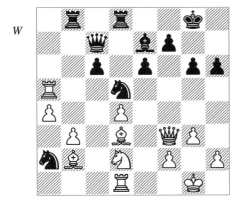

Petrosian – Guimard
Interzonal tournament, Gothenburg 1955

White has an extra pawn, but his b-pawn is backward and his d-pawn is isolated and blocking in his dark-squared bishop. Moreover, his a5-rook is in trouble. Petrosian's response is to sacrifice the exchange in order to straighten out his pawns and open his bishop's diagonal.

35 ♖c5! ♗xc5 36 dxc5 ♘ab4 37 ♗c4 f5 38 ♖e1 ♕e7 39 ♕e2 ♖e8 40 ♘f3 ♔h7 41 ♕e5 ♕c7 42 ♕e2 ♕e7 43 h4!

Finally, Petrosian decides that he will attack. The portents are good. His bishops are aiming at the black king, and Black's pawn-structure is decidedly loose. The attack leads to a Petrosian rarity: a spectacular king-hunt.

43...♘f6 44 ♗xe6 ♘e4 45 ♘d4 ♖bd8 46 h5! ♖xd4 47 hxg6+ ♔xg6 48 ♗xf5+! ♔xf5 49 ♕h5+ ♔e6 *(D)*

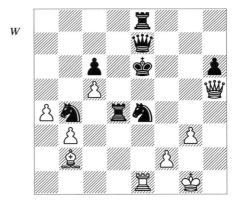

50 ♕g4+

Maybe Petrosian shared Alekhine's beauty compulsion, otherwise he might have been satisfied with the safe material advantage that he could force by 50 ♗xd4 ♔d7 51 f3.

50...♔d5 51 ♕f5+ ♕e5 52 ♕d7+ ♔xc5 53 ♖c1+ ♘c3 54 ♖xc3+ ♔b6 55 a5+! ♔xa5 56 ♕a7+ ♔b5 57 ♕b7+ ♔a5 58 ♖c1! ♖d1+ 59 ♖xd1 ♕xb2 60 ♕a7+ ♘a6 61 b4+ ♔xb4 62 ♕b6+ 1-0

Black is mated after 62...♔c3 63 ♕d4+ ♔b3 64 ♖d3+ ♔a2 65 ♕a4+ ♔b1 66 ♖d1+.

At the start of a game, we are furnished with a pair of rooks, so it is possible to sacrifice two exchanges in one game. The double exchange sacrifice is comparatively rare, but it is worth looking at a few examples to show

how two rooks can be dominated by the side with minor pieces.

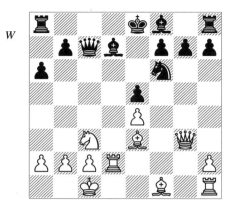

A.D. Martin – Ravikumar
Hastings 1984/5

White has sacrificed a pawn, but Black is ready to castle to queenside safety. Andrew Martin gives up one exchange to keep the king in the centre.

15 ♖xd7!? ♕xd7 16 ♗h3 ♕e7 17 ♖f1 h6

A little passive, but Black faced the threat of 18 ♗g5 followed by ♘d5. Martin decides that he will win the d5-square for his knight, even at the cost of another exchange.

18 ♖xf6! gxf6

18...♕xf6 leaves the e-pawn vulnerable. After 19 ♘d5 ♕d6 20 ♗b6 Black cannot protect it against 21 ♗c7 followed by 22 ♕xe5+, since 20...f6 21 ♕g6# is mate.

After the move played, White settles into the weak squares and the rooks can find no squares to call their own. Ravikumar eventually gives back an exchange, but falls victim to the attack on his king.

19 ♘d5 ♕d6 20 ♗b6 h5 21 ♘c7+ ♔e7 22 ♘d5+ ♔e8 23 b4 ♕c6 24 ♘c7+ ♔e7 25 ♘d5+ ♔e8 26 ♕g1! ♖c8 27 ♗xc8 ♕xc8 28 ♘xf6+ ♔e7 29 ♘d5+ ♔d7 30 ♕f1 ♕c6 31 ♕xf7+ ♔c8 32 ♗c7 ♗h6+ 33 ♔b2 ♖f8 34

♕h7 ♗e3 35 ♘e7+ ♔xc7 36 ♘xc6+ ♔xc6 37 ♕g6+ ♔d7 38 ♕g7+ ♔e8 39 ♕xe5+ ♔d7 40 ♕g7+ ♔e8 1-0

Rooks often have trouble dealing with connected passed pawns, so double exchange sacrifices to bring them about can be well worth considering.

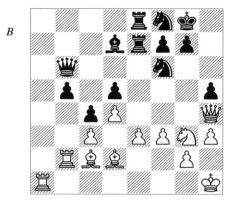

Lilienthal – Ragozin
Moscow 1935

White is ready to play e4, and Black decides to sacrifice one exchange to prevent it.

27...♖xe3! 28 ♗xe3 ♖xe3 29 ♘xh5 ♘xh5 30 ♕xh5 ♗c6 31 ♕g5

It appeared that the c-pawn could not be defended, but White has set a trap...

31...♖xc3!

...into which Black gladly falls! His rook is trapped, but the real point – to establish two connected passed pawns – is now revealed. The rooks cannot cope with the pawns, and White's attempted counterattack fails to land an effective blow.

32 ♕d2 ♖xc2! 33 ♖xc2 ♘e6 34 ♖d1 b4 35 ♖b2 b3 36 ♕c3 ♘c7 37 ♖e2 ♕a7 38 ♕b4 ♘b5 39 ♖e7 ♕a3 40 ♕e1 c3 41 ♖e8+ ♗xe8 42 ♕xe8+ ♔h7 43 ♕xf7 ♕a8 44 ♖e1 ♘d6 45 ♕c7 c2! 46 ♕xd6 b2 47 ♕f4 ♕c6 0-1

Now for some exercises. The first two exchange sacrifices are easy to see; all you need to do is to identify their purpose.

Exercise 16

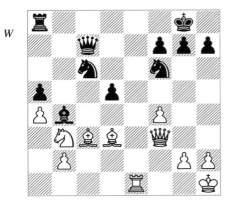

W

Level 1

What exchange sacrifice does White play here, and why?

Exercise 17

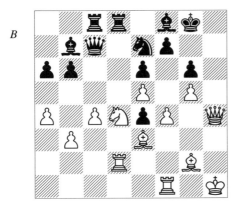

B

Level 2

Black played **32...⟂xd4**. Why?

Exercise 18

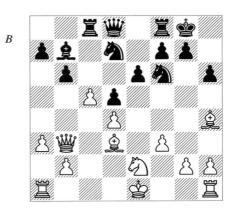

B

Level 3

Karpov has been one of the great players with rooks. His understanding of the rook's value has led him to make many exchange sacrifices. Most had fairly straightforward positional purposes, but this one is quite complex. In this position Karpov is Black, to play, and it is not even clear how he can sacrifice the exchange. How does he do it, and what compensation is he seeking? You will need to do some nifty analysis.

The solutions start on page 215.

The All-Powerful Queen?

Some of us have a problem with our queen. We know that it is worth approximately nine pawns, but we don't feel capable of attacking without it. It's bad enough having to exchange the queen – we'd be willing to give up ten or eleven points to capture our opponent's queen, but we certainly don't want to give up our own unless we receive a small fortune in return.

To sacrifice (or exchange) or not to sacrifice? Here is a personal reminiscence that demonstrates which side I would instinctively fall on that question.

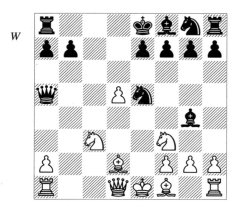

LeMoir – J. Flood
British Clubs Ch 1967

It was my 17th birthday, and my opponent has just offered me the chance to go for glory by sacrificing my queen. In my head I analysed 10 ♘xe5 ♗xd1 11 ♗b5+ ♚d8 12 ♘xf7+ ♚c8, when 13 ♖xd1 followed by 14 ♘xh8 enables me to emerge with a rook and two pieces for the queen. Should I do it or not?

In my mind's eye, I saw scattered white forces and Black still with his all-powerful queen. I stopped analysing and agonized instead. If you have the resulting position on the board (or in your head) you will know that White is winning. It takes very little time for the knight to re-emerge from h8, and Black's king will soon come under heavy fire.

I was already a practised sacrificer, and yet I chickened out, playing instead **10 ♗b5+ ♘d7 11 ♗xd7+ ♗xd7 12 0-0 ♘f6 13 ♘e5 g6 14 ♕f3 ♗g7 15 ♘e4 ♕d8 16 ♘g5 0-0 17 ♗b4 h6** and now I gave up two knights for a rook by **18 ♘gxf7?! ♖xf7 19 ♘xf7 ♚xf7**. Not a good transaction, but at last the adrenaline was flowing and my unsound attack soon crashed through.

Next morning I looked at the queen 'sacrifice' and stopped at the position after 10 ♘xe5 ♗xd1 11 ♗b5+ ♚d8 12 ♘xf7+ ♚c8 *(D)*.

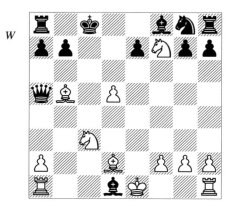

It took me seconds to see that I don't even need to recapture the bishop (let alone capture the rook) and that 13 ♖c1! is winning for White.

The threat is to move the knight, simultaneously discovering attacks on the king and the queen. The obvious move to save the queen is 13...♚b8, but then 14 ♗f4+! ♚c8 15 0-0 leaves Black totally helpless against a discovered check by the knight. Nothing comes close to saving the day for Black. There is no need for White to seek a material equivalent for the queen.

What a birthday present that would have been. I learned my lesson the hard way, on a sacrifice that could be calculated out to a clear win (if only I had been capable on the day). In order that you can learn the lesson the easy way, I offer below some examples to show how effective a well-judged queen sacrifice can be. They are all long-term sacrifices.

It is not my purpose to categorize queen sacrifices, but I have noticed some common factors that may help you when opportunities for queen sacrifices arise. Many are played because the opposing king will be extremely vulnerable to the sacrificer's pieces. Often, the two bishops and at least one rook play a part in the attack.

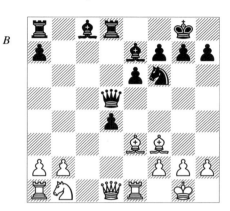

Borgo – Lanzini
Caorle 1985

Black has the choice between losing the exchange or his queen. He chooses to let his queen go because he can open up the white king's position by force.

14...dxe3!! 15 ♗xd5 exf2+ 16 ♔xf2 ♗c5+ 17 ♔e2

Black has only two pieces and a pawn for the queen, but the white king is out in the open and at the mercy of the black pieces. Notice how the queen can do nothing to reduce the power of the rook and bishops working in combination.

17...♗a6+ 18 ♔f3 ♖xd5 19 ♕c2 ♗d3 20 ♕d2 ♖f5+ 21 ♕f4

21 ♔g3 allows 21...♗d6+ 22 ♔h3 ♖h5#.

21...♖xf4+ 22 ♔xf4 ♘d5+ 23 ♔f3 ♗d4! 0-1

The next example is one of Keres's most celebrated games. What makes it most notable is his insistence on keeping the two bishops

when he could on several occasions cash them in at a profit.

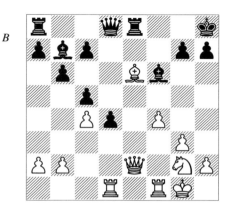

Euwe – Keres
Match (game 9), Rotterdam 1939/40

22...d3! 23 ♖xd3 ♕xd3!! 24 ♕xd3 ♗d4+ 25 ♖f2

After 25 ♔h1 ♖xe6, White can do nothing about 26...♖ae8 followed by 27...♖e2. He must mollify the black forces by offering back a rook for a bishop.

25...♖xe6 26 ♔f1 ♖ae8!

Now Black does threaten 27...♗xf2, as 28 ♔xf2 ♖e2+! wins the g2-knight. White is helpless against the combination of rooks and bishops, as illustrated by the line 27 ♖d2 ♗e4 28 ♕b3 ♗f5 29 ♕d1 ♗h3 30 ♖c2 g5! intending 31...gxf4 32 gxf4 ♖e4 and 33...♖xf4+. He desperately seeks some kind of distraction.

27 f5 ♖e5 28 f6 gxf6

Euwe's idea was 28...♗xf2 29 ♔xf2 ♖e2+? 30 ♕xe2 ♖xe2+ 31 ♔xe2 ♗xg2?? 32 f7, when the pawn promotes! Now the white rook escapes from f2, but Keres switches his light-squared bishop to another diagonal and is even willing to sacrifice the exchange himself to bring the white king to its knees.

29 ♖d2 ♗c8! 30 ♘f4 ♖e3 31 ♕b1 ♖f3+ 32 ♔g2 ♖xf4!! 33 gxf4 ♖g8+ 34 ♔f3 ♗g4+ 0-1

After 35 ♔e4 ♖e8+ 36 ♔d5 ♗f3+, it is mate next move.

The next example is less exciting, but demonstrates how difficult the defence can be, even when the defender's king is not fully exposed to the elements. Here, the two bishops are assisted by some far-advanced passed pawns.

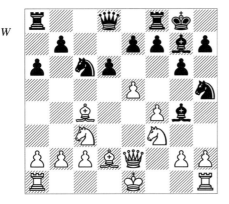

Hinks-Edwards – Rowson
Richmond International 1994

White makes what appears to be a rash advance.

12 e6!? ♘d4 13 exf7+ ♔h8 14 ♕d3!? ♗f5 15 ♕xd4! ♗xd4 16 ♘xd4

White has won two minor pieces and a pawn for the queen, removing the fianchettoed bishop in the process so that he might have kingside attacking chances later on. Black's king is far safer than in our previous examples, but the f7-pawn is such a nuisance that he resolves to give up the exchange for it.

Notice how the two white bishops stand quietly in the wings, awaiting their chance for a grand entrance.

16...♘g7 17 0-0-0 ♖c8 18 ♗b3 ♖c5 19 h3 g5 20 ♘xf5 ♖xf5 21 g4 ♖5xf7 22 f5! ♘e8 23 ♘e4 ♖g7 24 ♘xg5 e5

The king doesn't look so safe any more. Black turns the opposing f-pawn into a passed pawn in order to give his king some protection.

White repeatedly refuses to take the offered exchange, preferring to wait until he has a lethal follow-up ready.

25 ♘e6 ♕e7 26 ♖hf1 ♖fg8 27 ♘xg7 ♖xg7 28 g5 ♕f8 29 h4 ♖d7 30 ♗c3 ♖c7 31 f6 ♖c8 32 h5 h6 33 f7 ♘c7 34 ♖f6 1-0

A second pawn has arrived at f7, and Black is helpless to prevent the rook from forcing it home by ♖g6 and ♖g8+.

In the following example, a passed pawn again joins in the attack on the defender's king.

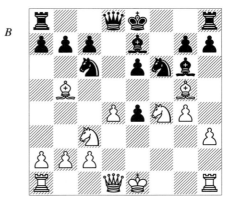

R. Bates – G. Wall
Richmond rapidplay 1998

Black starts with an invitation to White to win the exchange.

12...0-0! 13 ♘ce2

Black's idea was 13 ♘xe6 ♕d6 14 ♘xf8 ♕g3+ 15 ♔d2 ♘d5! 16 ♗xe7 ♕e3#. With that sacrifice refused, Wall tries offering his queen. This one is accepted.

13...♘d5!? 14 ♘xe6 ♗xg5!! 15 ♘xd8 ♗h4+ 16 ♔d2 ♗g5+ 17 ♔e1 ♖axd8

Black has only two pieces for his queen, but the white king is caught in the centre facing not only Black's rampant pieces but also the passed e-pawn.

18 ♗c4 ♘cb4 19 h4 e3 20 ♗b3 ♗e4 21 ♖h2 ♖f2! 22 ♖xf2 ♗xh4! 23 a3?

Better is 23 ♔f1 exf2 24 ♕d2 ♘xc2 25 ♖c1, when Black has two pieces and two pawns for the queen, with plenty of play. After the move played, Black wins the exchange and a pawn, and his attack remains undiminished.

23...exf2+ 24 ♔f1 ♘xc2! 25 ♕c1 ♘xa1 26 ♕xa1 ♔h8 27 ♕c1 ♖f8 28 ♗xd5 ♗xd5 29 b3 ♗g5!?

29...♗f3! 30 ♘g1 (or 30 ♘c3 ♖e8, coming in to e1) 30...♗c6 31 ♘e2 ♖e8 32 ♕c4 ♗f3 would be decisive, but this little repetition is harmless and provokes an error.

30 ♕b1 ♗h4 31 ♘c3? ♖e8 0-1

Even without the possibility of attacking the king, a passed pawn can offer convincing compensation for a queen, as John Nunn demonstrates in the next example.

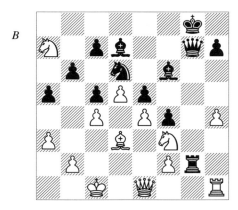

Piket – Nunn
Wijk aan Zee 1990

Black gives up his queen in order to establish a passed pawn at g2.

28...♕g4 29 ♗f1 ♕xf3 30 ♗xg2 ♕xg2 31 ♖g1 f3 32 ♘b5 ♘xb5 33 ♖xg2+ fxg2 34 cxb5?

In *John Nunn's Best Games*, Nunn states that 34 ♕g1! ♗h3 35 cxb5 ♗xh4 leads to a draw. That is not important for our purposes – the two bishops and passed pawn easily compensate for the sacrificed queen – and White's difficulty is highlighted by the fact that Nunn covers no fewer than five pages of his book with analysis and comment to prove that White can reach the draw!

34...♗xb5 35 ♕g1 ♗f1

At h3, as it was in the above line, the bishop would block the advance of the black h-pawn. With the bishop on f1, the h-pawn's eventual advance will be decisive. White does not wait to be shown, preferring to try for perpetual check, but he cannot achieve it.

36 ♕h2 ♗xh4 37 ♕xh4 g1♕ 38 ♕d8+ ♔g7 39 ♕xc7+ ♔h6 40 ♕xb6+ ♔h5 41 b4 ♗d3+ 42 ♔d2 ♕xf2+ 0-1

43 ♔xd3 loses the queen to 43...c4+.

It sometimes happens that, after a queen sacrifice, the defender is so hamstrung that he can only wait for the axe to fall.

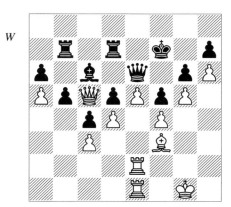

A. Eadington – J. Dobson
Cleveland 1995

White appears to have no way through.

41 ♕xc6!! ♕xc6 42 e6+ ♔f8 43 exd7 ♖xd7?

This loses. Black can save himself by continuing 43...♕xd7 44 ♖e6 ♕d8 (not 44...♖a7? 45 ♖f6+ ♔g8 46 ♗xd5+! ♕xd5 47 ♖e8#) 45 ♖1e5 ♖d7 46 ♖f6+ ♔g8 47 ♖xa6 ♖d6 48 ♖a7 ♖d7 49 ♗xd5+!? ♖xd5 50 ♖ee7 (apparently decisive, but...) 50...♖xd4! 51 cxd4 ♕xd4+ 52 ♔g2 ♕d2+ 53 ♔g3 ♕c3+! 54 ♔h4 ♔f8! preventing mate, and tying the rook to the e-file to cover the queen check at e1. Black will follow up with 55...♕f3, forcing perpetual check.

44 ♖e8+ ♔f7 45 ♖h8 ♕d6 46 ♖ee8 ♕a3 47 ♔f2 ♕b2+ 48 ♔g3 ♕a3 *(D)*

Black must cover f8 to avoid mate, and he needs his rook on d7 to prevent ♗xd5+.

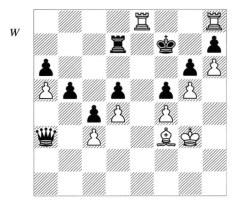

49 ♔h3!! 1-0

The black king has no move, there is no safe move on the a3-f8 diagonal for the queen, and the only 'safe' rook move that protects the d-pawn is 49...♖d6, but it blocks the queen's diagonal and allows 50 ♖hf8#. So, with queen and pawn for only rook and bishop, Black is in zugzwang.

Here is another example of a queen given up for a rook and a minor piece. The defender is hampered by his weak light squares and the power of his opponent's bishop and rooks.

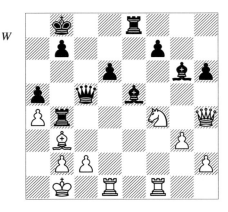

Spassky – Zhukhovitsky
USSR Ch semi-final, Leningrad 1957

Black's pieces are aggressively placed, with uncomfortable pressure on the c2-square, but Spassky's queen sacrifice transforms the position.

31 ♘xg6! ♖xh4 32 ♘xh4

Suddenly Black finds that two of his most aggressive pieces have disappeared, while the others have no targets. The dark-squared bishop can only defend pawns, and the lack of a light-squared bishop allows his opponent's pieces free access to key squares in the centre and on the queenside near the black king.

32...f6 33 ♘f5 h5 34 ♖d5 ♕c7 35 ♖b5 b6 36 ♘e3 ♗d4 37 ♘d5 ♕d8 38 ♖f4 ♗c5

The bishop cannot defend both pawns, so Spassky is able to re-establish nominal material parity. Tired of having nothing to do, the black rook charges off to attack a few pawns...

39 ♖xf6 ♖e2 40 ♖f7 ♖f2 41 ♖h7 ♖xh2 42 ♘xb6!

...but finds that it was needed back at home! The rook could have prevented the coming ♖b7(+), but not from h2.

42...♗xb6 43 ♗d5! ♔c8 44 ♖b7 ♕e8 45 ♖5xb6 ♕e1+ 46 ♔a2 ♖xc2 47 ♖a6 ♖c7 48 ♖b8+! ♔d7

48...♔xb8 49 ♖a8# is mate. Spassky drives home his attack, stopping off on move 51 just long enough to repel Black's counterattack.

49 ♖f8 ♕b4 50 ♖f7+ ♔d8 51 ♖f4! ♕d2 52 ♖f8+ 1-0

Sometimes, long-term queen sacrifices defy categorization. In our final example, young Bu Xiangzhi's opponent finds that he is unable to cope with the threats which buzz simultaneously around his queen, king and bishop.

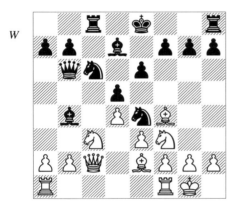

Bu Xiangzhi – Seres
Budapest 1999

In this ordinary-looking position, it is hard to believe that White has an effective sacrifice available. He is able to exploit the fact that Black has not castled and simultaneously to prove that the black queen and dark-squared bishop are exposed and vulnerable. The first trick is to recognize that Black has set a trap for the attempted pawn win on e4 – and to fall into it deliberately.

12 ♘xe4!! ♘xd4 13 ♕xc8+ ♗xc8 14 ♘xd4 dxe4 15 ♖ac1

For the time being, White has only rook and knight for queen and pawn, but he has calculated that his threats of 16 ♖xc8+ and 16 ♗c7! (winning back the queen) will not only prevent castling, but also force Black to return the pawn in order to give his queen an escape route.

15...♔d8 16 ♘b5 e5 17 ♗xe5 ♔e7

On this square the king blocks the bishop's retreat.

18 a3 a6 19 ♘c7

19 ♖c7+ may be even better, since after 19...♗d7 20 ♖d1 ♖d8 21 axb4 axb5 22 ♗g4 White wins the d7-bishop.

19...♕a5 20 ♗xg7 ♖g8 (D)

20...♖d8! prevents the knight's return via d5, and after 21 axb4 ♕g5! 22 ♗d4 ♗h3 Black wins back an exchange, leaving him with only a slight disadvantage. White would do better with 21 ♖c4!, as 21...♕g5 22 ♖xe4+ ♔d7 23 ♖d1+ ♔xc7 24 ♗e5+ ♔b6 25 ♖xb4+ leaves White with a material advantage and pressure against the black king.

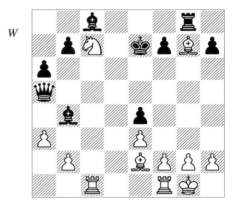

21 ♖fd1! ♗d2

After most other moves, including 21...♖xg7 and 21...♕g5, 22 ♘d5+ lets loose the rooks in a lethal attack on the black king. Now Bu sets about winning the errant bishop.

22 b4 ♕xa3 23 ♖a1 ♕b3 24 ♖ab1 ♕a3

Here the queen is exposed to a bishop retreat. If it moves instead to a2 or c2, then the trap closes on the d2-bishop; e.g., 24...♕a2 25 ♖b2 ♕a4 26 ♘d5+ ♔e6 27 ♘f4+ ♔e7 28 ♗d4, and the bishop is lost.

25 ♘d5+ ♔d6 26 ♗b2 1-0

Exercise 19

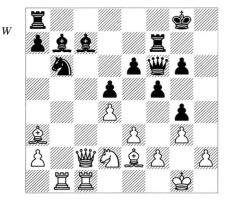

W

Level 1

In this position, White sacrificed his queen by **20 ♕xc7 ♖xc7 21 ♖xc7**. What compensation did he gain for the sacrificed material?

Exercise 20

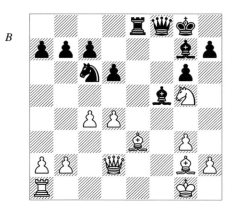

B

Level 2

How can Black sacrifice his queen here? What is his compensation, and why is it sufficient to win?

Exercise 21

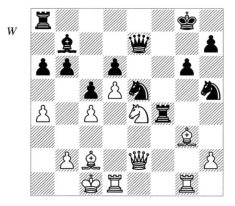

W

Level 3

White's queen sacrifice is fairly obvious, but can you prove that it wins in all variations? Further sacrifices may be required.

The solutions are on page 216.

7 You and Me

So what does all this mean to players like you and me?

We can motivate ourselves to be Deadly Tacticians, and some of the key secret ingredients are:

- a love of beauty in chess; if we have a huge desire to create beauty (the beauty compulsion) then all the better, as that is likely to make us daring when we most need to be
- the ability to resist reflex actions, which we can develop by understanding how and when they can strike
- a comfort with being behind on material, and an understanding of how and why we can expend pawns, rooks can struggle against minor pieces, and queens are not always all-powerful.

We can all do it. Let me introduce you to my old friend George Leyton. He had all of these ingredients, and it turned him from a fairly ordinary chess-player into one who not only loved his chess but who, every now and again, could achieve wonderful feats, including beating some of the best players around. Back in the 1970s, when he was in his prime, he defeated players rated up to 40 points above him on the BCF scale (equivalent to around 300 Elo points) such as Murray Chandler and Danny Wright (on the same day of a weekend tournament) and Michael Basman, the last two in violent sacrificial fashion. Here is the last of these games – it is well worth a detailed look.

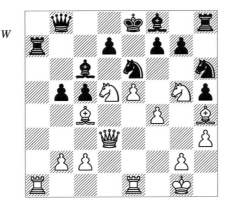

W

Leyton – Basman
Islington 1975

At the time of this game, Basman was rated in the UK's top ten players, with an Elo rating of 2395 and a 226 BCF grade. Leyton was around the 180s BCF, roughly equivalent to 2100 Elo.

Basman, a genius with the knack of creating and exploiting unusual positions, has lured Leyton's pieces forward until they are precariously placed.

22 ♘xe6! fxe6

From here onwards, each of the players is walking a tightrope. Thorough calculation is impossible; each player must simply hope that his intuition is correct or that his opponent will make the first error.

Basman gets the first key decision right: he naturally rejects 22...bxc4 as after 23 ♖xa7!, 23...cxd3 allows 24 ♘(either)c7+ with mate next move, and 23...dxe6 24 ♕a3 exd5 25 e6! lets the white rooks loose against the black king.

White also gains the advantage following 22...dxe6, since the open d-file gives White

mating threats on d8. White replies 23 ♖xa7, and now:

a) 23...♕xa7 24 ♘c3! wins the b-pawn thanks to the threat of mate on d8.

b) After 23...bxc4, simply 24 ♘c7+ ♕xc7 25 ♖xc7 cxd3 26 ♖xc6 is good enough to win, although 24 ♕a3 may be even better.

23 ♕g6+ ♘f7 24 f5!?

Leyton leaves two pieces *en prise* in order to break through to the e6-square. If Black exchanges rooks by 24...♖xa1, then one beautiful line is 25 fxe6!! ♖xe1+ 26 ♗xe1 bxc4 (or 26...dxe6 27 ♕xe6+ ♔d8 28 ♗a5+ mating) 27 ♗a5!!, when Black cannot escape mate.

This line demonstrates that it is essential for Black to hold the e6-square, and Nunn points out that White could have broken through on that square with 24 ♘b4!! cxb4 (or 24...♖h6 25 ♘xc6 dxc6 26 ♕e4) 25 ♗xe6! ♗c5+ 26 ♔h1 dxe6 27 ♕xe6+ ♔f8 28 ♕xc6 ♗b6 29 e6 with a winning attack.

24...♖h6!

Now the game seems to be up for White. Surely the queen must retreat, when White's brief attacking sally will be just a memory?

25 fxe6!!

Not for Leyton. Now 25...♖xg6 26 ♘c7+! ♖xc7 27 exf7# is an appropriate end for such an inspired pawn-dash.

25...dxe6 26 ♕e4! (D)

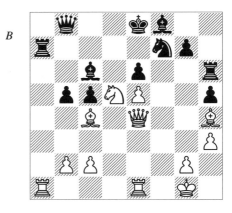

B

This is the key position. White has opened the d-file and his pieces stand poised. His big threat is 27 ♘f6+! gxf6 28 ♕xc6+ ♔d8 (or 28...♖d7 29 ♖a8 winning the queen) 29 ♖ad1+ with a huge attack.

There appear to be two reasonable defensive ideas: taking the threatening knight at once, or doing something about the veiled threat to the c6-bishop while holding the e6-square. In *CHESS* magazine, Basman suggested the latter, giving 26...♗d7 as winning. I didn't believe it, and subsequently found the lovely variation 27 ♖xa7 ♕xa7 28 ♖f1!! bxc4 (28...exd5 29 ♕xd5 ♖e6 30 ♗xb5! leaves Black amusingly helpless) 29 ♕f4! ♗c6 30 ♘e7!!, interfering with the queen's defence of f7 and winning at once.

However, there is another way to hold e6, namely 26...♘d8!, which also protects the bishop, moves the vulnerable knight and gives the black king an escape-square at f7. It gives rise to a whole new set of ideas. White probably plays 27 ♗xd8 and now it seems that only 27...♔xd8! *(D)* keeps Black in the game.

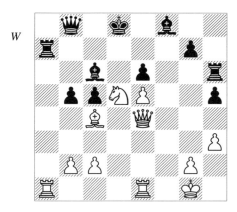

Even today, and even with the help of *Fritz*, I cannot quite work out what is going on. My latest verdict is that best play starts with 28 ♖ad1 exd5 29 ♗xd5 ♗xd5 30 ♖xd5+ ♔c7, and that Black should be able to save the game.

There is a bewildering array of complex variations hidden under the surface, which is just the way a Deadly Tactician like George Leyton likes it.

It all put Basman under terrible pressure. He had run horribly short of time, and decided to take the knight.

26...exd5 27 ♗xd5 ♗xd5 28 ♕xd5 g5

In playing this move, Basman lost on time. A better defence is 28...♗e7, but the consequences of conceding the e6-square are highlighted by the line 29 e6 ♘d6 30 ♕c6+ ♔f8 31 ♕f3+ *(D)*, and now:

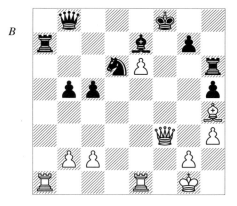

a) 31...♗f6 32 e7+ ♔g8 33 ♖xa7 ♗d4+ 34 ♔h1 ♕xa7 35 c3 ♗f6 36 ♕d5+ wins everything.

b) 31...♔e8 32 ♗xe7 ♔xe7 33 ♕g3! ♖xe6 34 ♕xg7+ ♘f7 35 ♖f1 and White wins the knight.

c) After 31...♖f6 32 ♗xf6 gxf6 33 ♕xh5 the attack continues to rage against the exposed black king.

After Basman's move he is lost, as White can play 29 e6 ♘d6 30 ♗xg5, threatening 31 ♕c6+ mating, and the black pieces cannot keep defending each other.

A short time later, George thoroughly mauled Danny Wright who, at the turn of the

1970s, had been one of England's top players.

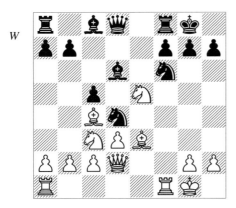

Leyton – Wright
Borehamwood 1977

White has well-placed pieces, so the breakthrough on f7 comes as no surprise.

14 ♗xd4 cxd4 15 ♘xf7! ♖xf7 16 ♘e4 b5 17 ♗b3 a5

Black has no time for 17...♔f8, as the white pieces surround the king by 18 ♘g5! ♗b7 (or 18...♖e7 19 ♘xh7+ ♔e8 20 ♖xf6! gxf6 21 ♘xf6+ ♔f8 22 ♕h6+ ♖g7 23 ♕h8+ mating) 19 ♖ae1! and White wins back his piece after 19...g6 20 ♘e6+ ♗xe6 21 ♖xe6 ♗e7 22 ♕h6+ ♔e8 23 ♖fxf6 with a winning position.

18 a3 ♖aa7 19 ♘g5 h6 20 ♘xf7 ♖xf7 21 ♖ae1 ♗c7 22 ♕e2

22 ♖xf6! is a little stronger. After 22...♕xf6 (not 22...gxf6 23 ♕xh6 with the threat of 24 ♕g6+) 23 ♖e8+ ♔h7 24 ♗xf7 ♕xf7 25 ♖xc8 White is the exchange ahead.

22...♔f8 23 ♗xf7 ♗g4 (D)

A little too clever, but 23...♕xf7 24 ♕h5+ ♔g8 25 ♕xb5 gives White a comfortable advantage; for example, 25...♕d6?! (25...♔h7 is better) 26 ♖xf6! ♕xh2+ 27 ♔f1 ♕h1+ 28 ♔e2 ♕xg2+ 29 ♔d1 ♗g4+ 30 ♔c1 gxf6? 31 ♕e8+ ♔g7 32 ♖e7#.

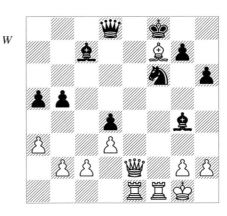

24 ♕e4!?

The queen sacrifice is a nice idea, but the temporary queen sacrifice 24 ♕e8+! would be even better, as after 24...♘xe8 25 ♖xe8+ ♕xe8 White has the unexpected *intermezzo* 26 ♗g6+!, and he emerges the exchange and a pawn ahead. Nonetheless, the text-move wins comfortably enough.

24...♘xe4 25 ♖xe4 g5

The threat was 26 ♗d5+, winning back the queen at once. White emerges with two rooks and a pawn for the queen, with his attack still raging.

26 ♗h5+ ♗f4 27 ♗xg4 ♔g7 28 g3 ♗e3+ 29 ♔g2 b4 30 ♗h5 ♕d5 31 ♖f7+ ♔g8 32 ♔f1 ♕c6 33 ♖f5 b3 34 ♗f7+ ♔g7 35 ♗xb3 g4 36 ♖e7+ 1-0

We shall meet George Leyton again later on, as he has played some inspiring chess in his life. To him, being a Deadly Tactician is not only the means to an end, it is an end in itself. Sharing his motivation could help you to create games that you can treasure.

I too am a player who delights in tactical play. Particularly in my earlier days, I played daring attacking chess with little concern for the material situation on the board. As I got older (I've now passed the half-century), I started to believe that my tactical flair was receding faster than my hairline. Oddly, I think I was wrong. Let me explain.

One of the basic tenets of this book is that by being exposed to a large body of sacrificial chess, my readers should start instinctively to look for sacrificial opportunities in their games, and can build the confidence required to play them. I spent a lot of time during the summer months of 2001 building a database of sacrifices for this book. With the end of the summer my chess season started.

Within my first nine games (up to the time of writing these lines), I had played five sacrificial efforts. In one, I was lucky to get away with a draw. Another one was (for me) a stunning conception against Owen Hindle, which will appear on page 193. The other three I will show you briefly here.

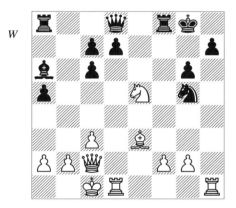

LeMoir – R. De Coverley
English Counties Rapidplay 2001

There is more than one quick win here. My beauty compulsion was hard at work, so the one that I decided to play involved sacrificing a rook and a knight.

19 ♖xh7! ♘xh7

19...♔xh7 20 ♕xg6+ ♔h8 21 ♖h1+ is mate in two more moves. Black cannot hold out much longer by 19...♕e8 as 20 ♗xg5!

♔xh7 21 ♖xd7+ ♔g8 22 ♕b3+ ♔h8 23 ♕a4 ♔g8 24 ♕h4 wins the queen and more. After the move played there is a forced mate.

20 ♕xg6+ ♔h8 21 ♖h1 ♕e7 22 ♘f7+! ♖xf7 23 ♗d4+ ♖g7 24 ♕xh7# (1-0)

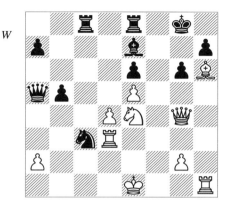

LeMoir – J. Heppell
Norfolk Ch 2001

24 ♕xe6+ ♔h8 25 ♗g7+! ♔xg7 26 ♖xh7+! ♔xh7 27 ♕f7+ 1-0

28 ♖h3+ will be mate in two.

Those were relatively straightforward combinations, although it is always extremely pleasant to sacrifice a rook and a minor piece for mate. The next example is a more complex long-term sacrifice (*see diagram on following page*).

Black is the exchange and a pawn down following a sacrifice in the opening. A move of the attacked knight allows White to expose the black king by 17 f5, so I preferred to leave the knight to be captured in the interests of developing a quick attack.

16...♕h3!? 17 gxf5

The best defence appears to be to sacrifice the knight for the e-pawn, but the timing is critical. White should play it now, since 17 ♘xe4! dxe4 18 ♗xe6+ ♔xe6 19 gxf5+ gxf5

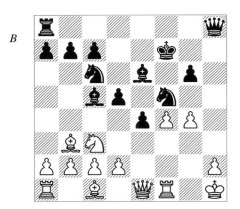

M. Hindle – LeMoir
Norfolk 2001

20 c3! (cutting out ...♘d4) 20...♗g1! 21 ♕e2 ♗xh2 22 ♕g2 forces Black to seek a draw by 22...♕d3! 23 ♔xh2 ♔f7! 24 ♕h3 ♕e2+ 25 ♔h1 ♖h8! 26 ♕xh8 ♕xf1+ with perpetual check. This is a rare example of a counter-sacrifice coming before accepting the sacrifice that it is designed to counter.

17...gxf5 18 ♗xd5

If White plays the 18 ♘xe4 sacrifice now, Black can avoid 18...dxe4, and play the apparently disastrous 18...fxe4!:

a) The point is that 19 f5 can be met by 19...♖g8!! 20 fxe6++ ♔e8!, when White is oddly defenceless: 21 ♕e2 (21 ♖f2 ♗xf2 22 ♕xf2 ♖f8 wins the queen) 21...♘d4 22 ♕f2 ♘f5! is decisive, as 23 ♕e2 ♘g3# is mate.

b) 19 c3 (covering d4) doesn't stop the knight getting around to the kingside, since it can now use the f5-square; e.g., 19...♖g8 20 ♖f2 ♘e7 21 d4 ♘f5! 22 dxc5 ♘g3+ 23 ♔g1 ♘f1+ 24 ♔h1 ♘xh2 25 ♖xh2 ♕f3+ 26 ♖g2 ♕xg2#.

18 ♕e2 is probably best, but the attack continues with 18...♖g8! and a typical conclusion is 19 ♖d1 ♘d4 20 ♕f1 ♕h5 21 d3 ♘f3 22 ♖d2 ♘xh2! 23 ♖xh2 ♕f3+! 24 ♕g2 ♖xg2 25 ♖xg2 ♕h3+ and mate next move.

18...♗xd5 19 ♘xd5 ♖g8 20 ♕e2? *(D)*

The obvious defence, but it loses quickly.

20 ♖f2 is better, but it fails to 20...♗xf2 21 ♕xf2 ♘d4, and now:

a) 22 ♘e3 ♘f3 23 ♘f1 loses to 23...♕h4!! 24 ♕c5 (24 ♕e3 ♕e1! is the lovely point) 24...♕e1 25 ♕xf5+ ♔e7 26 ♕h7+ ♔d6 27 ♕h6+ ♔d7 28 ♕h7+ ♔c6 29 ♕h6+ ♔b5 30 a4+ ♔b4 31 c3+ ♔b3 32 ♕e6+ ♔c2 and the king has escaped from the checks.

b) 22 ♘f6!? has the point 22...♗xf6 23 ♕xd4+ ♔e7 24 ♕f2 ♕h5 25 ♕f1, but Black can win with 22...♖g7! 23 ♘d7 ♘f3 24 ♘e5+ ♔g8 25 ♘xf3 exf3 followed by ...♖g2.

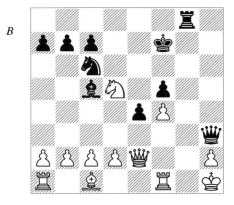

20...♘d4 21 ♕f2 ♘f3 22 ♕e2 ♘xh2!

This is sufficient for a quick mate, but 22...♕g3!! 23 hxg3 ♖h8+ 24 ♔g2 ♖h2# is more scenic.

23 ♖f2 ♘f1+ 24 ♖h2 ♖g1# (0-1)

I can only explain the sudden rash of sacrificial opportunities by the continual exposure to brilliant and inspiring play over the preceding months. Whatever the case, my flair for sacrifice had not deserted me, it only needed to be re-awakened. Hopefully, exposure to the brilliant play in this book will help you, too, to discover (or reawaken) your own sacrificial flair.

Part Two: Imagination

8 Simple Silent Sacrifices

Apart from pawn sacrifices, most sacrifices are made with a capture. For instance: the black king's defensive pawn-shield is on f7, g7 and h6; we line up bishop on e3 and queen on d2 and capture that h-pawn with the bishop. Our queen ends up on h6, and gobbles the king alive. Or maybe Black has fianchettoed his king's bishop; we play h4-h5, and when Black captures with his knight from f6, we take it with our rook from h1 – the sacrifice enables us to assault the h7-pawn and the g7-bishop.

Captures are easy for us to see, and also to calculate, as they normally compel our opponent to recapture. If they are easy for us, they are also relatively easy for our opponents to foresee, calculate, and possibly to avoid. If we play sacrifices without captures, they are normally checks that drag the king into a knight fork or onto a square where we can drive it towards checkmate. Checks, with or without captures, are often easy to calculate because, as with captures, they force specific action from the defender.

The Deadly Tactician's sacrifices catch defenders by surprise because they are not always captures or checks. They often compel action from the defender because they have a threat – such as mate or winning the queen. That helps the attacker's calculations, but is of less help to a defender taken by surprise.

If we can become familiar with the Deadly Tactician's sacrifices, then we will start to look for them in our own games. If we understand the mechanics of his sacrifices, then we will be able to find them more easily. Finally, if we experience and practice large numbers of his sacrifices, our imagination will become filled with ideas and we will be inspired to perform similar feats.

Larry Christiansen, author of *Storming the Barricades* and the player of many brilliant attacking games, has written that he spent many happy hours as a child with Fred Reinfeld's *1001 Sacrifices and Combinations*. In my early years as a player, I too consumed combinations by the barrow-load, and found that my imagination became particularly fired by the less obvious sacrifices. Many opponents still suffer today from the direct results of my wish to entertain myself with the beautiful side of chess. Rewarding study does not have to be unpleasant work!

"The sacrifice without a capture and without check" is a long name to keep repeating throughout this book, so I will use the term **silent sacrifice** instead. The Deadly Tactician has other specialities, as we shall see later, but the silent sacrifice is one he uses in many of his best combinations. You might like to go back to the examples and exercises in Part One to identify the many silent sacrifices contained in them.

Inside the Silent Sacrifice

Let's get inside the silent sacrifice and look at its mechanics.

The purpose behind a sacrifice is called a **motif**. In chess literature, many names exist to describe sacrificial motifs. Some are a little too vague for my purposes here, while sometimes there is more than one alternative name for a motif. I have tried to use some easy-to-remember names in what follows. If they appear to clash with naming systems that you have read elsewhere, then I trust that you will not become confused.

First, consider the original square from which the sacrificed piece moves.

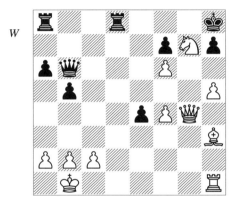

Short – Ljubojević
Reykjavik 1987

Short forced immediate resignation with **29 ♘e8!**. The knight jumps from g7 so that the queen can mate on this square. It lands on the only square that prevents the rook from playing to g8 to stop the mate, and it also protects f6 so that Black's defence 29...♛xf6 loses his queen. The motif of the sacrifice 29 ♘e8 is called **square clearance** because the square cleared by the sacrificed piece is used by the attacker later in the combination.

The square-clearance motif occurs relatively rarely. More often, it is the *line* that the piece moved from that is important, as the next diagram demonstrates.

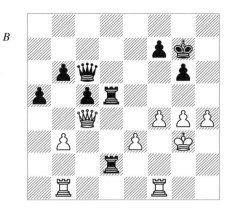

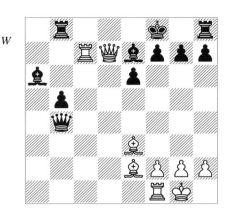

M. Belsten – LeMoir
Bristol League 1968/9

Sowray – T. Dickinson
British League (4NCL) 2000/1

Black forced immediate resignation with **29...罝5d4!**. When it was on d5, the rook blocked the diagonal of the black queen to g2 where, supported by the d2-rook, it could deliver checkmate. The rook move to d4 clears the diagonal and attacks the white queen, and White cannot defend against both threats. The motif is called **line clearance**.

When a sacrifice is accepted, the action by the defender of moving the capturing piece can provide the motif. Firstly, consider the original square from which the capturing piece moves (*see following diagram*).

The e7-bishop is in White's way. If it moves, then the seventh rank is opened and 豐xf7 will be mate. Therefore he played **23 奧c5!**, attacking both queen and bishop. Black gave up his queen by **23...豐xc5 24 罝xc5 奧xc5 25 豐c6** and then resigned. We shall call this motif – luring a piece away to open a line for our pieces – **deflection**.

The defender can decline a deflection sacrifice by leaving the defensive piece in place, so the sacrifice's purpose may not always be achieved. That observation can be made about most of the sacrificial motifs from here

onwards. Nonetheless, we shall still give the name *deflection sacrifice* (or *deflection* for short) to a sacrifice whose purpose is deflection, even if the defender does not allow his pieces to be deflected.

There is a second potential purpose behind luring a piece away from its original square. Each piece not only occupies its square (blocking a line, unless it's on a1, a8, h1 or h8), but it also performs a function by attacking or guarding squares. If that function prevents the attacker from carrying out his plans, then luring the piece away gives him a free hand.

In the diagram on the following page, White would like to mate by 39 罝h8+ 含d7 40 豐d8+ 含e6 41 罝e8# (or 41 豐d6#), but the black queen guards h8. So White played **39 罝a2!** and Black resigned as 39...豐xa2 allows the mate, and 39...豐d4 40 c3 forces the queen off the crucial diagonal anyway. We shall call this motif – luring a piece away so that it can no longer perform its preventive function – **diversion**.

In simple cases of deflection and diversion, the exact square to which the capturing

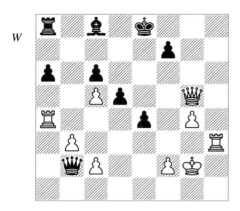

LeMoir – Swanson
Hertfordshire Open 1999

piece is lured is not of any great significance (apart from the fact that it is away from the action). Sometimes, however, this square is of critical importance, particularly when the capturing piece is in danger on its new square.

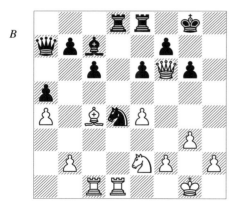

Jankovec – Fajer
Czechoslovakia 1968

Black played **1...♗e5!**, drawing the queen onto a square where it will fall victim to a knight fork. White resigned because not only

does 2 ♕xe5 lose the queen to 2...♘f3+, but 2 ♕g5 and 2 ♕h4 also fail for the same reason. I shall call this motif – luring a piece to a specific square or line where something nasty can happen to it – **decoy**.

There is another motif that depends on the square or line to which the capturing piece is lured. On its new square it may get in the way of one of its colleagues, a piece that needed an open line to perform its defensive function.

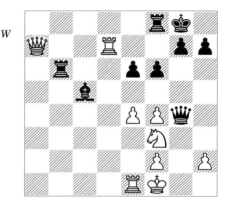

Speelman – Short
Phillips & Drew, London 1980

The black queen prevents White's intended mate starting with ♖xg7+, but **34 ♘g5!** gets in the way of that. If the f-pawn captures the knight, the queen's line remains blocked and White can carry out his mate. No other piece can defend against the mate threat, so Black resigned. We shall call this motif, where the capturing piece interferes with the line of action of another defensive piece, **interference**.

So far, we have looked at the sacrificed piece and the piece that captures it. With many silent sacrifices, the main idea behind the sacrifice is in the attacker's action of recapturing the piece that accepted the sacrifice. First we shall consider the specific piece that is recaptured.

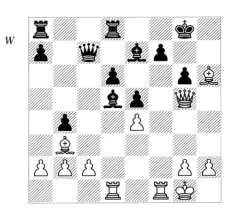

Rigo – Espig
Leipzig 1977

The e7-bishop covers the dark squares, on which White would like give checkmate.

24 ♖f6! ♗xb3

Black must decline the rook as 24...♗xf6 25 ♕xf6 eliminates the bishop, allowing the queen to mate on g7. However, White had another purpose in placing his rook on f6.

25 ♖xg6+! ♔h8

25...fxg6 allows 26 ♕xg6+ ♔h8 27 ♕g7#.

26 ♗g7+ ♔g8 27 ♗xe5+ fxg6 28 ♕xg6+ ♔f8 29 ♗g7+ 1-0

It is mate in a few moves.

We shall give the name **elimination** to the motif of eliminating a specific capturing piece in order to remove its defensive function. Elimination is a frequent motif in standard sacrifices, but is very rare in silent sacrifices as there would be little compulsion for the defender to accept the sacrifice.

Now we shall consider the specific piece that the attacker uses to make the recapture. If the piece previously blocked the line of one of the attacker's own pieces, the recapture can open a useful line.

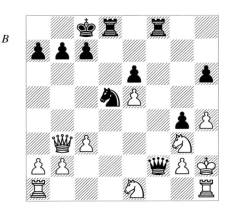

Schmid – Chigorin
Vienna 1882

Black played **21...♖f3! 22 ♘xf3 gxf3**. This recapture attacks the g2-pawn, but that can be defended, as White's reply shows. However, by capturing on f3 the pawn has cleared the g-file, which is now open from Black's side and can be occupied by a rook, leaving White defenceless.

After **23 ♖hg1 ♖g8** White resigned, as he cannot defend the knight, and moving it allows the breakthrough on g2. I shall call this motif – clearing a line by the move of the recapturing piece – **secondary line clearance**. It happens most often when, as in this example, the recapturing piece is a pawn, enabling a file that was previously closed to be opened. It is a key element of many knight sacrifices on the fifth rank, which we shall consider in the next chapter.

Another important idea behind a silent sacrifice can be to establish a specific piece on a given square. When that square is currently guarded, often by a pawn, the answer is to play a silent sacrifice of another piece on the square in order that the desired piece can occupy it by making the recapture.

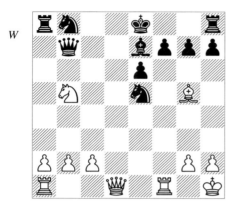

Rigo – Busu
Romania 1978

With the black queen on b7 and the king on e8, White would like to play his knight to d6. Unfortunately, the e7-bishop would then exchange it, so White played **17 ♕d6!!** intending to meet 17...♗xd6 by 18 ♘xd6+ ♔d7 19 ♘xb7 with a material advantage. Facing the threat of 18 ♘c7+, Black must lose material anyway and he resigned on move 26. We shall call this motif – establishing the recapturing piece on the square where the original sacrifice took place – **substitution**.

The process of recapturing can also open a line for the recapturing piece. Consider the next diagram.

This example features a standard mating combination in which a queen is sacrificed to blast open a line for a mere bishop. White continues **1 ♕f6!**. After **1...gxf6**, the f6-pawn blocks the bishop's diagonal. The recapture **2 ♗xf6#** opens the line with fatal effect. I shall call the motif involving in grabbing an open line by making the recapture **line-grabbing**.

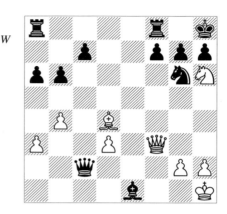

Sikorski – Anon
Gleiwitz 1934

Exercise 22
Level 1
Here are two silent sacrifices in the same game. What is the motif of each?

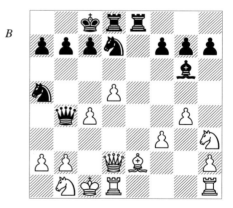

Kuijf – Hodgson
Wijk aan Zee 1989

16...♕b3!!
The first silent sacrifice must be declined in view of 17 axb3 ♘xb3#.

17 ♗d3 ♕xa2 18 ♕b4

Black threatened 18...♘b3+. Now comes the second silent sacrifice.

18...♖e2! 19 ♗xe2 ♘b3+ 20 ♕xb3 ♕xb3 21 ♖d2 ♕e3 0-1

Exercise 23

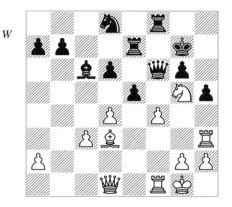

Level 2

22 ♘h7! is a silent sacrifice. What is the motif, and what is best play after the sacrifice is accepted?

The solutions start on page 216.

Square Clearance

We shall now see each silent sacrifice motif in action. To help you to understand the motif clearly, most of the examples will feature sacrifices with only one single motif. Many of the hardest sacrifices to foresee combine more than one motif, and you will find many examples in Chapter 9, 'Complex Silent Sacrifices'.

The first motif is square clearance, which is fairly rare. The Deadly Tactician database contains around 350 silent sacrifices from various sources, and only five of them are square clearances. As we might expect, their rarity doesn't prevent them from being beautiful. Here is one of Tal's offerings.

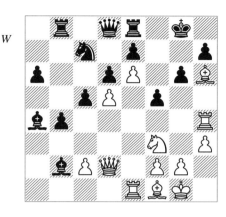

Tal – Benko
*Candidates tournament,
Bled/Zagreb/Belgrade 1959*

Tal wants to use his queen in the attack on Black's king.

23 ♗f8!!

The bishop makes room on h6. Benko now decides to give up his rook, but he cannot stave off mate.

23...♖xf8

After 23...♔xf8 24 ♕h6+ ♔g7 25 ♕xh7 Black has no defence to the threat of ♕xg6 followed by mate.

24 ♕h6 ♖f7 25 exf7+ ♔xf7 26 ♕xh7+ ♔g7 27 ♖h6 ♔g8 28 ♕xg6+ ♔f8 29 ♘g5 ♕xd5 30 ♖h8+! 1-0

This unusual silent sacrifice motif gave a suffering British chess public some welcome cheer in the pre-Fischer-Spassky era (*see diagram on following page*).

The dark squares in the black king's camp are horribly weak. The position cries out for a knight or rook sacrifice on h5, but the white queen cannot follow up with a check as g5 is

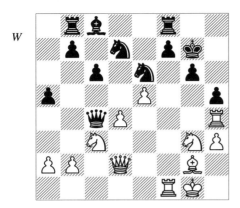

Markland – Hort
Hastings 1970/1

covered by a black knight. Markland sees that his queen could use the g2-square if only his bishop were somewhere else. He finds a good 'somewhere else'.

23 &d5!

The main line of the combination is truly sparkling as the white major pieces run riot: 23...cxd5 is answered by 24 ♘xh5+! gxh5 (or 24...♔h8 25 ♘f6+ ♔g7 26 ♖h7#, while 24...♔g8 loses to 25 ♕h6! gxh5 26 ♖xh5) 25 ♕g2+ ♔h6 26 ♖f5! (not 26 ♕g4?? ♕xd4+!, when Black wins!) 26...♘g7 *(D)*.

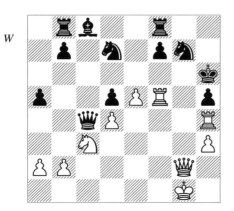

Now White mates by 27 ♕xg7+!! ♔xg7 28 ♖g5+ ♔h7 29 ♖hxh5#.

Hort prefers to give up his queen, but mate is not far off.

23...♕xf1+ 24 ♔xf1 cxd5 25 ♘xd5 b6 26 ♘f4 ♘xf4 27 ♕xf4 &a6+ 28 ♔g1 &d3 29 ♕g5 ♔h8 30 ♕h6+ 1-0

30...♔g8 loses to 31 ♖xh5! gxh5 32 ♘xh5, mating.

Exercise 24

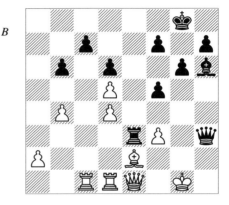

Level 2

Black has already sacrificed a rook. Now he is looking for mate. ...&e3+ would be decisive if the rook were somewhere else. Where was 'somewhere else' in this case? Analyse it out to a forced win.

The solution is on page 217.

Line Clearance

In contrast to square clearance, line clearance occurs fairly often, featuring in 75 out of 350 silent sacrifice positions in the Deadly Tactician database. It is an effective, and frequently startling, way to bring into the attack the pieces that lurk in the rear, as the next diagram illustrates.

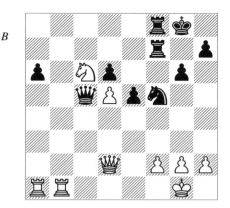

Bacrot – Ivanchuk
Cap d'Agde rapidplay 1998

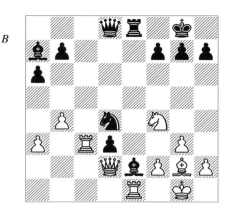

Smirin – Grishchuk
FIDE Knockout, New Delhi 2000

The f2-square is Black's target, with a queen (directly) and two rooks (indirectly) trained upon it. However, if he moves his knight to just any square, White will defend with ♖f1 or ♖a2. There is only one square that covers f1 without getting in the way and also allows an effective answer to the reply ♖a2.

28...♘g3!!

Most of us can only dream of landing a piece on such a square with complete impunity. Now 29 ♖a2 loses to 29...♖xf2! 30 ♕xf2 ♖xf2 31 ♖xf2 ♘e4, while 29 ♕e3 ♕xe3 30 fxe3 ♘e2+ 31 ♔h1 ♘c3 32 ♖e1 ♘xd5 simply costs White a second pawn. In desperation, Bacrot gives up his queen, but his position is quite lost.

29 hxg3 ♖xf2 30 ♘e7+ ♔g7 31 ♕xf2 ♕xf2+ 32 ♔h2 ♖f3 33 ♖b7 ♕xg3+ 34 ♔g1 ♕f2+ 35 ♔h1 ♕h4+ 36 ♔g1 ♖f7 0-1

In the following diagram, the piece waiting in the rear is ready to sacrifice itself.

Black is the exchange behind for a passed d-pawn, and that pawn appears to be decisively attacked. However, the a7-bishop is itching to sacrifice on f2, and only its own knight is in the way. The knight has to sacrifice itself, but does so in a way that compels action from White – it attacks the white queen:

28...♘b3!! 29 ♖xd3

Smirin prefers to give rather than take. Accepting the sacrifice by 29 ♖xb3 allows Black to play 29...♗xf2+! 30 ♔xf2 (or 30 ♔h1 ♗xe1 31 ♕xe1 d2 and the pawn wins the queen) 30...♕d4+ and mate next move.

29...♗xd3 30 ♖xe8+ ♕xe8 31 ♕xd3 ♕e1+ 32 ♕f1 ♗xf2+ 33 ♔h1 ♕xf1+ 34 ♗xf1

Black won with his extra pawn.

Boris Spassky has long been one of the great attacking players. His attack in the next example features several surprising moves, two of which are silent line-clearance sacrifices.

In the diagram overleaf, the 1969-72 World Champion has two pieces *en prise* – the a1-rook and the h6-bishop – and faces the threat of back-rank mate. He has foreseen, however, that his next move buys him time to pursue his attack on the black king.

19 ♘c3!

Line clearance, opening the back rank to prevent mate. Now 19...♗xc3 allows 20 ♗e3, attacking the queen and threatening mate on

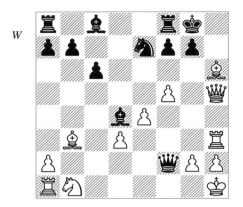

Spassky – Barua
New York Open 1987

the h-file. In his turn, Black has prepared a clever defence using the fact that his c8-bishop pins the white f-pawn against the h3-rook.

19...g6! 20 fxg6! ♗xh3 21 gxh3 ♕f6 *(D)*

21...♗xc3 would again allow 22 ♗e3!, a line-clearance sacrifice that attacks the queen and threatens mate on h7, so the queen scampers back out of danger, lending its king some defence in the process.

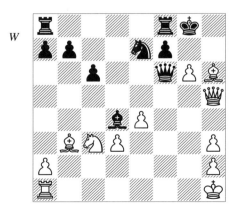

However, White's bishop is not to be denied.

22 ♗e3! 1-0

This line clearance sacrifice attacks the black bishop, and thereby ensures that the queen is dragged away after all. As the threat is 23 ♕h7#, Black is forced to play 22...♘xg6, when 23 ♗xd4 ♕xd4 24 ♕xg6+ ♕g7 25 ♕f5! threatens 26 ♖g1 and after 25...♕xc3 26 ♖g1+ White wins the queen anyway. Black preferred not to give his opponent the opportunity for yet another sacrifice.

Exercise 25

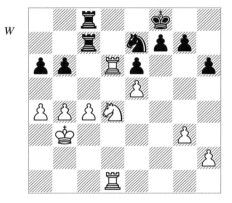

Level 1

White is to move. Find a silent sacrifice based on line clearance that will win material.

The solution is on page 217.

Deflection

Sacrifices use the deflection motif to open a line that was previously occupied by one of the defender's pieces. When that line is the back rank, the finish is often a sudden mate.

In the diagram on the next page, Fischer has been engaging in a little brinkmanship, tempting Reshevsky to threaten both mate, starting ♕xf7+, and the e8-rook. Fischer

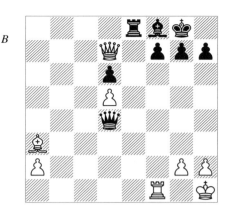

Reshevsky – Fischer
Interzonal tournament,
Palma de Mallorca 1970

played **30...♕f2!** and his opponent, realizing the error of his ways, resigned on the spot. 31 ♖xf2 opens the back rank, allowing 31...♖e1+ and mate next move, while 31 ♖g1 allows 31...♖e1, which also leads to mate.

In the next example, the deflection opens a diagonal.

White reckons that he will have a winning attack if only he can get his queen down to f7.
26 ♖e7!
The idea is to deflect the knight from d5 to open the a2-g8 diagonal for his bishop. After 26...♘xe7 27 ♕xf7+ the attack would crash through; e.g., 27...♔h6 28 ♕f4+ ♔g7 29 ♕e5+ ♔h6 (it is a quick mate after 29...♔f8 30 ♕f6+ ♔e8 31 ♕f7#) 30 ♕g5+ ♔g7 31 ♕xe7+ ♔h6 32 ♗e6! ♘xe6 (or 32...♕b8 33 g4 ♖h8 34 ♕g5+ ♔g7 35 ♕e5+ ♔h6 36 g5+ ♔h5 37 ♕e2+ ♔xh4 38 ♕g4#) 33 ♘xe6 ♖d5 34 g4! ♕g8 35 ♕g5+! ♖xg5 36 hxg5#.

Faced with the threat of mate from the combined force of queen and rook, Black is bound to lose at least a pawn; e.g., 26...♖f8 27 ♗xd5 ♘xd5 (or 27...cxd5 28 ♘d7) 28 ♖xb7.

26...♕f5 27 ♕xf5 gxf5 28 ♗xd5 ♘xd5 29 ♖xb7
White won the endgame.

When a sacrifice offers two of the defender's pieces the option of opening lines, we talk of a **double deflection**. In the next example, Black avoids a beautiful double deflection but falls victim to a decisive single deflection.

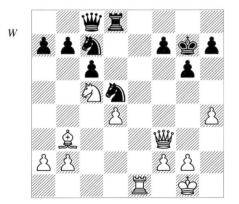

Davies – Lalić
Redbus Knockout, Southend 2000

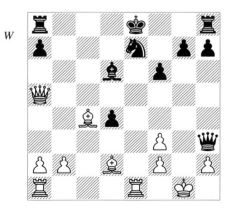

Ma. Tseitlin – Krutiansky
USSR 1971

20 ℤxe7+! ♔xe7

Tseitlin's combination opens with an exchange sacrifice, and Black recaptures with his king. The most attractive line follows the recapture with the bishop: 20...♗xe7 21 ♕d5 (given by Tseitlin in *Informator*, but 21 ℤe1 is also very good) 21...ℤb8 22 ♕c6+ ♔f8 *(D)* (or 22...♕d7 23 ♗f7+ ♔d8 24 ♗a5+ ℤb6 25 ♕a8+ ♕c8 26 ♕xa7, winning the rook).

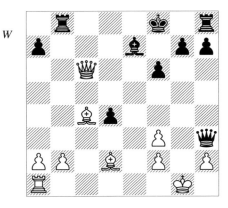

W

Now the move 23 ♗b4!! is a double deflection. 23...♗xb4 opens the seventh rank, allowing the double attack 24 ♕c7 threatening mate and the rook, while 23...ℤxb4 opens the back rank so that playing 24 ♕a8+ leads to mate.

21 ℤe1+ ♔f8

21...♗e5 loses to 22 ℤxe5+ fxe5 23 ♕xe5+ ♔d7 24 ♕d5+ and now 24...♔c7 25 ♗f4+ ♔b6 26 ♕b5# or 24...♔e7 25 ♗g5+ ♔f8 26 ♕f7#.

After the text-move, White appears to be in difficulties as Black threatens mate starting with 22...♗xh2+.

22 ♗f4!!

This deflection prevents Black's mate.

22...g6

White delivers his own mate after 22...♗xf4 23 ♕c5+.

23 ♕d5! 1-0

The only defence to mate on f7 is 23...♕d7, but that allows 24 ♗h6+ ♔g7 25 ♕xd6#.

So far, we have considered positions where major and minor pieces are deflected. However, in the majority of cases (over 75% of the deflections on the Deadly Tactician database) it is pawns that are deflected.

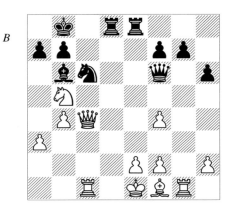

B

Ftačnik – Szeles
Zalaegerszeg 1979

...♕xf2 would be mate, but there is a pawn in the way.

20...♘e5!

The knight attacks the white queen, and it is immune in view of 21 fxe5 ♗xf2#.

The queen is stuck for good moves as 21 ♕c2 ♘f3# is mate, and after 21 ♕b3 both 21...♘d3+ and 21...♕xf4 win easily.

21 ♕e4 ♘d3+ 22 exd3 ℤxe4+ 23 dxe4 ♗xf2+! 0-1

After 24 ♔xf2 (24 ♔e2 ♕xf4 mates soon), 24...♕xf4+ 25 ♔g2 ℤd2+ leads to mate.

Here is a famous example of a pawn deflection combination (*see diagram on following page*):

Alekhine has been trying to untangle himself on the queenside, where the black queen

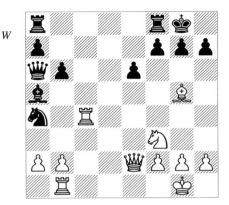

W

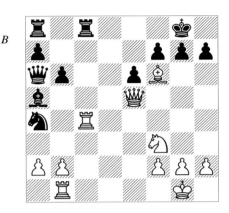

B

Alekhine – Sterk
Budapest 1921

pins his rook against his queen. On the other hand, Black's own queen is unprotected. With that in mind, Alekhine has prepared a sudden shot on the other side of the board.

23 ♗f6!!

Now the deflection of Black's g-pawn by 23...gxf6 would open the g-file and lose the black queen to 24 ♖g4+.

Sterk soon found that deflection of the g-pawn was not the only point of Alekhine's idea. There is a threat of 24 ♖g4! ♕xe2 25 ♖xg7+ ♔h8 26 ♖g6#, and although Black has many defensive tries, none of them work:

a) 23...h6 is met by 24 ♘e5 threatening simply 25 ♕g4.

b) 23...h5 doesn't save Black as 24 ♖g4!! follows and White mates after 24...♕xe2 25 ♖xg7+ ♔h8 26 ♘g5 followed by 27 ♖h7++ ♔g8 28 ♖h8#.

c) 23...♘c5 protects the queen and thus draws the sting from 24 ♖g4. White would reply 24 ♘e5!, with a very strong attack.

23...♖fc8

Black decides to move his f8-rook, but Alekhine is soon able to bury the black king.

24 ♕e5! *(D)*

24...♖c5

The three captures all fail:

a) 24...♕xc4 25 ♕g5 ♔f8 26 ♕xg7+ ♔e8 27 ♕g8+ ♔d7 28 ♘e5+ ♔c7 29 ♕xf7+ ♔b8 30 ♘d7+ and White mates in three further moves.

b) 24...♖xc4 fails to 25 ♕g5 ♖g4 26 ♕xg4 g6 27 ♕xa4 with an extra piece.

c) 24...gxf6 allows White to win by 25 ♖g4+ ♔f8 (or 25...♔h8 26 ♕xf6#) 26 ♕d6+ ♔e8 27 ♖g8#.

25 ♕g3 g6 26 ♖xa4 ♕d3 27 ♖f1 ♖ac8 28 ♖d4 ♕f5 29 ♕f4 ♕c2 30 ♕h6 1-0

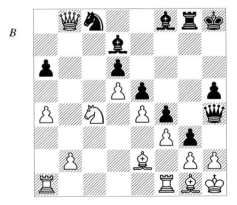

B

Summerscale – Friedland
Metropolitan Open, London 1998

The last two examples featured the opening of a file so that a major piece could fire along it. Another purpose for clearing a file can simply be to let a pawn advance on it. The diagram on the previous page shows a simple but drastic example.

Black has allowed White to gobble up a rook on the queenside. Now comes the payoff.

29...♗h3!

The first idea is that 30 gxh3 (deflection from the g-file) allows 30...g2#. The second idea is that Black threatens 30...♗xg2+ 31 ♔xg2 gxh2+ 32 ♔h1 hxg1♕#, against which White has no reasonable defence.

30 ♖f2 gxf2 31 gxh3 ♕xh3! 0-1

There is no defence to mate on the g-file.

Here is an example of a pawn deflection to open a rank.

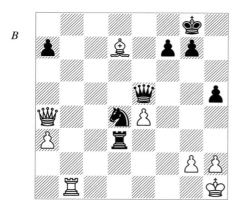

Ståhlberg – Keres
Bad Nauheim 1936

Keres forced open the seventh rank with **27...♘f3!** and Ståhlberg resigned because 28 gxf3 ♖d2 leads to mate on h2.

A pawn deflection can also be used to open a diagonal, but in that case it often involves additional motifs. Here is a simple example.

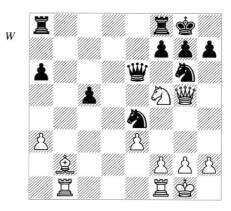

I. Rabinovich – Goglidze
Leningrad/Moscow 1939

23 ♕h6! 1-0

23...gxh6 is forced, but it opens the diagonal of the b2-bishop so that the black king cannot move to h8 or g7. Then 24 ♘xh6# recaptures the pawn and establishes itself on h6 (the substitution motif) with checkmate.

Exercise 26

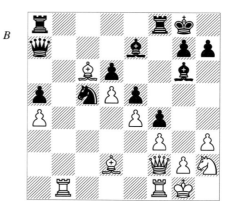

Level 1

Black, to play, uses a major-piece deflection to win material by exploiting the fact that his queen is on the same diagonal as the white king. At the same time, he is able to win some extra material as his light-squared bishop is on the same diagonal as a white rook.

Exercise 27

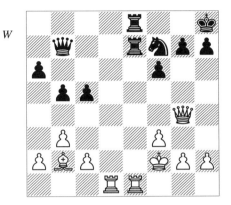

Level 2

White, to play, sees that ♖xe8 would be mate if the black e7-rook were out of the way. What should he do about that? Find Black's best reply to White's deflection sacrifice, and the little combination that White must find in order to emerge a pawn ahead.

Exercise 28

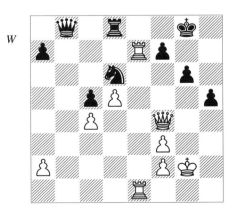

Level 1

White (to play) is already the exchange ahead. He would like to end the game with checkmate on g7. What pawn deflection can he use to bring it about? (Note that the black knight is effectively pinned against the queen because if queens are exchanged the white rooks can win various pawns on the queen-side.)

Exercise 29

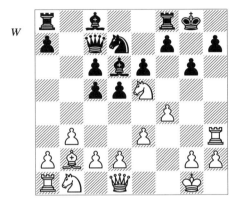

Level 2

What pawn-deflection sacrifice does White use to work up a sudden attack? After Black's best defence, see if you can find White's stunning reply which eventually leads to Black giving up material to avoid mate.

The solutions start on page 217.

Diversion

A diversion sacrifice involves luring a piece away so that it cannot continue to guard or attack certain squares, allowing the attacker to carry out his intentions. Here is a simple diversion of a piece, which aims at achieving a back-rank mate.

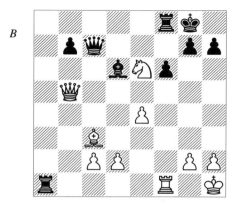

Popov – Neikirkh
Belgrade 1947

As the black queen and both rooks are attacked, White might expect 1...♖xf1+ 2 ♕xf1 ♕ moves 3 ♘xf8, when he is a pawn ahead in the endgame. However, the white queen protects the f1-rook and so prevents mate, which enables Black to play **1...♕d7!**, with the point 2 ♕xd7 ♖xf1#. The white queen must move, leaving the e6-knight *en prise* after the exchange of rooks on f1. Black emerges a rook up, not a pawn down.

In the diagram at the top of the next column, it is a pawn that is diverted, allowing the attacker's queen to invade on the square that it once guarded.

After **21...♖e3!** White resigned because the black queen invades decisively whether he accepts the rook (22 fxe3 ♕g3+ 23 ♔h1 ♖f2! and mate next move) or declines it (22 ♕d2 ♖xh3 and now both 23 f3 ♕g3+ 24 ♕g2 ♕h4! and 23 f4 ♕e6 24 f5 ♕e4! 25 ♕g2 ♕e3+ lead to a win for Black).

I once devised a combination with two silent diversion sacrifices, the first of which diverted a pawn, while the second was intended to divert the queen. Unfortunately, my

opponent rather spoiled things by resigning before I could play the second sacrifice.

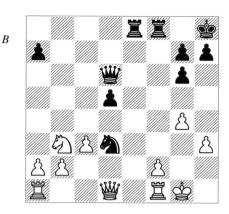

Harley – S. Williams
British League (4NCL) 2000/1

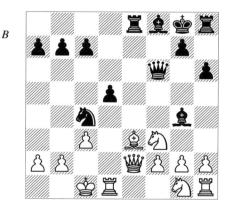

K. Shaw – LeMoir
Norfolk Ch 1999

What I really wanted to play was 15...♗f5 intending ...♕xc3+! with ...♗a3# to follow, but White can play 16 ♖xd5, grabbing a pawn and freeing d1 for his king. I had played for this position with a less artistic combination up my sleeve, and decided to play it.

15...♗a3!

The bishop diverts the b-pawn, which is protecting the c3-pawn.

16 bxa3 ♕xc3+ 17 ♕c2 ♕xa3+

Now I intended 18 ♔b1 ♗f5! (diverting the queen from the protection of b2) 19 ♕xf5 ♕b2#. White decided to be a party-pooper and resigned.

The next example also features multiple sacrifices, only one of which is a diversion, but it is the key link in a brilliant combination.

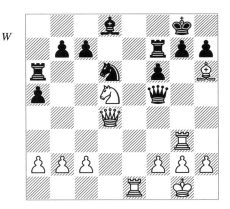

Koremar – Poliak
Ukrainian Ch 1937

White wants to bring about the sequence ♖e8+ ♖f8, ♖xg7+ ♔h8, ♖xf8#, but it is prevented by Black's d6-knight, which guards e8. The white queen will sacrifice itself for the knight, but White's own knight needs to clear the queen's line to d6 with a gain of tempo.

1 ♘b4! axb4 2 ♕xd6! ♕d7

Black has prevented mate, but White's response is stunning. He nudges the queen back from one attacked square to another.

3 ♕d5!!

The mate is still on if Black accepts the sacrifice, and meanwhile the queen pins the rook and so threatens 4 ♖xg7+.

3...♔f8

3...g6 fails to 4 ♖ge3! (still leaving the queen *en prise*), when Black is defenceless against the threat of 5 ♖e8+, so Black moves his king in order to unpin the rook. However, he is hit by another queen sacrifice which leads to a lovely back-rank mate.

4 ♖xg7!! ♕xd5

4...♖xg7 loses to 5 ♕xd7 since the g7-rook is pinned.

5 ♖g8+! ♔xg8 6 ♖e8+ ♖f8 7 ♖xf8# (1-0)

Sometimes, the piece that we wish to divert is doing more than simply guarding a square or a piece. In the next example, it is pinning a key attacking piece.

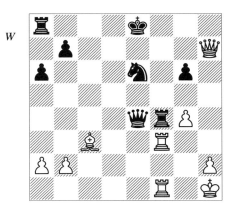

LeMoir – R. Franks
London League 1971/2

In this position, Black cannot castle as his king has already wandered to g8 and back. He has a nasty pin on the f3-rook, and expects me to deliver perpetual check. Instead, he is rocked by an unexpected diversion sacrifice.

30 ♗b4!!

The aim is to unpin the rook.

30...♕xb4

Since 30...♘f8 31 ♕e7+! ♕xe7 32 ♖xf4 ♕e2 33 ♖e1 ♕xe1+ 34 ♗xe1 ♖d8 35 ♗b4 gives White an ending a pawn ahead, Black decides to take the bishop.

31 ♕xg6+ ♔d7

31...♔e7 allows 32 ♖xf4 ♘xf4 33 ♕g5+, winning the knight.

Now I should have regained my piece by 32 ♖xf4 ♘xf4 33 ♕f7+ with an easy win, but for some reason I played **32 ♖d1+?**. Even that move eventually forced Black to return the piece and I won the endgame.

Here is an example of a deeply mysterious diversion sacrifice.

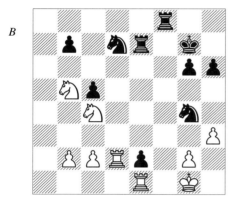

Bologan – Nunn
Bundesliga 1992/3

Nunn would like to play 30...♖f1+ 31 ♖xf1 e1♕. It looks decisive, but White can respond 32 ♖xd7! to divert the e7-rook from the defence of the new queen. After 32...♕xf1+ (or 32...♕e6 33 ♖xe7+ ♕xe7 34 hxg4) 33 ♔xf1 ♖xd7 34 hxg4, White would have a material advantage in the endgame.

White's counter-sacrifice will fail if the new black queen can escape with a check on move 32. The only square available for a queen check is e3, but that is currently guarded by the c4-knight. Knowing all this, Nunn's move is no longer so mysterious.

30...♘b6!!

Now White must lose material.

31 ♖dxe2

31 ♘xb6 ♖f1+! 32 ♖xf1 e1♕ 33 ♖d7 ♕e3+ 34 ♔h1 ♖xd7 35 ♘xd7 ♕e2 is a comfortable win for Black.

31...♖xe2 32 ♖xe2 ♘xc4 33 hxg4 ♘xb2

Nunn won the endgame with his extra pawn.

We can also divert a piece with a sacrifice of low value to make it release its guard on a piece of high value. This happens quite often with sacrifices that capture something, as the sacrificer wins material even if the sacrifice is declined. It is very rare for an effective silent sacrifice to have this kind of diversion as its sole motif, as there is little compulsion involved for the defender. The next diagram shows the only convincing example that I can find, and even then it is unusually complex for a sacrifice with one single motif.

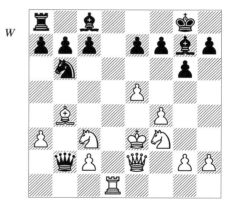

Adorjan – Wright
England 1975

Adorjan would like to play 20 ♖d8+ ♗f8 21 ♗xe7 ♕xc3+ 22 ♔f2, but then his attempted breakthrough on f8 is foiled by 22...♗f5! 23 ♖xa8 ♘xa8, retaining the extra piece. On the other hand, if that knight were diverted from its protection of the a8-rook, the c8-bishop would be pinned against the rook and unable to move.

20 ♞a4!! ♞xa4 21 ♖d8+ ♗f8 22 ♗xe7

Now there is no way for Black to avoid the capture on f8, as 22...♗f5 simply loses the a8-rook. White's attack turns out to be decisive.

22...♞b6 23 ♖xf8+ ♚g7 24 ♖d8 ♗g4 25 ♗f6+ ♚h6 26 ♖xa8 ♛c3+ 27 ♚f2 ♗xf3 28 gxf3 ♞xa8 29 ♚g3 c6 30 ♛f1 1-0

Another variant of the diversion motif is the **double diversion**, where the same move involves two diversions. In the first example, one piece, the black queen, is diverted from the protection of two important squares.

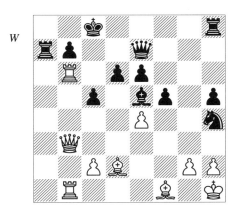

LeMoir – S. Williams
West of England Ch, Cheltenham 1977

White has been piling up the pressure on the b7-pawn, and now we might expect to see the sacrifice 32 ♗a6. It is very good, but there is a quicker breakthrough by using the other bishop to divert the black queen from the protection of both b7 and e6.

32 ♗g5! ♛xg5 33 ♖xb7

Now 33...♖xb7 leads to mate after 34 ♛xb7+ ♚d8 35 ♛b8+ ♚e7 36 ♖b7+ ♚f6 37

♛xh8+, etc. In desperation, Black decides to threaten mate himself.

33...♛f4

Indeed, he wins if White stops to defend as 34 g3?? ♛xe4+ is mate in a few moves. However, the second square left unprotected by the black queen proves to be decisive.

34 ♛xe6+ 1-0

It is mate next move.

The other form of double diversion, the diversion of *two pieces* at once, is even more impressive.

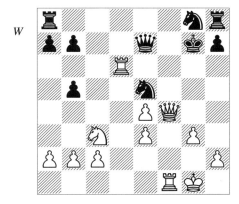

Berndtsson – Bengtsson
Copenhagen 1916

The e5-knight is the cornerstone of Black's defence, and it takes a remarkable move to get it out of the way.

20 ♖d7!!

White aims to divert either the knight or the queen.

20...♞xd7

20...♛xd7 loses to 21 ♛xe5+ ♚g6 22 ♞d5! threatening 23 ♞f4+ followed by 24 ♞e6 with a rapid mate. Now the finish is even swifter.

21 ♛g4+ ♚h6 22 ♖f5 1-0

Mate is unavoidable.

Exercise 30

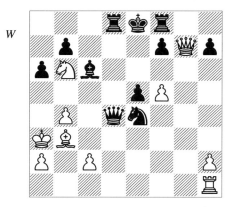

Level 1

White is a whole rook down, but ♕xe5 will be mate if only she (Judit Polgar) can divert the black queen. How does she do that?

Exercise 31

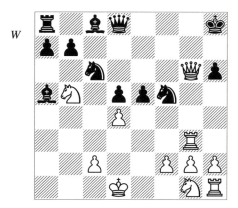

Level 2

White (to play) has sacrificed two pieces, but his attack appears to have run into a dead end, and meanwhile his g3-rook is under attack. However, he is able to force his opponent to resign after two more moves. How?

Exercise 32

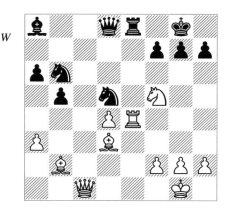

Level 3

This game was played in the good old days when a player could announce 'mate in x moves' without his opponent thinking that he had a computer up his sleeve. White announces mate in seven moves at most, and somewhere in there is a powerful silent diversion sacrifice (which must be declined).

The solutions are on page 218.

Decoy

When a piece is decoyed to a square where it is in danger, the true nature of that danger is not always immediately obvious. Our first example is a little beauty that illustrates the point well (*see diagram on next page*).

White can reply to 31...♕h1+ with 32 ♖g1. That reply would lose material if the g2-rook were pinned against something on the h1-a8 diagonal. Ivanchuk seeks to provide that 'something'.

31...♖f3!! 32 ♕d2

32 ♕xf3 loses the queen to 32...♕h1+ 33 ♖g1 ♕xf3. After the move played, the white queen no longer guards the h3-square.

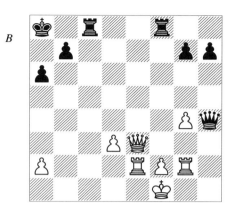

Shirov – Ivanchuk
*Sicilian theme tournament,
Buenos Aires 1994*

32...♕h1+ 33 ♖g1 ♕h3+ 0-1

After something like 34 ♖g2 ♖xd3 35 ♕e1 ♕h1+ 36 ♖g1 ♕d5, more pawns will disappear.

In the next example, the piece that is decoyed by the first sacrifice is exposed by a second, diversionary sacrifice.

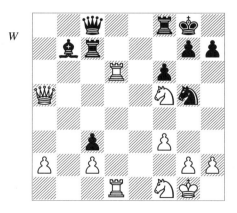

Bangiev – Cherepkov
USSR 1974

White would like to find an excuse to play ♘e7+, forking king and queen. By capturing the knight, the c7-rook would open the line of the white queen and expose the d8-square. Unfortunately, if White plays 26 ♘e7+ ♖xe7 27 ♖d8, Black does not have to continue 27...♖xd8??, which loses his queen after 28 ♖xd8+, but escapes simply by moving his queen forward. On the other hand, the queen is stuck on c8 right now, and moving it away would endanger the c7-rook.

White exploits all of these factors by playing the moves in a different order.

26 ♖d8!! ♖xd8

This is forced since 26...♕e6 loses the c7-rook, as does 26...♕xd8 27 ♖xd8 ♖xd8 28 ♕xc7.

27 ♘e7+! ♔f7 *(D)*

Black must give up his queen as 27...♖xe7 28 ♖xd8+ is even worse. The game ends neatly.

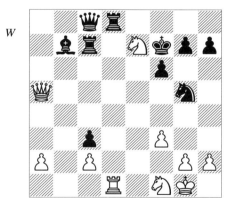

28 ♘xc8 ♖dxc8 29 ♖d8! ♘e6?

Better is 29...♖c5 30 ♕b6 ♖xd8 31 ♕xd8, but White has a winning material advantage.

30 ♕h5+ 1-0

In my early years as a chess-player, it was a mysterious decoy sacrifice that helped to fuel my own love of silent sacrifices.

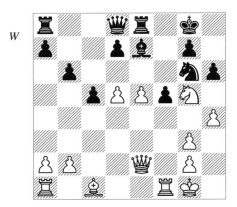

LeMoir – D. Thomas
Bristol League 1965/6

If the white knight retreats then Black can assault the e-pawn with 19...♗f6. If I play 19 ♕h5 then Black has 19...♘xe5. I wanted to capture the f-pawn without losing my e-pawn and realized that if the black king were at f7 and my queen at h5, then ♖xf5+ would win the knight as well as the pawn.

A little more analysis convinced me that Black could only avoid the loss of material by allowing weaknesses in his kingside, so I went ahead.

19 ♘f7!! ♔xf7

After 19...♕b8 20 ♖xf5 ♗d6, White is able to tear the black kingside to shreds with a cascade of sacrifices: 21 ♘xh6+! gxh6 22 ♕g4 ♔g7 23 ♗xh6+!! ♔xh6 24 ♕h5+ ♔g7 25 ♖f7+! ♔xf7 26 ♕h7+ ♔f8 27 ♖f1+ and mate next move.

20 ♕h5!

Now Black must allow his kingside to be weakened without any material compensation.

20...♗f6

20...♗xh4, attempting to remain a pawn ahead, loses rapidly to a sacrificial breakthrough starting with 21 ♖xf5+ ♗f6 22 exf6 gxf6 23 ♗g5!.

21 exf6 gxf6 22 ♖xf5 ♖h8

22...♖e1+ 23 ♔h2 ♕e7 is better, but White replies 24 b3 followed by ♗b2, ganging up on the weak f-pawn.

23 b3 ♔g7 24 ♗b2 ♖f8 25 ♖af1 ♕e8 26 ♖xf6 ♖xf6 27 ♖xf6 ♔h7 28 ♕f5 1-0

In the next example, a white rook finds a square deep inside the black position where it is completely immune from capture, since the defender cannot allow his queen to be decoyed to that square.

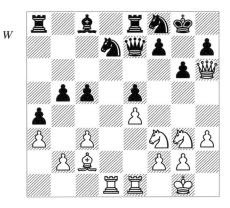

Ivkov – Gufeld
Sarajevo 1964

White is able to double rooks on the d-file in a particularly powerful way.

22 ♖d6! c4

On 22...♖xd6, 23 ♘h5! forces 23...gxh5 24 ♕xd6, as 23...♘e6 allows 24 ♘g5 ♘df8 25 ♘f6+ ♔h8 26 ♘xf7#.

23 ♖ed1 ♘c5 24 ♘xe5!

White wins a pawn as 24...♕xe5 25 ♖1d5 ♕e7 26 ♖xc5! ♕xd6 27 ♘h5! repeats the idea. Black declines the sacrifice again, but White finishes brilliantly.

24...♗e6 25 ♘c6 ♕c7 26 e5 ♗d7 27 ♖1d5 ♘d3 28 ♖xd7! ♘xd7 29 ♖xd7! ♕xd7 30 ♘e4! ♖e6 31 ♘f6+ 1-0

Exercise 33

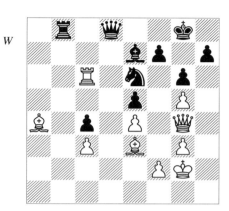

Level 1

White (Fischer) played **39 ⟨R⟩xe6!** intending 39...fxe6 40 ⟨Q⟩xe6+ ⟨K⟩f8 41 ⟨Q⟩xe5 with a winning attack. Black's reply **39...⟨Q⟩c8** appeared to catch Fischer in a trap, as the rook is pinned against the white queen. What decoy sacrifice had Fischer prepared that forced immediate resignation?

Exercise 34

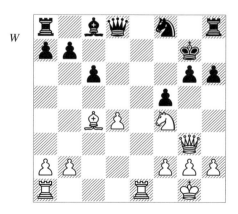

Level 2

How can White make full use of his knight?

Exercise 35

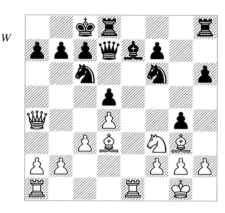

Level 3

White plays **16 ⟨N⟩e5**, apparently intending after **16...⟨N⟩xe5** to play 17 ⟨Q⟩xd7+ ⟨N⟩exd7 18 ⟨R⟩xe7 with some pressure. Instead, his 17th move comes as a nasty shock to Black, who only lasts another five moves. What is White's idea?

The solutions start on page 218.

Interference

Interfering with the line of a defending piece often has an immediately terminal effect, particularly when mate, or pawn promotion, can no longer be prevented. Here is a simple example of a silent sacrifice using interference to promote a pawn (*see diagram on following page*).

We come in at the beginning of the winning sequence. White is the exchange for a pawn down, but his aim is to promote his b-pawn.

1 b6 c5

Black envisages 2 b7 ⟨N⟩c6 controlling the queening square.

2 ⟨N⟩a5!

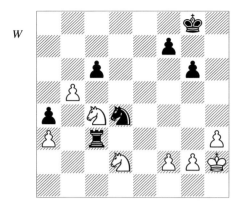

Chernenko – Bazonyin
USSR 1968

White puts an end to that thought. Now the rook is forced to prevent promotion by occupying the b-file.

2...♖c2 3 b7! ♖b2 4 ♘db3!! 1-0

The rook's line is blocked. Black can prevent the b-pawn from promoting by returning the exchange, after 4...♖xb3 5 ♘xb3 ♘c6 6 ♘xc5 ♘b8 7 ♘xa4 he is three pawns down.

Interference can be employed to allow a player to pursue his dreams of mate undisturbed, as White does in the next example (*see following diagram*).

Black has given up a piece in order to win the white rook in the corner. White sees a mate with a sequence commencing ♕xe4+, but the black queen protects e4 and prevents that possibility. An interference sacrifice is called for.

13 ♘f3!!

Black is invited to take his pick between capturing both rooks or satisfying himself with a knight. All danger of mate can be averted by 13...0-0, but White will save his rook and remain a piece ahead, so Black decides to demand proof.

13...♕xh1+

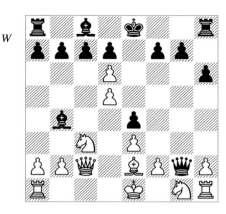

Maes – Huba
Leuven 2000

13...exf3 allows 14 ♕e4+ with the same winning sequence.

14 ♔d2 ♕xa1 15 ♕xe4+ ♔f8 16 ♕e7+ ♔g8 17 ♕e8+ ♔h7 18 ♗d3+ 1-0

It is mate by 18...g6 19 ♕xf7#.

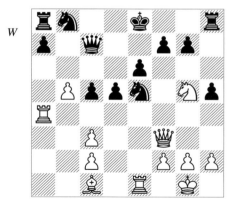

D. Johnston – A. Punnett
British League (4NCL) 2000/1

This example is unusual. White works out a sequence that mates or wins the black queen, but Black can deliver mate first. White's response is to play an interference sacrifice that prevents the mate and enables his own plans to go ahead.

White kicks off his combination by forcing his queen in to f7.

17 ♖xe5! ♕xe5 18 ♕xf7+ ♔d8

Now he would like to play 19 ♗f4, but 19...♕e1# is mate.

19 ♖e4!!

This interference sacrifice blocks the black queen's line to e1 with a gain of time.

19...dxe4 20 ♗f4 ♕xg5

The queen has to give up its life for the knight or bishop, when Black's king is fatally exposed.

21 ♗xg5+ ♔c8 22 ♕xe6+ 1-0

Simple interference sacrifices, like the examples above, are comparatively rare. Generally, other motifs are also involved, and can result in some of the most beautiful of combinations. We will enjoy some in the next chapter. For now, let us consider what happens when two interference motifs are combined, in other words when we have a **double interference**. Here is a simple example.

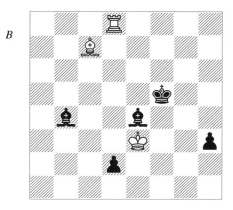

Nenarokov – Grigoriev
Moscow 1923

Black wants to promote one of his pawns, but the white bishop prevents ...h2, and the rook prevents ...d1♕.

1...♗d6!! interrupts the line of both pieces. White resigned because 2 ♗xd6 allows the d-pawn to promote, and after 2 ♖xd6 h2 both pawns have reached the seventh rank and the rook must allow one of them to promote.

It is possible to cause an interference between pieces that move in the same way. For instance, we can simultaneously interfere with two rooks, or queen and rook, as long as one is working on a rank and the other's influence is on a file. A sacrifice at the point of intersection of the rank and the file can cause mutual interference. Here, as proof, is one of the most famous double interferences in history.

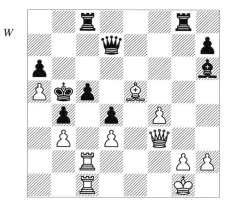

Tarrasch – Allies
Consultation game, Naples 1914

White has two mating ideas: one is ♖xc5# and the other is the sequence ♕b7+ ♔xa5, ♖a1+ and mate. At the moment, the black rook prevents the first idea by its action along the c-file and the queen prevents the second by acting along the second rank. Tarrasch realizes that, if either defending piece is on the c7-square, it will get in the way of the other, and he can play a diversion sacrifice to force mate.

1 ♗c7!! 1-0

The bishop interferes with the queen's line to the b7-square and the rook's line to the c5-square.

Now 1...♕xc7 blocks the rook's defence of c5, so Black must reply to the diversion sacrifice 2 ♖xc5+!! with 2...♕xc5. The queen is then no longer guarding b7, so 3 ♕b7+ is mate next move.

The alternative is 1...♖xc7, which blocks the queen's defence of b7, so Black must reply to the diversion sacrifice 2 ♕b7+!! with 2...♖xb7. The rook is then no longer guarding c5, so White can play 3 ♖xc5#.

The next example has the appearance of a treble interference, but that is deceptive.

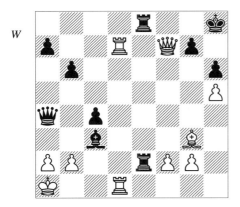

Miles – Pritchett
Lloyds Bank Masters, London 1982

White's two mating ideas are ♕xe8+ (followed by ♕g6+ and a back-rank rook check) and ♕xg7#. The mutual protection of the rooks prevents the first mate, while the bishop prevents the second. Tony Miles's decisive **34 ♗e5!!** *(D)* cuts the lines of communication for all three pieces, and Pritchett resigned at once.

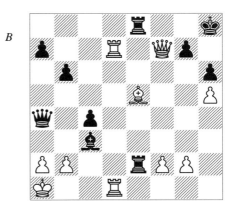

The bishop landed at the intersection of the lines of two rooks and a bishop, but the move is only a double interference. The interferences that matter are to the lines of the e2-rook (which protects the e8-rook) and the bishop (which guards g7). The blocking of the line of the e8-rook has no effect.

Exercise 36

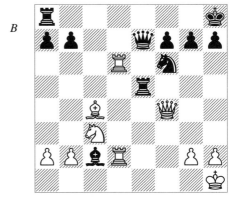

Level 1

Black to play and win. 25...♖e1+ fails to 26 ♗f1. If you pretend you are Tony Miles, you should be able to work out how Black overcomes that problem.

Exercise 37

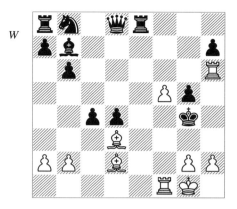

Level 2

White has given up his queen to drag the black king all the way up the board. How does he slam the door shut on the king's prison cell?

Exercise 38

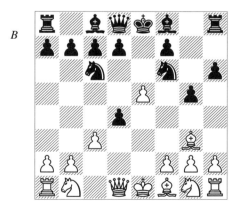

Level 3

A little joke. Who is winning after **7...dxc3 8 exf6** ?

The solutions are on page 219.

Elimination and Secondary Line Clearance

We shall skip over silent sacrifices with the elimination motif, because they occur so rarely.

Secondary line clearance is also extremely rare as a sole motif for a silent sacrifice. However, as we shall soon see, it can be a major motif in complex sacrifices such as knight offers on the fifth rank (see the section '♘d5 and All That' in the next chapter).

Substitution

The substitution motif happens when the attacker wants one of his pieces to occupy a certain square that is currently guarded by one of the defender's pieces. By sacrificing another piece on that square, and allowing it to be captured, the desired piece is established where it is needed.

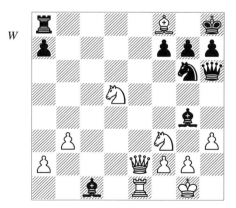

Tal – Holm
European Team Ch, Kapfenberg 1970

Several pieces are *en prise*, but the crucial factor is the weakness of Black's back rank.

Tal's priority is to get a rook or queen there, so he plays **26 ♕e8!** and after **26...♖xe8 27 ♖xe8 ♗d7 28 ♖d8** Black resigned as there is no way to prevent mate.

The next example is more complex, and features a preparatory sacrifice to make the substitution sacrifice possible.

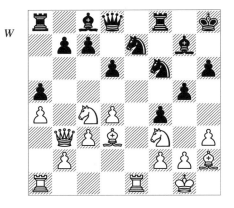

Ribli – Wl. Schmidt
Zonal tournament, Baile Herculane 1982

White wants to get a knight to g6 to torment the black king. Two obstacles must be overcome before one of them can get there, the first being that Black's e7-knight guards the g6-square. The combination starts with an exchange sacrifice to remove it.

18 ♖xe7! ♕xe7

e5 is the only feasible stepping-stone to g6, but the black d-pawn is guarding that square, so the combination continues with a substitution sacrifice.

19 ♘ce5!!

White's point is 19...dxe5 20 ♘xe5, and now if Black blocks the white queen's diagonal with 20...♕e6 he loses his queen to 21 ♘g6+ ♔g8 22 ♗c4, while if 20...♕d8 White mates by 21 ♘g6+ ♔h7 22 ♘e7+! ♔h8 23 ♕g8+! ♘xg8 24 ♘g6+ ♔h7 25 ♘xf8+ ♔h8

26 ♘g6+ ♔h7 27 ♘e5+ ♔h8 28 ♘f7#. Other queen moves allow White to regain material and keep the attack.

Black declines the knight but White has several further shots in his locker.

19...♕e6 20 d5! ♕e8

20...♕xd5 loses the queen immediately to 21 ♘g6+ ♔g8 22 ♘e7+, and 20...♘xd5 loses it to the more complex sequence 21 ♘g6+ ♔g8 22 ♖e1 ♕f7 23 ♖e7! ♘xe7 24 ♘xe7+ ♔h8 25 ♘g6+ ♔g8 26 ♗c4.

21 ♘g6+ ♔g8 22 ♖e1 ♕d8 23 ♘xf8 ♕xf8 24 h4!

Material is equal, but the black position is falling apart.

24...♘g4 25 hxg5 hxg5 26 ♘xg5 ♗e5 27 ♘f3 ♕g7 28 ♕c4 ♘xh2 29 ♔xh2 ♗d7 30 ♘xe5 dxe5 31 d6+ 1-0

Silent sacrifices with the single motif of substitution are fairly rare and, like the one above, most of the examples that I have seen lead to complex play, even though the basic idea may be quite simple. In the next example the substitution sacrifice is combined with the offer of a rook, but otherwise it is about as simple as it gets.

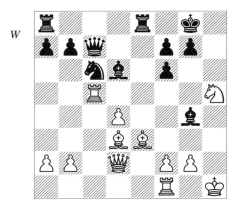

W. Watson – Weidemann
Britain vs W. Germany (universities) 1984

White has a rook under attack on c5, but his aim is to mate on g7 or h7. He needs to get his queen to h6 quickly.

19 ♗h6!!

With a black pawn on h6, this move would come as less of a surprise, but the square is empty so the sacrifice is silent and therefore shocking.

19...♗xh5

Black cannot capture the rook because after 19...♗xc5 20 ♗xg7 ♗xh5 21 ♕h6, mate is unavoidable, and he must also decline the bishop as 19...gxh6 20 ♕xh6 (substituting the queen for the bishop) also leads to mate.

With the text-move, Black tries unsuccessfully to stop a white piece landing on g7. He could achieve this aim better with 19...♗f8!, but I think that White can still win by 20 ♘xf6+! gxf6 21 ♖g5+! fxg5 22 ♕xg5+ ♔h8 23 ♗xf8 f6 24 ♕xf6+ ♔g8 25 ♗h6 ♕d7 26 ♗c4+ ♖e6! (or 26...♗e6 27 d5) 27 f3 b5 28 ♕g5+ ♔h8 29 ♗xe6 ♗xe6 30 d5 ♗xd5 31 ♖d1 ♘b4 32 ♖d4, when the mating threats win material.

20 ♖xh5 g6 21 ♖h3 ♕a5? (D)

21...♕d8 is better, but White wins by 22 ♗g7! g5 23 ♗h6!, intending ♕d1 followed by ♕h5 with a quick mate.

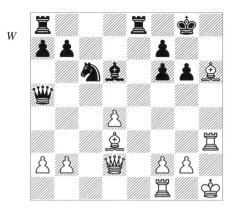

W

22 ♗g7!!

This decoy sacrifice forced resignation as Black faces mate from 22...♔xg7 (or 22...♕xd2 23 ♗xf6 mating) 23 ♕h6+ ♔g8 24 ♕h8#.

Exercise 39

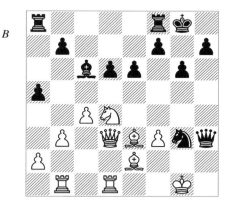

B

Level 2

Black has sacrificed a piece for the three pawns and an attack. His next move is a beautiful substitution sacrifice that forces a decisive material gain.

The solution is on page 219.

Line-Grabbing

With the line-grabbing motif, the recapturing piece opens a line for its own use. It is a relatively rare motif for silent sacrifices, so we will look at just a few examples. In the first, the sacrificing piece makes an unexpected switch in direction (*see diagram on following page*).

White is threatening 30 ♘a6, winning the black queen, while Black's eye is on the f2-square. With a white pawn on e3, the next move would be easier to spot because it would be a capture.

29...♗e3!

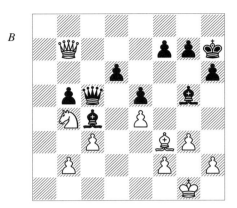

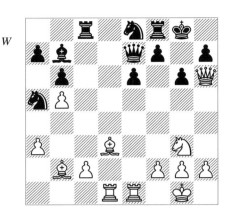

Blackstock – LeMoir
Spalding 1970

Spielmann – Hönlinger
Match, Vienna 1929

Black switches the direction of the bishop's attack with the simple intention of ripping open the white king's position. Now after 30 fxe3, the recapture 30...♕xe3+ grabs the a7-g1 diagonal and White is soon mated: 31 ♔g2 ♕d2+ 32 ♔h3 (or 32 ♔g1 ♕e1+ 33 ♔g2 ♕f1#) 32...♗f1+ 33 ♔g4 ♕g5#.

White therefore tries to complicate the issue.

30 b3

This fails because Black can ignore the attack on his light-squared bishop and make hay with the other one. 30 ♘d5! is better as after 30...♗xf2+ 31 ♔h1 ♕a7 (31...♗xd5? 32 exd5 ♕e3 33 ♕xf7 gives White the stronger attack) 32 ♕xa7 ♗xa7 the ending would be difficult for Black to win.

30...♗xf2+ 31 ♔g2 ♗g1! 32 bxc4 ♕f2+ 33 ♔h3 ♕xh2+ 34 ♔g4 h5+ 35 ♔f5 ♕h3+ 0-1

Next we have a famous example of Spielmann's chess art (*see following diagram*).

White's first thought is to mate on h7, as his queen and bishop are lined up with only the g-pawn in the way. He rejects the deflection sacrifice 23 ♘h5 because, thanks to the defending knight on e8, it does not threaten mate on g7.

23 ♘f5!!

By contrast, this knight move threatens the black queen. The sacrifice must be declined since 23...gxf5 allows the bishop to grab the diagonal to h7 by 24 ♗xf5, and it is immune from capture as the black e-pawn is pinned against its queen. The only defence to mate at h7 is 24...f6, when 25 ♗xe6+ ♔h8 26 ♖d7 wins at once.

This means that the black queen is forced to move, but where? 23...♕c7 loses to 24 ♗f6!, when the bishop is immune due to mate on g7 and Black has no good defence to the threats of ♘e7+ and ♗e7. He needs to be able to prevent ♗f6 or to meet it with ...♖c7, but 23...♕d8 24 ♗f1 ♗d5 25 ♖xd5! exd5 26 ♖xe8! leads to mate.

The queen must come out to c5, whereupon Spielmann can demonstrate the full glory of his idea.

23...♕c5 24 ♖e5! ♗d5 25 ♘e7+!! 1-0

Black resigned because the knight clears the rook's line to h5 and the finish will be 25...♕xe7 26 ♕xh7+! ♔xh7 27 ♖h5+ ♔g8 28 ♖h8#.

Exercise 40

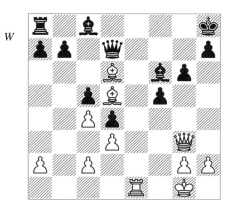

W

Exercise 41

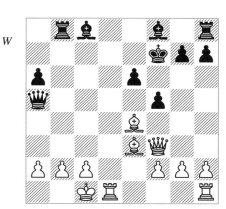

W

Level 1

White's combination starts with **22 ♖e7!**, intending 22...♗xe7 23 ♕e5+ followed by mate. Black replies **22...♕d8**, but White's line-grabbing follow-up sacrifice causes instant resignation. What is it?

Level 2

Without the e-pawn, the black king would be badly exposed. What long-term silent sacrifice did White find to remove it? Work out how White should conduct his attack after the sacrifice.

The solutions are on page 220.

9 Complex Silent Sacrifices

In the previous chapter, we considered silent sacrifices that generally had a single, or dominant, motif. Many silent sacrifices are more complex, and some combine as many as four motifs.

Deadly Tacticians love complex silent sacrifices because they can be very powerful, and they are often hard to foresee. Although it may not fully understand the mechanics involved, the chess public loves them because they can be very surprising and often spectacular. Before considering complex silent sacrifices in general, we shall look at the knight sacrifice on the fifth rank, a type that occurs remarkably often.

♘d5 and All That

The knight has a particular affinity to squares on the fifth rank. It can be tempted there despite the fact that a pawn is guarding its destination. Knights have been sacrificed on empty squares all the way across the fifth rank. The first example is a favourite from my personal collection (*see diagram on following page*).

The black rooks are lined up on the g-file in order to squeeze White's pieces into the corner.

23...♘g4!?

This is the point of Black's formation, exploiting the discomfort of White's kingside

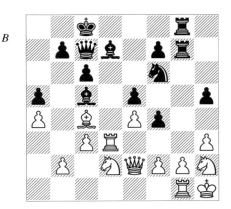

D. Lynch – LeMoir
London League 1974/5

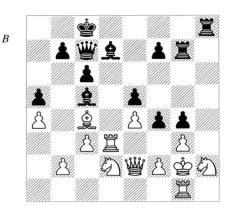

28...gxf3 29 Rxf3 Rh7+ 30 ♔g2 ♗h3+ 31 ♔h2 ♗f1# (0-1)

pieces. Black could also get away with playing 23...♛b6!, with the attractive possibility of 24 Rf3 ♛xb2 25 Rb1 Rxg2! 26 ♘g4 hxg4 27 Rxb2 Rg1+! 28 ♔h2 gxh3 29 Rg3 R8xg3! 30 fxg3 fxg3#.

24 hxg4 hxg4

The h-file is now completely open and, with his rooks well placed to occupy it immediately, Black is threatening 25...g3, winning back the piece at once. White would be best advised to let that happen and to respond by playing his other knight to f3.

25 g3

The attempt to block the advance of the black g-pawn is natural, but it allows a swift sacrificial breakthrough based on the bad position of the white king.

25...Rh8 26 ♔g2 *(D)*

26 Rd1 clears a square for the king, but Black has a very strong continuation in 26...f3 27 ♛e1 Rxh2+! 28 ♔xh2 ♛d8!, followed by ...♛h8+ and then ...Rh7 or ...♛h3.

26...Rxh2+! 27 ♔xh2 f3! 28 ♘xf3?

He overlooks the mate, but after 28 Rxf3 Black wins easily by 28...Rh7+ 29 ♔g2 gxf3+ 30 ♔xf3 ♛d6; e.g., 31 ♛e1 Rh2 32 Rf1 ♗h3 and White loses at least the exchange.

In terms of our silent sacrifice motifs, 23...♘g4 in this game is a complex sacrifice with multiple motifs: *deflection* of the white h-pawn to open the h-file at White's end, *secondary line clearance* (through the recapture by the black h-pawn) to open the same file at Black's end, and *substitution* of the knight with a black pawn at g4 that controls key squares and threatens to advance to g3. This is typical of many sacrifices of knights on the fifth rank.

These sacrifices are popular among tacticians because they often give the sacrificer benefits that can last for many moves – the compensation nearly always includes an open file for his major pieces and a clear space advantage.

The most popular knight-to-fifth-rank sacrifice is ♘d5 for White in Sicilian Defence and Hedgehog formations with a black pawn at e6 and white pawns at e4 and/or c4. The sacrifice is so popular, and its effects can be so lasting, that I decided to do a quick survey of a selection of games in *Mega Database 2001* to identify the main types of ♘d5 sacrifice. I looked at games from June to October 2000, picking out only games where the ♘d5 sacrifice was played by White, and which White went on to win. There were no fewer than 32 such games. (For the record, *Mega Database 2001* lists about 45,000 games in total over that period.)

Some ♘d5 sacrifices are temporary in nature, since the extra piece has to be returned at once, as in the first example below.

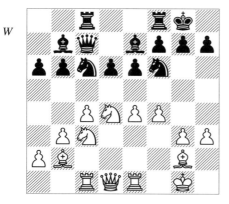

Bargad – Albarran
Argentine Ch semi-final, Ezeiza 2000

16 ♘d5!

Black cannot capture the knight because 16...exd5 17 cxd5 completely opens the c-file and pins the knight against the queen. White wins material after 17...♕d7 18 dxc6 ♗xc6 19 ♘xc6 ♖xc6 20 ♖xc6 ♕xc6 21 e5 ♕c5+ 22 ♗d4. Black therefore has to allow his dark-squared bishop to be exchanged, whereupon White's pressure on the dark squares gives him a strong initiative.

16...♕d8 17 ♘xc6 ♗xc6 18 ♘xe7+ ♕xe7 19 ♕d4 ♕b7 20 g4 ♖cd8 21 ♖cd1 ♖d7 22 ♕e3 ♘e8 23 ♖d2 b5 24 cxb5 axb5 25 b4 d5 26 e5 ♘c7 27 ♗d4 ♖a8 28 ♖c2 ♖a6 29 f5 ♕a8 30 ♖ec1 ♘e8 31 ♕f2 ♗b7 32 ♗f1 ♖c6 33 ♗xb5 ♖xc2 34 ♖xc2 ♖c7 35 fxe6 ♖e7 36 exf7+ ♖xf7 37 ♕e3 ♗a6 38 e6 ♖c7 39 ♖xc7 ♘xc7 40 ♕e5 1-0

When a white rook and black queen are both on the c-file and a black minor piece is on c6, as in this example, the Maroczy Bind formation enables the ♘d5 sacrifice to be temporary.

The same thing can also happen in the Morra Gambit, where there is no white c-pawn. When the white e-pawn recaptures on d5, a white rook on c1 will pin a minor piece at c6 in front of a queen at c7.

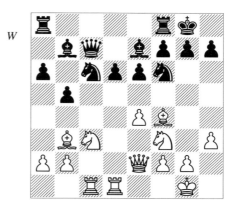

Garcia Romero – Diaz Sanchez
Spanish Team Ch, Barcelona 2000

14 ♘d5! exd5

Black can refuse the knight by 14...♕d8 but 15 ♘xe7+ ♘xe7 16 ♖xd6 equalizes material and leaves White with a dominant position on the central dark squares.

15 exd5 ♘d4

Played to avoid worse, because 15...♘xd5 16 ♗xd5 ♕d7 17 ♗xc6 ♗xc6 18 ♘e5 results in loss of material for Black. The rest of the game sees him facing a strong attack by White without having the comfort of a material advantage.

16 ♘xd4 ♕d7 17 g4 ♖fe8 18 ♕f3 ♖ec8 19 ♘c6 ♗f8 20 ♗g5 ♘e8 21 ♖e1 f6 22 ♗d2 ♘c7 23 ♗c2 ♖e8 24 g5 fxg5 25 ♗f5 ♖xe1+ 26 ♖xe1 ♕f7 27 ♗xh7+ 1-0

♘d5 can also be a temporary sacrifice for other reasons; for instance, if a recapture on d5 by the c- or e-pawn traps a piece that then has no escape.

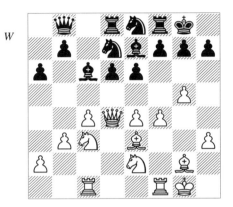

Pastor – M. Diaz
Pan American Women's Ch, Merida 2000

White exploits the c6-bishop's lack of a retreat square.

18 ♘d5! exd5 19 exd5

White at once regains the piece, and will soon exert strong pressure on the light squares.

19...♖c8 20 dxc6 bxc6 21 ♕e4 ♗d8 22 ♘d4 ♘c5 23 ♘xc6 ♘xe4 24 ♘xb8 ♖xb8 25 ♗xe4

Black has nothing for her pawn and White won on the 41st move.

White can also regain the piece if the e-pawn recaptures attacking one piece and discovering an attack on another on the newly-opened e-file (*see following diagram*).

18 ♘d5 exd5 19 exd5

The recapture hits both bishops at once. Black decides to keep his dark-squared bishop, but White retains a strong initiative.

19...♖e8 20 dxc6 bxc6 21 c4 ♖b8 22 b4 ♕d7 23 ♖ad1 h5 24 ♗d4 d5 25 ♗c3 ♕a7+ 26 c5 ♘g4 27 h3 ♘f6 28 ♖e5

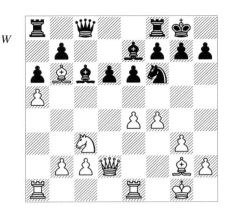

Am. Rodriguez – Corral Blanco
Spanish Team Ch, Barcelona 2000

By doubling rooks on the e-file, White achieved a dominating position, winning on move 59.

In the next example from the 32 *Mega Database 2001* games in my review, Black is obliged to decline the sacrifice because a bishop recapturing on d5 would skewer his queen on c6 to the a8-rook.

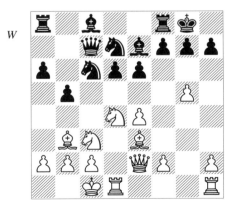

Arquie – Meynard
Cannes 2000

In this position, White can exploit the diagonal from d5 to a8 by playing 13 ♘d5! exd5 14 ♘xc6!, when 14...♕xc6 15 ♗xd5 costs Black the exchange, and meanwhile Black's central position is ruined. Instead, he plays his moves in the wrong order.

13 ♘xc6?! ♕xc6 14 ♘d5

Now Black is not forced to capture the knight on d5.

14...♗d8 15 ♖hg1 ♗b7 16 ♕h5

White continues to offer the knight, and now it is relatively safe to accept it.

16...exd5 17 ♗xd5 ♕c7 18 g6!? hxg6?

Black collapses in the face of some extremely aggressive play, allowing a fine finish. He should play 18...♘f6 19 gxf7+ ♖xf7 20 ♗xf7+ ♕xf7 21 ♕xf7+ ♔xf7 with a perfectly acceptable position.

19 ♖xg6 ♗f6 20 ♖h6!! gxh6 21 ♕g6+ ♗g7 22 ♖g1 1-0

The most important ♘d5 sacrifices are played with long-term compensation in mind. The opening of the e-file can lead to lasting pressure if the black king has not yet castled. When a white pawn arrives on d5 it not only cramps the black pieces for room, but it can also support a knight jumping in to the c6-square to increase the pressure on e7 and create havoc in the enemy ranks, as the next example demonstrates (*see following diagram*).

14 ♘d5!? ♘axb3+?

Black exchanges White's dangerous light-squared bishop, but chooses the wrong knight for the job. 14...♘cxb3+ retains the a5-knight, which guards the c6-square. He soon regrets his error.

15 axb3 exd5 16 exd5 ♗e7 17 ♗f4 ♖a7 18 ♘c6

Piling up the pressure on e7. Black is forced to return the piece and more.

18...♘e6 19 ♘xe7 ♘xf4 20 ♕e3 ♕xe7 21 ♕xf4 ♗e6 22 dxe6 0-0 23 exf7+ ♕xf7 24 ♕xb4 ♕xf2 25 ♕xd6

White won with his two extra pawns.

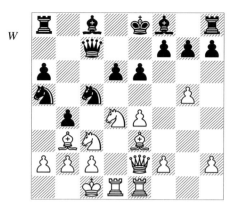

Leitão – Chemin
Zonal tournament, São Paulo 2000

In the example we have just seen, a black bishop on c8 prevented the remaining white knight from using the f5-square to reinforce the pressure on e7. Often, the bishop is on b7, or there is a black knight on d7. In either case, the knight is free to use the f5-square, which can be extremely useful in White's attack.

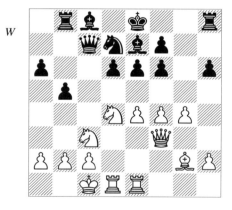

Porras Rodriguez – Z. Hernandez
Pan American Women's Ch, Merida 2000

14 ♘d5! exd5 15 exd5 ♔f8

White can now play 16 ♕e4, virtually forcing the reply 16...♘e5 as 16...♗d8 17 ♕e8+ ♔g7 18 ♘f5+ forces mate and 16...♘c5 17 ♕xe7+ ♕xe7 18 ♖xe7 ♔xe7 19 ♘c6+ leads to a good endgame for White. She prefers to give Black the option of retaining her extra piece at the cost of facing a strong attack.

White has to choose whether to use c6 or f5 for her knight. They are both reasonable, but Ms Porras Rodriguez chooses f5, since that creates more pressure on the kingside.

16 ♘f5 ♗d8 17 ♕e4 ♘e5

This is no longer completely forced, but an extremely reasonable decision. Trying to retain the piece by 17...♔g8 (D) allows White to demonstrate how hard it is to resist the slow build-up of the attack in positions like these.

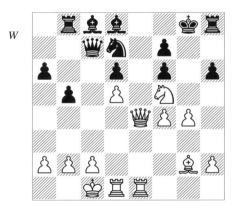

The game could go 18 ♖d3!, when the natural 18...♘c5 leads to a great finish: 19 ♕e8+ ♔h7 20 ♖h3!! ♗xf5 (or 20...♖xe8 21 ♖xh6+ ♔g8 22 ♖xe8#) 21 ♖xh6+!! ♔xh6 22 ♕xh8+ ♗h7 23 ♕f8+ ♔g6 24 h4 f5 25 h5+ ♔f6 26 g5#. The more circumspect 18...♘f8 forces White to progress more slowly, but the attack is still very dangerous; e.g., 19 ♖h3 ♗xf5 20 gxf5 ♔h7 21 ♗f1 ♖g8 22 ♕f3 ♕a5 23 c3 ♕xa2 24 ♕h5 and once Black runs out of checks White will break through on h6.

After the move played, White retains some attacking chances, but they are greatly reduced. Unfortunately, Black blundered before the game could become interesting.

18 fxe5 fxe5 19 ♔b1 ♗g5 20 ♖d3 ♗xf5 21 ♕xf5 ♖c8?? 22 ♖c3 1-0

There can be many variations on the e-file-attack theme. To illustrate just one, in the next example White has already pushed his f-pawn to f6. Its presence prevents Black from occupying the e7-square and makes it extremely unlikely that his king will find a safe haven on the kingside. On the other hand, he can block the e-file with ...♘e5 without being harassed by a white f-pawn. In this example, White also has a bishop on the h3-c8 diagonal, which makes it difficult for the black king to escape to the queenside.

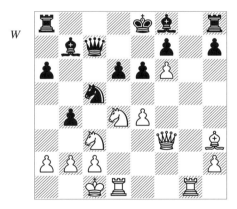

Barbier – Rajaobelina
Etang Sale 2000

In my selection of ♘d5 examples, three of the positions occurred in previous games in the 1.7 million game *Mega Database 2001*. One appeared no fewer than 44 times. The position in front of you occurs five times.

18 ♘d5 exd5 19 exd5 ♘d7 20 ♖ge1+ ♘e5 21 ♘c6 ♗xc6

This is very risky as it half-opens the d-file and gives White a second pawn on the sixth rank near the black king.

22 dxc6 ♖d8?

At this point Black has an interesting idea in 22...♗h6+ (making room for the king on f8) 23 ♔b1 ♖g8, hoping to catch White napping on the back rank after the apparently decisive blow 24 ♖xd6. Black replies 24...♕xd6 25 c7 ♖c8! 26 ♗xc8 ♖g1!! and now only 27 ♗d7+! ♔xd7 28 c8♕+ ♔xc8 29 ♕a8+ can save White. Instead, White could play 24 a3!? with the idea of aiming at the same line, but at the end (after ...♖g1) he can let his rook go (it is no longer back-rank mate) and play ♕b7!!, winning the black queen for the c-pawn.

The move played loses drastically.

23 ♖xe5+! dxe5 24 ♗d7+ ♖xd7 25 cxd7+ ♔d8 26 ♕a8+ ♕c8 27 ♕xc8# (1-0)

Following the ♘d5 sacrifice, an alternative method of play is to smash open the centre by playing e5 rather than exd5. The idea dates back to the early 1970s.

2001. White scored a huge 74%. In the same database, the position occurs a further 171 times without White playing the sacrifice. There can be no better advertisement for playing sacrifices such as ♘d5, theoretically sound or not, than the statistic that White only scored 51% in these 171 games.

12 ♘d5!? exd5 13 ♗f5! g6? *(D)*

Current opinion is that 13...♔f8! is good for Black. Another idea is 13...dxe4, which led to an interesting draw in Marinković-Kostić, Subotica 1992: 14 ♗xe4 ♘xe4 15 ♖xe4 ♗xe4 16 ♕xe4 0-0 17 ♘e7+ (17 ♗xe7 is a reasonable attempt to win for White) 17...♔h8 18 ♕xh7+! ♔xh7 19 ♖d3 ♕xc2+ 20 ♔xc2 g6 21 ♖h3+ ♔g7 22 ♗h6+ ♔f6 23 ♗xf8 ♖xf8 24 ♘d5+ ♔f5 ½-½.

In the early games that reached this position, Black often played 13...♗f8, and White went straight for the e5 breakthrough, as in Enevoldsen-Hamann, Esbjerg 1972: 14 e5 dxe5 15 fxe5 ♘xe5 16 ♘xg7+ ♗xg7 17 ♗f6 ♗xf6 18 ♕xf6 ♖g8 19 ♖xe5+ ♔f8 20 ♖de1 ♕c6 21 ♖e6 1-0.

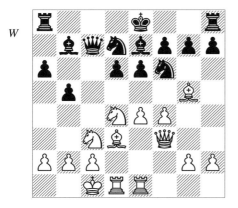

W

Sandoval Pinera – Ortiz
U-20 Girls Tournament, Guanare 2000

This is the position that appears, with the ♘d5 sacrifice, 44 times in *Mega Database*

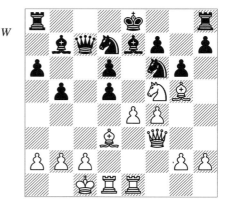

W

The text-move is no improvement, as the e5 breakthrough is still extremely powerful.

14 ♘xe7 ♔xe7 15 e5 dxe5 16 fxe5 ♘xe5 17 ♕xf6+ ♔d7 18 ♖xe5 ♖he8 19 ♖xe8 ♖xe8 20 ♕xf7+ 1-0

The long-term ♘d5 sacrifice is not restricted to situations where the black king has not yet castled. Leaving my study of the *Mega Database 2001* games on one side, here is an example of the sacrifice played when Black has castled queenside.

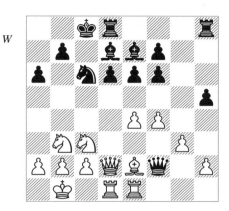

Velimirović – Ničevski
Skopje 1971

Dragoljub Velimirović has enriched Sicilian Defence theory with many imaginative ideas.

16 ♘d5! exd5 17 exd5 ♘a7 18 ♕c3+ ♚b8 19 ♗xa6! ♖he8

In *Informator* Velimirović gives 19...bxa6 20 ♖xe7 and simply states, without further analysis, that White has a decisive advantage. That statement seems a little sweeping, but White certainly has plenty of play against the denuded king, and his rook on the seventh rank is a powerful piece.

In the game, the main theme is White's enormous pressure on the e-file, which eventually leads to a mating attack.

20 ♕b4 ♗c8 21 ♖e2! ♕f3 22 ♖de1 ♖d7 23 ♗c4 ♖c7 24 ♘d4 ♕g4 25 a4 ♖d8 26 ♘b5 ♘xb5 27 axb5 b6 28 ♖xe7 ♖xe7 29 ♖xe7 ♕d1+ 30 ♚a2 ♕xc2 31 ♗b3 ♕xh2 32 ♕d4 1-0

Finally, when the black king is castled on the kingside, the ♘d5 sacrifice can give White space and lines that help him to build up a rapid attack. One good example is Tal-Larsen on page 31. Here is another dramatic example.

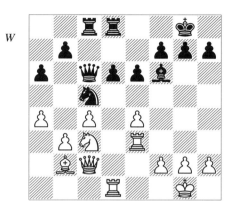

Tkachev – W. Watson
Lloyds Bank Masters, London 1993

20 ♘d5!

In terms of our silent sacrifice motifs, this move involves line clearance, as the knight clears the diagonal of the b2-bishop, and secondary line clearance, as the recapture opens two lines – not just the e-file, but also (and most significantly) the fourth rank. The recapture wins a tempo by establishing a white pawn on d5 that attacks the black queen, so he is bound to create doubled f-pawns, seriously weakening the black king's position.

20...exd5 21 exd5 ♕d7 22 ♗xf6 gxf6

Tkachev states in *Chess Monthly* that he originally intended to play here 23 ♖h3 f5 24 ♖g3+ ♚f8 25 ♕d2 ♘e4 26 ♕h6+ ♚e7 27 ♖e1 with a clear advantage, but then he saw a rather better finish.

23 ♖g3+ ♚h8 24 ♕xh7+!! ♚xh7 25 ♖d4! 1-0

That open fourth rank comes into play. Mate is unavoidable.

Exercise 42

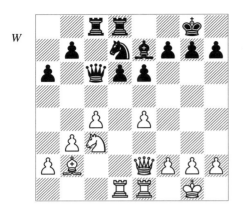

Level 1

What is the purpose behind **18 ♘d5**, and what should Black's reply be?

Exercise 43

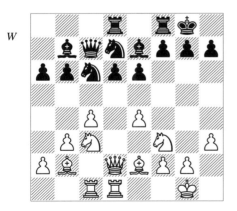

Level 2

Here is some post-sacrifice fun for you. After **15 ♘d5 exd5 16 cxd5**, Black must return the piece. The game continued **16...♘db8 17 ♘d4 ♕d7 18 dxc6 ♘xc6**, and now White played a snap attack that soon led to mate. See how far you can get with it.

Exercise 44

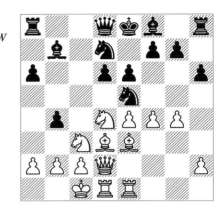

Level 3

After **14 ♘d5 ♘xd3+ 15 ♕xd3 exd5 16 exd5 ♗e7** how should White continue his attack? Black's response was weak, allowing a very nice combination. See if you can work out what happened.

The solutions start on page 220.

Multiple Motifs

With its relatives along the fifth rank, ♘d5 makes up a specific family of complex silent sacrifices. There are many other ways in which silent sacrifice motifs can be combined, although none occur quite so frequently. This gives us the excuse to look at individual instances of complex silent sacrifices, many of which are strikingly beautiful. Consider this lovely Alekhine effort (*see diagram on following page*).

Let's examine the move **27 ♘d7!**, which caused Steiner's immediate resignation.

It clears two lines, namely the bishop's long diagonal and the e-file. If the bishop captures, then it interferes with the rook's defence of the second rank and the bishop is

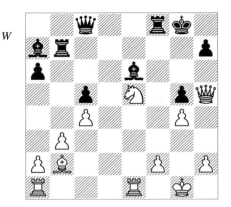

Alekhine – H. Steiner
Pasadena 1932

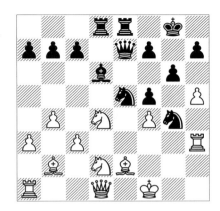

Taimanov – Vorotnikov
USSR 1978

deflected away from e6, leaving the e-file fully open. All four motifs contribute to the simple finish 27...♗xd7 28 ♕xg5+ ♔f7 29 ♕g7#. If the rook captures, then it interferes with the queen's defence of the e6-bishop, and this contributes to the variation 27...♖xd7 28 ♕xg5+ ♔f7 29 ♕g7+ ♔e8 30 ♖xe6+.

The finish after the queen capture mainly utilizes the two line clearances. The line goes 27...♕xd7 28 ♕xg5+ ♔f7 29 ♕f6+ ♔g8 30 ♕h8+ ♔f7 31 ♕xh7+ ♔e8 32 ♕g6+ ♔e7 33 ♖ad1 ♕c6 34 ♕g5+ ♔f7 35 ♕f6+ ♔g8 36 ♕g6+ ♖g7 37 ♕xg7#.

Two interferences, two line clearances and a deflection from one move – quite a haul!

In the next example, Vorotnikov appeared to be seeking some kind of record for the number of pieces to which he could place his knight *en prise* (*see following diagram*).

Black is a piece down and is trying to develop an attack in compensation. The square f3 is the most protected square in White's camp. In all, five pieces guard the square, and after **21...♘f3!!** four of them can capture the interloping knight – and the knight is completely unprotected.

If any piece other than the h3-rook takes the knight, the rook's line to e3 is interrupted, and 22...♘e3+ wins the queen. Meanwhile Black threatens 22...♘e3+, and if the queen moves away to avoid the check then it will relinquish its protection of the e2-bishop (and 22...♘xd4 will remove its last defender). However, capturing with the white rook diverts it from guarding the h4-square (letting the black queen in to h4), deflects it from h3 so that the queen can travel unmolested along the h-file from h4 to h1, and diverts the rook to a square from which it cannot prevent ...♕h1+, as the game continuation shows.

22 ♖xf3

White should play 22 ♘c4!, preventing the knight check at e3. Black's attack continues with 22...♘fh2+ followed by 23...♗xf4, but there is nothing immediately decisive.

22...♕h4! 23 ♖g3 ♕h1+! 24 ♖g1 ♘e3+ 25 ♔f2 ♕h2+ 0-1

It is mate in two more moves.

As with these two examples, many of the great multiple-motif silent sacrifices involve interference as a key component. Here is another classic case.

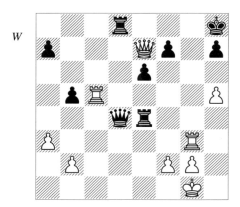

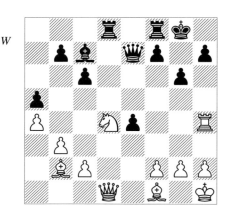

Eliskases – Hölzl
Austria 1931

Vuković – Anon
Simultaneous, 1937

White can mate on e8 or f8 if the d8-rook moves away from the back rank, on f6 if the queen moves from the a1-h8 diagonal, and on d8 if the queen moves off the d-file or its line is interrupted. One single move ensures that one of these events will happen.

1 ℤd5!!

It is double diversion plus interference. Two of the mates are 1...ℤxd5 2 ♕f8# (one diversion) and 1...exd5 2 ♕xd8+ followed by mate (interference). Black allows mate based on the second diversion.

1...♕xd5 2 ♕f6# (1-0)

In the initial position, there is another attractive way to win: 1 ℤe5! (single diversion plus interference), but Black can at least avoid mate by 1...ℤf4 2 ♕g5! ♕xf2+ 3 ♔h2 ♕xg3+ 4 ♕xg3.

In the next example, a multiple-motif sacrifice is prepared by a preliminary sacrifice of almost equal beauty to create a short combination that is hard to beat (*see following diagram*).

Black threatens to play 1...♕xh4. For his part, White's potential aims are mates by his knight on h6 and e7, by queen or rook on the

g-file and by the queen on g7. The opening move brings the knight onto its optimum square, but leaves both it and White's queen *en prise*.

1 ♘f5!! ♕xh4

There are three alternatives:

a) 1...ℤxd1 2 ♘xe7# or 2 ♘h6# achieves the desired knight mates.

b) 1...gxf5 2 ♕g4+! fxg4 3 ♕xg4+ ♕g5 4 ♕xg5# is the g-file mate.

c) 1...♕g5 2 ♕c1! ♕xh4 3 ♕h6!! ♕xh2+ (or 3...♕xh6 4 ♘xh6#) 4 ♕xh2 h5 5 ♕xc7 ℤd1 6 ♕e5 leads to the mate on g7.

Now Black threatens mate on h2 and expects 2 ♘xh4 ℤxd1 with an easy win, but here comes the real shocker.

2 ♕h5!!

White protects against mate on h2. There is interference on the h-file (2...gxh5 3 ♘h6#) and diversion of the queen from guarding the e7-square (2...♕xh5 3 ♘e7#). Black resigned.

That was a little-known old classic. The next example deserves to become a modern classic despite the small amount of material sacrificed.

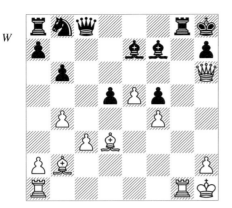

S. Hawes – S. Kerr
Lloyds Bank Masters, London 1979

White is trying to mate on the long diagonal. He must not allow Black to block it by occupying e6, so he played **25 e6!**, intending to meet 25...♕xe6 with 26 c4+ d4 27 ♗xd4+, mating. Black's defence was the ingenious **25...♕b7!**, threatening his own mate with 26...d4+. White could prevent the mate and create winning threats by 26 ♖xg8+ ♗xg8 27 ♖g1, but he preferred the stunningly artistic **26 ♗e4!!**.

The point is that neither pawn can capture the bishop. 26...dxe4 deflects the pawn from its line so that 27 c4+ cannot be met by 27...d4+. The other capture, 26...fxe4, interrupts the queen's diagonal, so that after 27 c4+, 27...d4 is no longer check. The game finished **26...♘c6 27 ♗xd5 1-0**, as c4+ by White can no longer be avoided.

The next example introduces a rare silent sacrifice motif that only applies when another motif is also present. I call it **partial interference**.

Full interference happens when a piece moves to a square where it interferes with the line of a defensive piece, but where the normal capture of the sacrificed piece continues to interfere with the defending piece's line. With partial interference, the piece whose line is blocked can make the capture itself, lifting the interference. The point of the sacrifice would then lie in the other sacrificial motif(s) in action.

A simple example was Short-Ljubojević, Reykjavik 1987 on page 70. The knight that cleared the g7-square landed on e8 where it interfered with the black rook's path to g8, from where it could have prevented the threatened mate. The rook could capture the knight, lifting the interference, but that would allow White to fulfil his square clearance motif with 30 ♕g7#.

Here is another example.

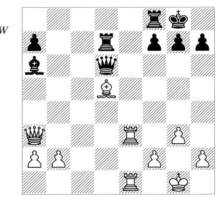

Lombardy – G. Kramer
USA Ch, New York 1957/8

Lombardy has spotted a very nice back-rank mate, but first he needs to deflect the black queen.

21 ♗c6!!

The bishop attacks the d7-rook and blocks the queen's defence of the a6-bishop (partial interference). The mating finish occurs if the queen is deflected to capture the bishop: 21...♕xc6 22 ♕xf8+! ♔xf8 23 ♖e8#. The exchange of queens loses rook for bishop, as

21...♕xa3 22 ♖xa3 leaves both bishop and rook attacked.

Black decided to lose the exchange while retaining queens, but soon gave up the struggle.

21...♗c8 22 ♗xd7 ♕xd7 23 ♖d3 ♕c7 24 ♕d6 1-0

Line clearance often works well in conjunction with other motifs. In our next example, the great Bent Larsen is the victim of a line clearance combined with decoy.

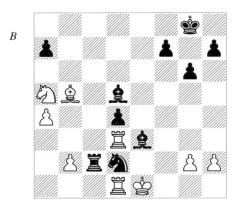

Larsen – Wl. Schmidt
European Team Ch prelims, Århus 1971

Black is the exchange down but his attack is very threatening. He reasons that ...♗f2 will be mate if he can lose the knight and keep the f1-square guarded. He can succeed if his light-squared bishop is on g2.

31...♘f1!!

Black clears the seventh rank and hopes to decoy the white king to f1. After 32 ♔xf1 he achieves his mate with 32...♗xg2+ 33 ♔e1 ♗f2#, and meanwhile he still threatens to play 32...♗xg2.

32 ♖xd4

White tries to return the extra exchange, hoping for 32...♗xd4 33 ♖xd4 ♘e3, when

the game is probably drawn. Black is not to be sidetracked.

32...♗xg2! 33 ♖d8+ ♔g7 34 ♗e2

Black was still threatening mate on f2, so White blocks the rank again.

34...♘xh2!

The threat is 35...♘f3+! 36 ♗xf3 ♗f2#, so White is forced to lose a move to make room for his king to escape.

35 ♖1d3 ♗b6!

Finally, Black forks knight and rook, forcing White to return the exchange and consequently leave his opponent with two extra pawns.

36 b4 ♗xd8 37 ♖xd8 ♗f3 38 ♗c4 ♘g4 39 ♖e8 ♔f6 40 ♗b3 ♖b2 41 b5 h5 0-1

In the next example, the line-clearance motif is combined with diversion, to ensure that a key defensive piece is not around to prevent further sacrifices that will force mate.

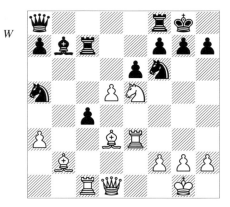

Kärner – Madl
Szolnok 1987

White needs to remove the black knight, which is the main defender of the kingside, so he sacrifices his knight to open the long diagonal for his bishop.

20 ♘d7!!

The knight can be captured by either of two pieces. If the knight captures, diverting it from the protection of h7, then White can play the well-known double bishop sacrifice which leads to a quick mate: 20...♘xd7 21 ♗xh7+! ♔xh7 22 ♕h5+ ♔g8 23 ♗xg7! f5 24 dxe6 ♔xg7 25 ♕g5+ ♔h8 26 ♖h3#.

Black prefers to capture with the rook, but the bishop can capture the defensive knight and, despite losing his d3-bishop, White is able to sacrifice his way through to mate on the kingside.

20...♖xd7 21 ♗xf6 cxd3 22 ♖g3 ♖c8

22...g6 allows 23 ♕h5!, when there is no defence to 24 ♕xh7+! ♔xh7 25 ♖h3+ ♔g8 26 ♖h8#.

23 ♖xg7+ ♔f8 24 ♖g8+! 1-0

White forces mate in three more moves: 24...♔xg8 25 ♕g4+ ♔f8 26 ♕g7+ ♔e8 27 ♕g8#.

In the next example, White similarly kicks off his combination by throwing his knight into the heart of his opponent's position with a line clearance and diversion. This time it must be declined, but its presence allows him to construct a pretty mating position.

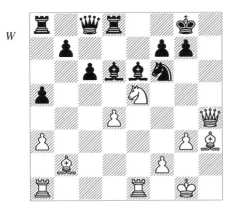

Taimanov – Kuzminykh
USSR 1950

1 ♘g6!! clears the line of the white rook so that if the f-pawn captures the knight (diversion and deflection) 2 ♗xe6+ will win the queen. The threat of mate at h8 apparently forces the reply **1...♘h7**, but White finishes gloriously with **2 ♖xe6! fxe6 3 ♕xd8+!! ♕xd8 4 ♗xe6# (1-0)**.

Those two tactical geniuses, Tal and Ale-khine, perpetrated some imaginative multiple-motif silent sacrifices. Here is the young Tal clearing a file by a move of his knight while simultaneously opening the same file and another diagonal by the deflection of one of his opponent's pawns.

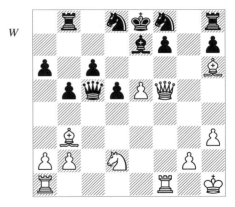

Tal – Teschner
European Team Ch, Vienna/Baden 1957

Tal seeks to deliver mate at f7, as he has three pieces trained on that square and it is only protected by the d8-knight. Naturally, he needs to get rid of the black d-pawn first, as it blocks his bishop's line to f7, and he needs to shift it away from the d-file so that his rook can prevent the king's escape via d8 or d7. There is another small problem that he must overcome, but we'll come to that detail in due course.

23 ♘e4!!

This move clears the d-file and aims to deflect the enemy d-pawn from the two lines that White wants open.

23...dxe4

Now after 24 ♖ad1, 24....f6 exploits the fact that White's e-pawn is pinned against his own queen by the black queen at c5. White can then continue with the spectacular 25 ♕h5+ ♘g6 26 exf6!!, with the point 26...♕xh5 27 f7+ ♘xf7 28 ♗xf7#. Black can prevent the mate by 26...♖f8, although with 27 ♖f5 White should win eventually.

Tal prefers a clean finish to something showy but slower, and forces Black to release the pin on his e-pawn.

24 ♖ac1! ♕b6 25 ♖cd1! 1-0

Only now does he threaten the mate, and Teschner resigned as he must give up most of his army to delay it.

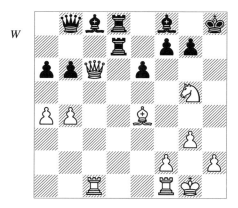

Alekhine – Rubinstein
Karlsbad 1923

Alekhine sees a mating attack if he can get his queen around to h7. For that to happen, he needs to have his bishop out of the way of the queen's path to the kingside, and for the mating attack to work he needs the black f-pawn to be removed or deflected (we shall see why).

25 ♗g6!!

He clears the e4-square for his queen and tries to deflect the black f-pawn.

25...♕e5

Rubinstein chooses to lose material.

If the sacrifice is accepted, mate comes quickly: 25...fxg6 26 ♕e4 (26 ♕g2, coming out at h3, also works) 26...♗d6 (the bishop must move to meet the threat of ♕h4+ {or ♕xg6} followed by ♕h7#) 27 ♕h4+ ♔g8 28 ♕h7+ ♔f8 29 ♕h8+ ♔e7 30 ♕xg7+ (here is why he needed the f-pawn out of the way) 30...♔e8 31 ♕g8+ ♗f8 32 ♕xg6+ ♔e7 33 ♕xe6#.

26 ♘xf7+ ♖xf7 27 ♗xf7 ♕f5 28 ♖fd1! ♖xd1+ 29 ♖xd1 ♕xf7 30 ♕xc8 ♔h7 31 ♕xa6 ♕f3 32 ♕d3+ 1-0

In the next example, Alekhine played a strange-looking long-term sacrifice which combines line clearance, diversion and, in one hidden variation, decoy motifs.

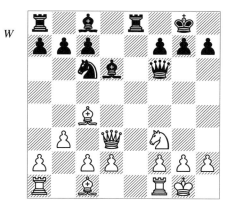

Alekhine – A. Rabinovich
Triangular Tournament, Moscow 1918

With the black queen out of the way, White could play ♘g5 with a double attack against h7 and f7. We might expect Alekhine to leave his rook *en prise*, but he prefers something more forcing.

13 ♗b2! ♛xb2

The queen has been diverted from guarding the g5-square, and Alekhine has also gained time for his attack by clearing the line for his a1-rook to come to e1. At some point in the future, Alekhine might play c3, cutting off the queen's retreat and making it ineffective as a defensive piece. In that respect, 13 ♗b2 is also a decoy sacrifice, since its success depends on the precise square to which the queen has been diverted.

14 ♘g5 ♗e6

14...g6 allows 15 ♗xf7+, when 15...♔g7 16 ♗xe8 ♛e5 17 ♛c3! ♘d4 18 f4! ♛f6 19 ♖ae1 retains the extra exchange for White, while 15...♔f8 16 ♗xe8 ♔xe8 17 ♖ae1+ gives White a strong attack with no material disadvantage.

15 ♗xe6 fxe6 16 ♛xh7+ ♔f8 17 ♖ae1

There is a quicker win with 17 c3!, cutting off the queen's retreat. In *My Best Games of Chess 1908-1923*, Alekhine gives the line 17...♛xd2 18 ♛h8+ ♔e7 19 ♛xg7+ ♔d8 20 ♖ad1 ♛f4 21 g3 trapping the black queen. After 17...♗e5 18 ♛h5 ♔g8 19 ♛f7+ ♔h8 he gives 20 f4 ♗f6 21 ♖f3 ♛xa1+ 22 ♔f2 ♗xg5 23 fxg5 with the statement that White is winning, missing the fact that 23...♛b1! defends perfectly adequately by giving up the queen for the rook. White should instead play 20 ♖ae1!, threatening both ♖e3 and ♖e4 followed by checking on the h-file. Then 20...♗f6 leads to a remarkable finish: 21 ♛h5+ ♔g8 22 ♛h7+ ♔f8 23 ♛h8+! ♔e7 24 ♖xe6+ ♔d7 25 ♛h3! ♗xg5 26 ♖fe1! and there is no defence to the discovered check.

17...♛f6 18 ♛h5 ♔g8 19 ♖e3! ♗f4

Black could minimize his disadvantage by 19...♘d4! 20 ♖h3 g6 21 ♛h7+ ♔f8 22 ♛d7 ♖e7 23 ♘h7+ ♖xh7 24 ♛xh7 ♖d8. Instead, he quickly subsided to defeat:

20 ♛h7+ ♔f8 21 ♛h8+ ♔e7 22 ♖xe6+ ♛xe6 23 ♛xg7+ ♔d6 24 ♘xe6 ♖xe6 25 d4 ♖ae8 26 c4 ♖8e7 27 ♛f8 ♖e4 28 ♛f5! ♖xd4 29 c5# (1-0)

Silent sacrifices which combine diversion and decoy of the same piece have a certain economy about them. The sacrificer diverts an enemy piece (which allows him to utilize a specific square that was previously guarded by that piece) but he also decoys it to a specific square where it is in danger. Here are two elegant examples, the first being a Tal effort from a 5-minute blitz tournament.

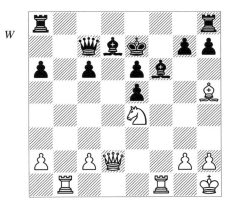

Tal – Quinteros
Blitz tournament, St del Esterol 1987

Tal wants to continue his attack by checking on d6 with his queen, but that square is guarded by Black's own queen. His solution is to divert the queen, and to decoy it to a square which allows the white knight the opportunity for a double attack.

20 ♖b7!! ♛xb7 21 ♛d6+ ♔d8 22 ♘c5!

This double attack regains a bishop for the sacrificed rook and tightens the noose around the black king's neck.

22...♛a7 23 ♖d1 ♔c8

23...♗e7 allows 24 ♘xe6+ ♔c8 25 ♛xe7, with a winning attack for White; for example, 25...♗xe6? 26 ♛xe6+ ♔b8 27 ♛d6+ ♔c7 28 ♖b1+ ♔c8 29 ♗g4+ and mate follows next move.

24 ♘xd7 ♛c7 25 ♛xe6 ♖d8 26 ♘xf6+

Tal misses a quicker win by 26 ♘xe5+ ♔b7 27 ♖b1+ ♔a7 28 ♘xc6+, but he is soon able to wrap up the game.

26...♔b7 27 ♖b1+ ♔a7 28 ♘e4 ♖ab8 29 ♖e1 ♖d4 30 ♗f3 ♖b2 31 h3 ♖xc2 32 ♖b1 h5 33 ♕b3 ♖cc4 34 ♕e3 ♕d7 35 ♘d2 1-0

The second example is from England's own tactical maestro, Julian Hodgson, and is very similar in its effect. Hodgson's bishop sacrifice lets his queen into the black defences and decoys his opponent's queen to a square where it is the target of a double attack from a white knight.

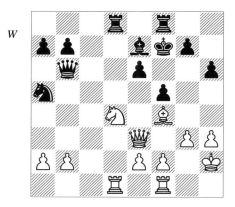

Hodgson – Van Wely
Olympiad, Moscow 1994

The first job is to divert the black queen from the defence of e6. Hodgson does so in a way that allows him to gain a later tempo with his knight.

25 ♗c7!! ♕xc7 26 ♕xe6+ ♔e8 27 ♕g6+ ♖f7 28 ♘e6! ♕b6

Now White finishes with mate.

29 ♘xg7+ ♔f8 30 ♘e6+ ♔e8 31 ♕g8+ ♖f8 32 ♘g7# (1-0)

We complete our look at multiple-motif silent sacrifices with a few examples of *multiple*

multiples – multiple sacrifices with multiple motifs. In the first case, Black plays four silent sacrifices, three of which White can decline. Finally, there comes a fourth – which he must accept with disastrous results.

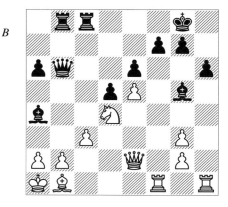

Kosashvili – Rechlis
Israeli Ch 1986

In order to increase the pressure on the b2-square, Black aims to eliminate White's d4-knight and replace it with his bishop. An exchange sacrifice is called for, but first he must bring his bishop round within reach of d4. He will exploit the fact that the white queen is tied to the defence of the b2-square by the threat of mate.

24...♗e3!

This single-motif diversion sacrifice threatens to win a pawn at d4.

25 ♖h4 ♖c4 26 ♗d3

White forces his opponent to choose between retreat or an exchange sacrifice. Black is happy to oblige.

26...♖xd4! 27 cxd4 ♗xd4 28 ♖b1 *(D)*

White's queen helps to defend the b-pawn but it is the only piece defending the e-pawn.

28...♗d1!!

This double-diversion sacrifice forces the win of a second pawn for the exchange, and in

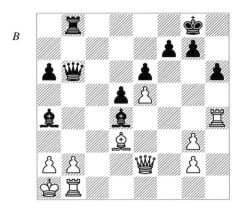

so doing lengthens the dark-squared bishop's diagonal.

29 ♕d2

After 29 ♖xd1 ♗xb2+ 30 ♔b1 ♗xe5+ 31 ♔c1 ♕c5+ 32 ♔c2 (or 32 ♗c2 ♕a3+ 33 ♔d2 ♕c3+ 34 ♔c1 ♖b1+! mating) 32...♕a3+ 33 ♔d2 ♖b2 the white queen is lost.

29...♗xe5! 30 g4 *(D)*

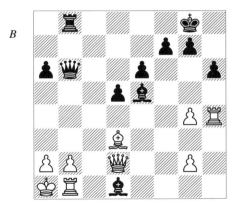

If allowed, White will increase the protection of his b-pawn by 31 g3 and 32 ♖h2, so Black acts quickly.

30...♗b3!!

Without the white a-pawn, Black can mate with his queen on a4 or a3. This sacrifice aims

to deflect the a2-pawn from the a-file and to substitute the queen for the bishop. After 31 axb3 ♕xb3, mate is inevitable.

White must try to give his king some air by moving his rook from b1. To make that possible, he needs to relieve some of the pressure on the b2-square by exchanging one of his rooks for Black's dark-squared bishop.

31 ♖h5 f5 32 ♖e1 *(D)*

The rook moves away from b1 in a vain attempt to eliminate Black's all-powerful dark-squared bishop.

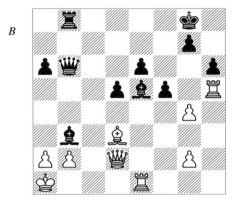

Black can win by dropping the bishop back to f6, but he finds an artistic way to exploit the rook's absence from b1.

32...♗c2!!

This silent sacrifice combines interference (33 ♗xc2 ♕xb2#) and line-clearance motifs, and also leaves the dark-squared bishop *en prise*. Black's pieces at last gain access to the b2-square, and the game is soon over.

33 ♕xc2 ♗xb2+ 34 ♔b1 ♕d4 35 a4 ♗a3+ 36 ♗b5 axb5 37 ♕b3 ♗b4 38 ♖d1 ♕xg4 39 ♖h3 bxa4 0-1

In our final example of silent sacrifices, Stuart Conquest demonstrates his remarkable imaginative powers by creating a blistering attack from an unlikely-looking starting position with the help of two brilliant complex silent sacrifices.

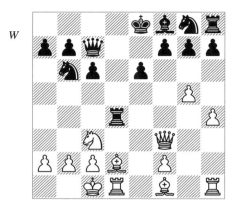

Conquest – Hodgson
Bundesliga 1995/6

The first sacrifice is reminiscent of the sixth game of the 1965 Tal-Larsen candidates match (pages 30-1).

15 ♘b5!!

The purpose is to open lines: the c-file and the queen's diagonal to b7 (both by deflection) and, for immediate use, the a4-e8 diagonal, which will be grabbed by the bishop when it recaptures on b5.

15...cxb5 16 ♗xb5+ ♘d7 17 ♗f4!!

A second stunning idea. Conquest clears the d-file for his rook with gain of tempo and aims to deflect the black rook from its protection of the d7-knight.

17...♖xf4

The sacrifice cannot be declined, because 17...♕b6 18 ♗xd7+ ♖xd7 19 ♖xd7 ♚xd7 20 ♖d1+ ♚e8 21 ♕d3 is fatal. The most natural defence is 17...♕xf4+ 18 ♕xf4 ♖xf4 19 ♖xd7 (threatening 20 ♖d4+ winning the rook) 19...♖b4, hoping to refute the combination by attacking the bishop that protects the rook. However, White can finish the job with 20 ♖hd1! (threatening 21 ♖d8++ ♚e7 22 ♖1d7#,

when White's g5-pawn comes in very handy) 20...f5 21 ♖d8+ ♚f7 22 ♗e8+ ♚e7 23 ♖1d7#.

18 ♗xd7+ ♕xd7 19 ♕xf4 ♕c8

Hodgson has met all the immediate threats and must have been feeling that the real game is only just beginning. In reality, it is nearly over, as Conquest produces a masterly rook manoeuvre...

20 ♖h3! ♘e7 21 ♖f3! ♘f5 22 ♖c3! ♗c5 23 ♖xc5!

...which ends with the rook sacrificing itself to drag the black queen off the back rank.

23...♕xc5 24 ♕b8+ ♚e7 25 ♕xb7+! 1-0

The finish would be 25...♚e8 26 ♕d7+ ♚f8 27 ♕d8#.

Exercise 45

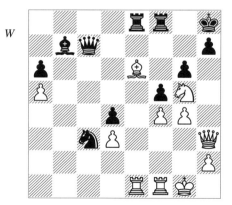

Level 1

White's next move combines line-clearance, diversion and partial interference motifs. That may sound complicated, but it wins at once.

Exercise 46

W

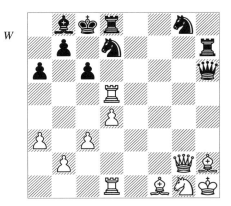

Level 2

Black threatens mate on h2. Yet White, to play, wins brilliantly with a complex silent sacrifice.

Exercise 47

W

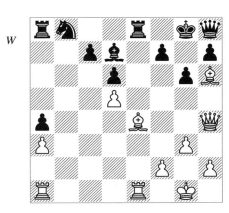

Level 3

White, to move, starts his combination with a complex silent sacrifice that must be declined. After Black's best defence, how does White continue his combination?

The solutions are on page 221.

10 Brilliant Blunders

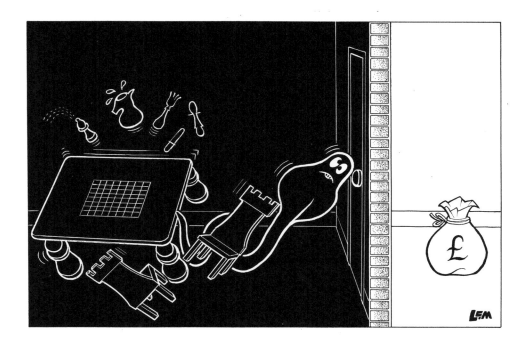

At times, we play like beginners. We overlook an attack on one of our pieces. We take the protection away from a previously guarded piece. We forget that there is a vulnerable and valuable piece that can be captured if we move its pinned colleague. We are so engrossed in our own plans that we forget to recapture when one of our pieces disappears, or we simply overlook the fact that we could have captured a piece for nothing. Sometimes, and this is more excusable, we overlook our opponent's plan and let him go ahead with little or no resistance.

In this chapter, playing like a beginner is not only allowed, it is positively encouraged.

We throw away those defensive reflex actions and start to think and act less like wimps and more like Deadly Tacticians, players who accept the challenge to look beyond the obvious.

Passive Sacrifices

One of the biggest shocks that a sacrificer can give his opponent is to leave a piece *en prise* when the defender attacks it. I shall call that a **passive** sacrifice (please note that this name does not imply that the move itself is at all passive, merely that the attacked piece waits passively to be captured). Many of the most famous and inspiring combinations have a passive sacrifice in there somewhere.

In my youth I saw the following amazing finish. Black had already sacrificed his queen, but his opponent returned it in order to construct a defence. The last two moves of the game, however, will stay in my memory forever.

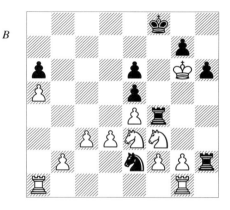

Hermann – Hussong
Frankfurt 1930

It is clear that the white king is in trouble. On the other hand, he has an extra piece and two pawns and meanwhile he is threatening the black rook on h2. Black sees that ...♘f4 will be mate as long as the white king cannot get to h7, and if the black rook can clear the f4-square without allowing the white king to escape.

On that basis, Black's decisive combination is easy to understand.

30...♔g8!! 31 ♘xh2 ♖f5!! 0-1

The first move is contrary to all of our chess-playing instincts. If a piece as valuable as a rook is attacked, it must surely move. Black allowed his imagination free rein as material is a very minor concern when mate is on the cards. Thanks to the threat of mate by

31...♖f6#, White was obliged to stop and accept the sacrifice.

The second move is of a type that we have already seen. It is a silent square-clearance sacrifice which forces mate because it threatens both 32...♘f4# and 32...♖g5# (on the square that was previously covered by the knight that captured the h2-rook). By moving to that specific square, the rook prevents the escape of the white king to h5. After 32 exf5 ♘f4#, it is now the knight that covers the h5-square, preventing the king's escape. Black has only one piece left, but is enough to give checkmate.

From that time onward, I have always remembered the alliterative adversaries and the work of art that they produced. I should note, reluctantly, that there is the artistic blemish that a brutal approach also works, namely 30...♖f6+ 31 ♔h7 h5 followed by ...♖h6#.

The idea of many passive sacrifices is simply to move the attack along at the fastest possible pace. They are played in situations where time is more important than material, and they can result in some good old-fashioned sacrificial orgies.

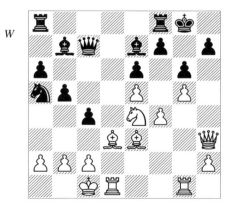

Pirisi – Van Wely
Sas van Gent 1988

White has in mind a mating pattern based on establishing a pawn on f6 and his queen on h6. It is worth the passive sacrifice of his d3-bishop in order to bring it about.

19 ♘f6+!! ♗xf6 20 gxf6 cxd3 21 ♖xd3

White's threat is now is a quick mate by 22 ♕h6, but Black can move his king into the corner and then play ...♖g8 to cover the g7-square. The result is a serious lack of breathing space for the black king, and White has seen that the white rook, having recaptured on d3, can play a decisive role by exploiting that fact in the final mating combination.

21...♖fc8 22 c3 ♔h8 23 ♕h6 ♖g8 24 ♗b6!

This silent sacrifice gains a tempo by attacking the queen. Its main purpose is to clear the rook's line to h3 in preparation for the final flourish.

24...♕xb6 25 ♕xh7+! ♔xh7 26 ♖h3# (1-0)

Passive sacrifices are often accepted – the defender has normally committed at least a tempo to attacking the piece in question and feels some compulsion to be consistent. However, as with silent sacrifices, the defender is not always obliged to accept. In a remarkable middlegame, John Nunn once left a knight *en prise* for thirteen moves as his opponent found one reason after another to spare its life. The next example is less extreme, but Bronstein is able to leave his knight unmoved for a couple of moves while he builds his attack around it (*see following diagram*).

Bronstein will leave his knight where it is on e5 because he can attack the g2-square without delay.

33...♖g6!! 34 ♘e1

34 fxe5 loses in short order to 34...♕h3 35 g3 ♖xg3+! 36 hxg3 ♕xg3+ 37 ♔h1 ♖c6 followed by mate. After the move played, Black could weaken his opponent's defence of g2 by exchanging knights, but that would allow the white queen to join in the defence of its king. Bronstein preferred to strike at once, leaving his knight *en prise* for a second move.

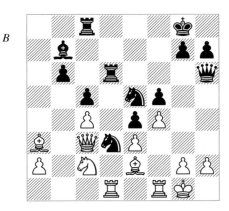

F. Olafsson – Bronstein
Alekhine Memorial, Moscow 1959

34...♕h3!! 35 ♗xd3

Against 35 ♔h1, Black can play the decisive silent sacrifice 35...♘f3!!. Then:

a) 36 ♗xf3 exf3 leaves White defenceless.

b) 36 ♖xf3 exf3 37 ♗xf3 ♗xf3 38 gxf3 allows 38...♘f2#.

c) 36 gxf3 loses prettily to 36...♕xf1+! 37 ♗xf1 ♘f2#.

After the text-move, Bronstein loses his consistency and relinquishes the chance to finish the game quickly and attractively. He should leave the knight on e5 for a little longer and play 35...exd3!, threatening mate on g2. The reply 36 ♖f2 loses to 36...♗xg2! 37 ♘xg2 ♘f3+ 38 ♔f1 ♘xh2+ 39 ♔g1 ♘f3+ 40 ♔f1 ♕h1#, while 36 ♖d2 ♗xg2! 37 ♘xg2 ♘g4 is also fatal.

Bronstein's choice is inferior, but it doesn't spoil the win.

35...♕xe3+?! 36 ♔h1 ♘xd3 37 ♕d2 ♕d4 38 ♘c2 ♕f6 39 ♘e3 ♖d8 40 ♕e2 ♖a8 41 ♗c1 ♖h6 42 g3 ♕f7 43 ♖g1 ♖d6 44 ♖df1 h5 45 ♖g2 ♗a6 46 ♕c2 ♘b4 47 ♕c3 ♖d3 48 ♕e5 ♗xc4 0-1

Some passive sacrifices are not played to speed up an attack, but to exploit the capture of the attacked piece. Here is a typical example, a famous mating combination by Alekhine.

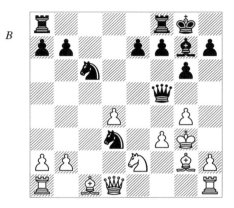

Potemkin – Alekhine
St Petersburg 1912

Alekhine has spotted a very pretty mate if he can get his c6-knight to f5. His queen is already on f5, attacked by the white g-pawn, so he played **16...♞xd4!!**, winning a pawn. White preferred to have an extra queen against his illustrious opponent, even for a short time, so he played **17 gxf5 ♞xf5+** and then resigned as 18 ♔g4 h5+ 19 ♔h3 ♞f2# is mate.

In the following diagram, Steiner plays passive sacrifices on three consecutive moves.

Black's f-pawn makes a beeline for the white king's position.

14...f5!

Now 15 fxe4 fxe4 opens the f-file for the black major pieces, and 16...♛f6 will spell disaster for the white king. Naturally, Eliskases declines, preferring to create an escape-square for his king.

15 ♛b3

This appears to gain a move by attacking the black d-pawn, but Black can ignore it and leave his knight for the taking one more time.

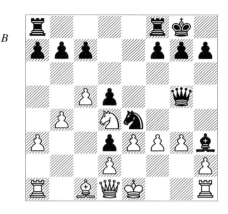

Eliskases – L. Steiner
Budapest 1933

15...f4!! 16 exf4

Eliskases attacks the queen by capturing the f-pawn.

If White instead continues 16 ♛xd3, Black breaks through on the kingside with 16...fxg3. 16 fxe4 loses to 16...fxg3 since 17 ♛xd5+ ♛xd5 18 exd5 g2 19 ♖g1 ♖f1+ leads to mate while 17 ♖g1 is answered by 17...gxh2! 18 ♖xg5 ♖f1#.

White is better off playing 16 ♖g1! at once, when Black will experience difficulty in breaking through.

16...♖ae8!!

This passive sacrifice of both queen and knight exploits the newly-opened e-file.

17 fxg5

17 fxe4 loses nicely to 17...♖xe4+ 18 ♔f2 ♖fxf4+ 19 gxf4 ♛g2#, so Eliskases captures the queen in the hope that he can emerge a piece ahead.

17...♞xc5+ 18 ♔d1 ♞xb3 19 ♞xb3 ♗g2

This is decisive, now that the white knight has been lured away from the defence of f3.

20 ♞d4 ♗xh1 21 f4 ♖e4 22 ♗b2 ♖fe8 0-1

The two main purposes of passive sacrifices, to buy time for the attack and to exploit the threat to the attacked piece in a functional way, are not mutually exclusive. It often happens that both purposes can be served.

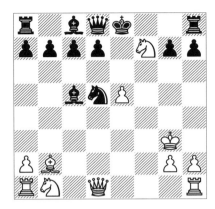

Hoffman – A. Petroff
Match, Warsaw 1844

In this famous old position, Black works out that he can mate White's exposed king if he can grab the f-file. The king will be stuck on the side of the board with nowhere to hide. With that in mind, Black ignores the threat to his queen and plays a double passive sacrifice.

12...0-0!! 13 ♘xd8

White can capture either the queen or the knight. If 13 ♕xd5 ♖xf7 14 ♕xc5, then the fact that Black has castled allows him to use the time gained to start a mating attack with 14...♕g5+ 15 ♔h3 d6+.

The move played allows Black to display the functional purpose of his sacrifice. It opens the f-file (deflection) so that he can play for mate with his remaining pieces

13...♗f2+ 14 ♔h3 d6+ 15 e6 ♘f4+ 16 ♔g4 ♘xe6 17 g3 ♘d4+ 18 ♘e6 ♗xe6+ 19 ♔h4 ♘f5+ 20 ♔h3 ♘e3+ 21 ♔h4 ♘g2+ 22 ♔h5 g6+ 23 ♔g5 ♗e3# (0-1)

The fact that passive sacrifices can be used to gain time makes them particularly useful at

the beginning of long-term attacks. The extra tempi allow the sacrificer's pieces to pour into the attack.

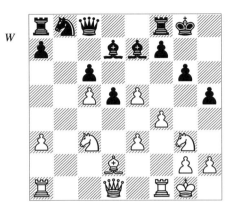

Illescas – Morozevich
Madrid 1996

There is a logjam of black pieces on the queenside, so White decides to strike at once at the black king.

18 e4! d4

18...♗xc5+ takes the bishop away from the defence of its king. The move played seems to gain a move, but Illescas presses on with his preparations, ignoring the threat to his knight.

19 f5! dxc3 20 ♗xc3 ♘a6 21 ♘xh5!

Already the attack breaks.

21...♘xc5

Black must decline the second knight as 21...gxh5 22 ♕xh5 leaves his unsupported king at the mercy of White's well-supported queen.

22 ♘f6+ ♗xf6 23 exf6 ♗xf5 24 exf5 ♘e4 25 ♕c1! g5 26 ♕d1!

The end comes with an elegant sidestep which ensures that the queen penetrates on the kingside.

26...♘xc3 27 ♕h5 ♘e4 28 ♕h6 ♘xf6 29 ♕xg5+! ♔h7 30 ♖f3! 1-0

For the defender, the shock of having his threat to capture a piece completely ignored is only exceeded by being presented with the option to capture a piece with check. Leaving a piece to be captured with check is rare, but nearly always beautiful. The only occasion on which I played such a sacrifice was in a correspondence game. In this book, I have avoided using sacrifices played in correspondence games because it is unlikely that they could be foreseen by most of us over the board. As any such sacrifice is a rare and wonderful thing, I am making an exception in this case.

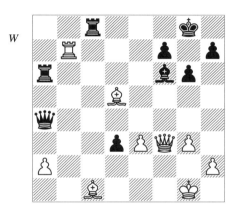

LeMoir – R. Tracy
Correspondence 1968

White has already sacrificed the exchange and is struggling to get some attack on the black king before Black forces through his passed d-pawn. Black threatens to capture the dark-squared bishop with check, so White must strike now or never.

25 ♖xf7!! ♖xc1+ 26 ♔g2 ♖c2+

There is no escape:

a) Shifting the king by 26...♔h8 loses to 27 ♖xf6 ♖c2+ 28 ♔h3 ♕d7+ 29 g4 ♕xd5 30 ♕xd5 ♖xf6 31 ♕d4 ♖f2 32 g5, winning a rook.

b) Returning the rook home simply results in it being lost: 26...♖c8 27 ♖c7+ ♔h8 28 ♖xc8+, and White still has a mating attack.

c) Forcing White to prove his attack by 26...d2 27 ♖xf6+ ♔g7 28 ♖f7+ ♔h6 results in mate by 29 ♖xh7+!! ♔xh7 30 ♕f7+ ♔h6 31 ♕f8+ ♔h7 32 ♗g8+ ♔h8 33 ♗e6+ ♔h7 34 ♕g8+ ♔h6 35 ♕h8+ ♔g5 36 h4+ ♕xh4 37 gxh4#.

27 ♔h3 d2 28 ♖xf6+ ♔g7 29 ♖xa6 ♕d7+

29...♕xa6 allows White a quick mate by 30 ♕f7+ ♔h6 31 ♕f8+ ♔g5 32 ♕f4+ ♔h5 33 ♕h4#.

30 g4 ♖c1 31 ♕f6+ ♔h6 32 ♕f8+ 1-0

Even in a correspondence game, being able to leave a piece to be captured with check is a great feeling. Over the board, I once managed to play a sacrifice which shed a mere pawn with check, and even that felt very good. I hope you get the chance to play one in your lifetime. The pride and beauty comes from the realization that after apparently gaining a move with a check, the defender is helpless to do anything with his extra move.

Let me introduce to you Rashid Nezhmetdinov, a Soviet player who played most of his chess from the end of the Second World War to the mid-1960s. Although only an international master, he could beat just about anyone on his day – his plus score against Tal includes three wins from the latter's heyday, two of which were truly brilliant, and he also beat Spassky twice.

For the chess fan, most important was the style of his wins which was brilliant and daring – even into his middle age. Tal said that the wonderful game that he lost to Nezhmetdinov in the 1961 USSR Championship made him truly happy. Nezhmetdinov was nearly fifty at the time. He was clearly a great inspiration to Tal himself, as he was capable of flights of fancy that became the great man's own trademark. Here is his great version of this sacrifice idea.

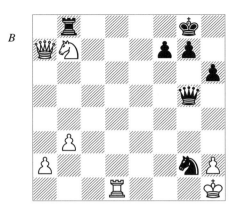

Kosalopov – Nezhmetdinov
Kazan 1936

We are at the end of a sequence of moves in which Nezhmetdinov has tried to break through on the g2-square. His opponent has met all of the threats and now confidently expects his attack on the rook to lead to an early draw. Nezhmetdinov's skill is evident in the fact that he almost certainly foresaw this position, and the winning idea, several moves ago.

29...♘f4!! 30 ♕xb8+ ♔h7

OK, so the threat is mate, but White has a spare move in which to organize a defence. Surely, with an open board and so few pieces left, he can avoid mate without giving up a lot of material? The answer is no, and that is not only a tribute to Nezhmetdinov's imagination but also to the power of queen and knight to cooperate in mating attacks.

White plays his only defence to the mate threat.

31 ♖d2 ♕g4!

Now White faces the threat of 32...♕f3+ 33 ♔g1 ♘h3#. Nezhmetdinov has taken into account the fact that the position of the white knight on b7 prevents the white queen from defending the light squares, and that the only realistic defence of the f3-square, 32 ♖f2, allows mate in two by 32...♕d1+. Therefore

White must give his king room by moving his h-pawn.

32 h4 ♕h3+

32...♕xh4+ is a quicker win, but that is just a detail. After the move played, Nezhmetdinov regains his rook without relinquishing the mating threats.

33 ♔g1 ♕e3+ 0-1

White loses at least his queen, as after 34 ♔f1 ♕xd2 35 ♕e8 ♕d1+ 36 ♔f2 ♘d3+ 37 ♔g2 (or 37 ♔e3 ♕e1+ winning the queen) 37...♕g4+ 38 ♔h2 ♕f4+ 39 ♔g2 ♕f2+ 40 ♔h1 ♕f3+ 41 ♔h2 ♘f4!, mate is unavoidable.

There is a variant on the passive sacrifice, which is the **unguarding sacrifice**. The effect is the same – an attacked piece allows itself to be captured – but the sacrifice takes the form of desertion by the attacked piece's protector. The threatened piece was protected by one of its fellows, but that piece goes off to take part in attacking operations.

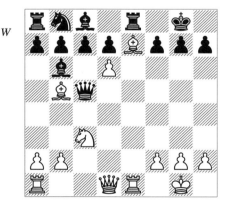

Grossbach – Emerich
Vienna 1899

White espies an opportunity to sacrifice his knight and queen for mate. The knight is needed for his attack, but it currently guards the b5-bishop.

15 ♘e4!! ♛xb5 16 ♘f6+! gxf6

After 16...♚h8 17 ♛c2 g6 the most attractive finish is 18 ♛c3 ♝a5 19 ♘h5+! ♝xc3 20 ♝f6+ ♝xf6 21 ♖xe8#.

17 ♛g4+ ♛g5 18 ♝xf6!! 1-0

It is mate after 18...♖xe1+ 19 ♖xe1 ♛xg4 20 ♖e8#.

The passive or unguarding sacrifice allows one of the attacker's pieces to be captured at once. A further rare variant is the **invitation sacrifice**, which allows material to be captured in the future. The invitation sacrifice might allow a fork, a pin or a skewer, or some other form of material-winning manoeuvre. Let us invite Tal to demonstrate.

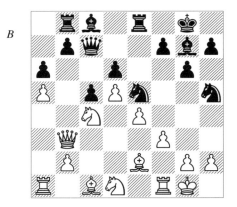

Tukmakov – Tal
USSR Ch, Moscow 1969

Black is getting nowhere on the queenside, owing to the combined efforts of the white knight and queen at c4 and b3 respectively. White's kingside is less well defended, but after the thematic 16...f5 17 exf5, it appears that Black must recapture with the g-pawn, as capturing with the bishop allows his knight and bishop to be forked. Nonetheless, with typical disdain for convention, Tal presses ahead.

16...f5! 17 exf5 ♝xf5! 18 g4 ♘xc4 19 ♝xc4 b5 20 axb6 ♖xb6

One of Tal's points is that the f5-bishop prevents the queen from taking up its natural defensive post at c2.

21 ♛a2 ♝d4+ 22 ♚g2 ♛g7!

This is the other key point. If White captures either bishop or knight, then the g-file becomes open through secondary line clearance, just like with the ♘d5 sacrifices that we saw earlier, where it was the c- or e-file that was opened. In this case, the white king could not survive:

a) 23 gxf5 gxf5+ 24 ♚h1 (or 24 ♚h3 ♖e4!! 25 ♛a5 ♝f6! threatening 26...♖h4#) 24...♚h8! and White must give up material to prevent mate on g1.

b) 23 gxh5 gxh5+ 24 ♚h1 ♝h3 is immediately fatal for White.

Tukmakov is obliged to decline both pieces, but the attack remains too strong for him to survive.

23 ♘c3 ♝d7 24 ♝d2 ♖eb8 25 ♖ab1 ♘f6 26 ♖fc1 ♛f7 27 b3 ♘xg4! 28 ♘e4

28 fxg4 allows 28...♛f2+ with a quick mate.

28...♘e5 0-1

White is a pawn down and his kingside cannot hold out under the pressure.

The passive sacrifice, along with its variants, is practised by players with hyperactive imaginations, and its high priest was Mikhail Tal. In the Deadly Tactician database, there are 48 games in which Tal played such sacrifices. Here are two further examples that show the sheer range of ideas of which he was capable.

In the following diagram, Tal is a pawn down, and he cannot capture the c2-knight in view of mate on f1. The white rook is under attack from the knight, and 20 ♖xe1 ♘xe1 21 ♛xe1 ♛e5! 22 ♝e3 d4 leaves Black the exchange ahead, while 20 ♖d1 c6! 21 g3 ♖f2 forces White to exchange his dangerous

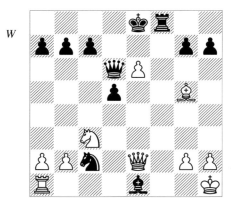

Tal – Miller
Simultaneous, Los Angeles 1988

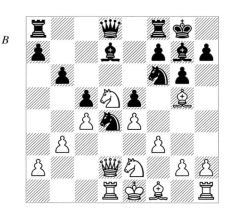

T. Bjornsson – Tal
Reykjavik 1964

passed pawn. It seems that it is Tal, for a change, who is under the tactical cosh. The idea of 20...♛e5 (with the point 21 ♛xe5 ♜f1#) appears to be decisive, and yet Tal chooses to encourage it.

20 ♘b5! ♛e5! 21 h4!!

In reply to Black's silent queen sacrifice, Tal plays a passive queen sacrifice. At this moment, his bishop is more important than his queen, and Tal's move also releases the threat of back-rank mate. Naturally, Black isn't going to fall for 21...♛xe2 22 ♘xc7#, but Tal's idea goes deeper than that.

21...♛g3 22 ♜d1!

Allowing an apparently decisive double attack, and also planning to meet 22...c6 with 23 ♜d3 ♛b8 24 ♜f3!. After this passive sacrifice of the knight, which has the point 24...cxb5 25 ♛xb5#, Black would be lost. Apart from using his rampant e-pawn, White has ideas like 25 ♛f1 aiming to deliver mate on f7.

22...♜f2 23 ♛xf2!! ♝xf2 24 ♜xd5!

Black can only prevent mate on d8 by giving up his queen.

24...♛xh4+ 25 ♝xh4 ♝xh4

White soon won.

Any advantage in this blocked position is with White. Certainly, Tal faces a long slow grind to get anything out of the game. He comes up with a crazy idea: invite White to win material to unbalance the game.

13...♘e6?!

One of Tal's apparently naïve moves. By opening the d-file, he allows White the choice of two ways to win material.

14 ♘xf6+ ♝xf6 15 ♝h6!?

White chooses to win the exchange. He could win a piece by 15 ♝xf6 ♛xf6 16 ♛xd7, but shies away from it, as 16...♜fd8 17 ♛b7 ♜xd1+ 18 ♚xd1 ♜d8+ leaves his queen out of play while Tal's pieces are ready to strike along the d-file. He may have done better to take that option, as his choice leaves him so weak on the dark squares that Tal is able to build his attack at leisure.

15...♝h4+ 16 ♘g3 ♝c6! 17 ♝xf8 ♛xf8 18 ♝d3 ♝g5 19 ♛f2 ♛h6 20 ♘f1 ♜d8 21 g3 ♘d4 22 h4 f5

Black is already on the verge of breaking through.

23 ♜h2 ♝c1 24 ♘d2 ♝xd2+ 25 ♜xd2 fxe4 26 ♝xe4 ♝xe4 27 fxe4 ♜f8 28 ♛g2 ♛e3+ 29 ♚d1 ♛c3 30 ♜xd4 exd4 31 ♛h3

♕a1+ 32 ♔d2 ♕xa2+ 33 ♔c1 ♖f1+ 34 ♕xf1 ♕a1+ 0-1

Our final examples show other imaginations feverishly at work. In the first, a modern problemist plays an unguarding sacrifice as the prelude to a startling silent decoy sacrifice.

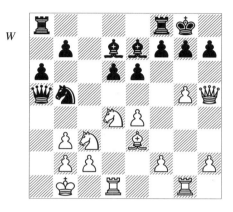

Afek – Kogan
Israeli Team Cup (semi-rapid) 1999

The d4-knight is firmly protected, and yet Afek neutralizes both guards in one fell swoop. His idea is to drive the queen back to d8 in order to tempt it back out to a5 again.

17 ♗d2!! ♘xd4

17...♕c7 is perfectly playable, but Black can be forgiven for missing the complex silent sacrifice that White has in mind.

18 ♘d5 ♕d8 19 ♗a5!! ♕e8

Only now does Black understand. Accepting White's sacrifice brings the queen to a5 (decoy) and diverts it from the defence of the e7-bishop. After 19...♕xa5, 20 g6!! opens the line of White's own queen to a5, allowing him to win the black queen after 20...fxg6, by 21 ♘xe7+ ♔f7 22 ♕xa5, while 20...hxg6 opens its line to h8 so that 21 ♘xe7# delivers mate.

Even with the careful move played, the sacrifices are not at an end.

20 ♘f6+! 1-0

Black faces 20...gxf6 21 gxf6+ ♔h8 22 ♖g7 or 20...♗xf6 21 gxf6 g6 22 ♕h6 with inevitable mate in either case.

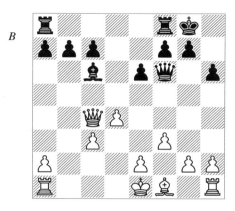

Beilin – Lipnitsky
Dzintari 1951

The diagram shows the position well before the passive sacrifice was played, so that we can view Black's idea from a distance. He will tempt White to accept his c-pawn and his bishop while he moves his own pawn from e6 to e3 in order to block the development of White's kingside. The fact that the white d-pawn will advance, and the c-file will open, will expose White's c-pawn so that Black can penetrate with his major pieces to attack the hemmed-in white king.

13...e5! 14 d5?! ♗d7 15 ♕xc7 e4! 16 ♖c1 e3!! 17 ♕xd7 ♖ac8 18 ♕a4

18 ♕b5 ♖xc3 19 ♕b2 seems to cover everything, but the extremely neat 19...♖c5! unhinges the white defence: 20 ♕a3 (20 ♕xf6 ♖xc1#; 20 ♖xc5 ♕xb2 mating; 20 ♕b1 ♕d4 and Black will soon mate) 20...♕h4+! 21 g3 (the alternative defence 21 ♔d1 loses to both 21...♖xd5+ and 21...♕d4+ 22 ♕d3 ♖fc8! 23

♖xc5 ♕xc5, with mate) 21...♕b4!! 22 ♕xb4 ♖xc1#.

18...♖xc3 19 ♖d1 ♖fc8 20 g3 ♖c1 21 ♗h3 ♖xd1+ 22 ♕xd1 ♕c3+ 23 ♔f1 ♕d2! 24 ♔g2

Escaping just in the nick of time?

24...♖c1!! 0-1

Another silent sacrifice brings down the curtain. After 25 ♕xd2 exd2 the pawn promotes, while 25 ♕xc1 ♕xe2+ is mate next move.

Finally, we see a player attempting a world record for the number of pieces he can offload in consecutive moves, starting with a passive sacrifice of both rooks.

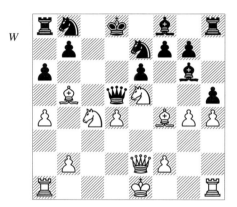

W

Cohn – Chiszar
1944

As we shall see, White only needs his queen and light-squared bishop (and some pawns) to build a mating-net, so he sacrifices the rest one by one, starting with a double rook sacrifice to drag the queen away from the defence.

1 ♘b6!! ♕xh1+ 2 ♔d2 ♕xa1 3 ♘xf7+!

White clears the line of the dark-squared bishop...

3...♗xf7 4 ♗c7+!

...so that it can be sacrificed to decoy the king to a square allowing a white queen check.

4...♔xc7 5 ♕e5+ ♔xb6

Black might as well capture the fifth piece in five moves in view of 5...♔d8 6 ♕d6+ ♘d7 7 ♕xd7#. Now the sacrifices are over and White mates in two moves.

6 ♕c5+ ♔a5 7 b4# (1-0)

Exercise 48

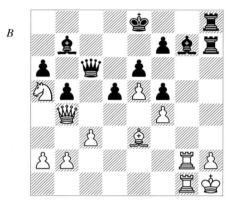

B

Level 1

Black (to play) has both his queen and his light-squared bishop under attack. As this is a passive sacrifice, one of them will be sacrificed as Black forces a quick mate.

Exercise 49

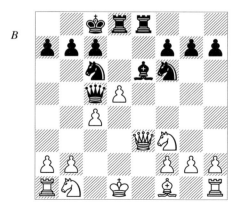

B

Level 2

Black's queen is under attack. Does he leave it *en prise* in the search for mate, or is there another passive or unguarding sacrifice in this position? How does the game finish?

Exercise 50

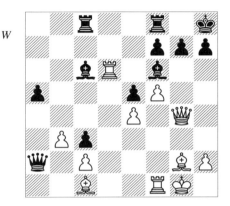

W

Level 3

White to play. The passive sacrifice doesn't come at once, as only a couple of White's pawns are under attack. So when and how does it happen? Be ready for a striking finish.

The solutions start on page 221.

The Unpinning Sacrifice

Passive and unguarding sacrifices involve leaving a piece alone on a square where it is under attack. The opponent is surprised because he automatically expects the normal action of protecting or moving the attacked piece.

The same applies to the **unpinning sacrifice**. A pin normally involves trapping a piece in front of a unit of higher value. The opponent can continue his analysis on the assumption that the piece will not move, and there is generally a strong element of surprise when it

does. Everyone knows the most famous unpinning sacrifice, Legall's Mate, in which a white knight on f3 is pinned against its queen by a black bishop coming to g4. It commits suicide on behalf of the queen by jumping to e5, then takes part in a mate when its queen is captured by the bishop.

Here is a more advanced example.

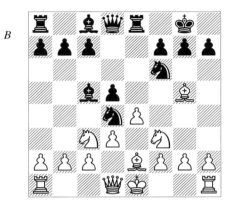

B

Nicifor – E. Kramer
Celje 1921

White is a pawn ahead, but has not yet castled. Black takes aim at the white king before it can get away.

9...♘xe4!! 10 ♘xe4?

The immediate capture 10 ♗xd8? loses to 10...♘xf3+, and now:

a) 11 ♗xf3 ♘xc3+ and Black emerges a piece ahead.

b) 11 gxf3 ♗xf2+ 12 ♔f1 ♗h3#.

c) 11 ♔f1 ♘ed2+ and White must give up his own queen.

White can emerge in relative safety if he is not greedy; e.g., 10 dxe4 ♘xf3+ 11 ♗xf3 ♕xg5 12 ♕xd5, when Black has some compensation for his pawn. However, White wants that queen.

10...dxe4 11 ♗xd8 exf3 12 ♗h4 fxg2 13 ♔d2

As 13 ♜g1 allows 13...♘f3#, the white rook must allow itself to be swallowed up and the king is forced to wander around. The black pieces soon mount an invasion force to surround the white king.

13...gxh1♛ 14 ♛xh1 ♜xe2+ 15 ♚d1 ♗g4 16 ♛xb7 ♜xc2+ 17 ♚e1 ♜e8+ 18 ♚f1 ♗h3+ 19 ♚g1 ♘e2+ 20 ♚h1 ♘c1! 21 f4 ♜ee2 22 ♛b8+ ♗f8 23 ♗g3 ♜ed2 24 ♛xa7 ♜d1+ 0-1

Nowadays we are very aware of the possibility of our opponent sacrificing his queen on its home square in this way, but there are still occasions when it happens. It should have happened to Flood in his game against me on page 56. In the next example, Tony Miles fell for an unusual version, the purpose of which was a double knight mate.

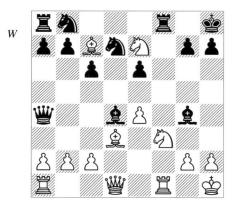

de Firmian – Miles
USA Ch, Cambridge Springs 1988

16 ♘g5!!

The idea is 16...♗xd1 17 ♜xf8+ ♘xf8 18 ♘f7#. Black can prevent mate, but the spared white queen is released from its cage and soon penetrates Black's kingside with decisive effect.

16...h5 17 ♜xf8+ ♘xf8 18 ♛f1 ♘bd7 19 ♛f7 ♘f6 20 e5 1-0

Another famous unpinning pattern happens when a queen is on the eighth rank, apparently pinning the opponent's minor pieces against an unprotected rook in the corner. Many a famous 19th-century masterpiece featured the spectacular release of the minor piece (e.g., Fleissig-Schlechter on page 18). The queen would disappear into the corner and its owner's king would subsequently be hacked to death. I remember being surprised (and delighted) when I saw the following game in which two 20th-century players as sophisticated as Réti and Euwe created a particularly fine example of the genre.

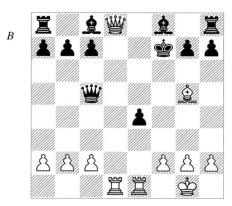

Euwe – Réti
Match (game 1), Amsterdam 1920

Euwe has sacrificed a piece for a massive lead in development and the chance to hound the wandering black king. Réti has other ideas. His unpinning sacrifice invites the white queen into one corner...

14...♗d6! 15 ♛xh8 ♛xg5 16 f4 ♛h4 17 ♜xe4 ♗h3!

...then an identical offer buries it in the opposite corner. The end comes rapidly with a third sacrifice that exposes the white king.

18 ♛xa8 ♗c5+ 19 ♚h1 ♗xg2+! 20 ♚xg2 ♛g4+ 21 ♚f1 ♛f3+ 22 ♚e1 ♛f2# (0-1)

There is even a fine example from two top-class modern grandmasters, although it is very complex.

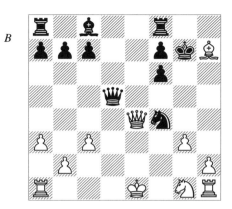

Topalov – Bareev
Linares 1994

White's assault on the black king has gone wrong, though after 16...♕xe4+ 17 ♗xe4 ♖e8 18 gxf4 ♖xe4+ 19 ♔f2 ♖xf4+, Black would only have a slight advantage. The fate that befalls White is far worse. First his queen will be dragged by the hair all the way up the board to the 8th rank.

16...♖e8!!

In the language of our silent sacrifices, Black decoys the queen to a square that can be exploited (as we shall see) and also deflects it from the black queen's diagonal to h1.

17 ♕xe8 ♗f5!!

This unpinning sacrifice is the point of the previous silent sacrifice. While the queen is away on a8, the black pieces will get to work on the white king.

18 ♕xa8 ♕e4+ 19 ♔f2

19 ♔d2 allows 19...♕g2+! with similar play. The king is dragged over to be executed on the queenside.

19...♕g2+ 20 ♔e3 ♘d5+ 21 ♔d4 ♕d2+ 22 ♔c5 ♕e3+ 23 ♔c4 ♘b6+ 0-1

It's mate in three. This throw-back to the 19th century deservedly won Bareev a brilliancy prize.

Another typical pattern is the white queen on a4 with its knight or bishop on b5 attacked by a black a6-pawn (or the same idea on the kingside). Sometimes ...axb5 can bury the queen for several moves. In the next example, the result was its untimely death.

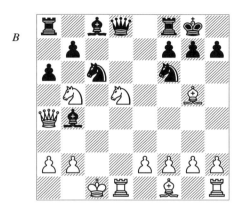

Heller – Rechlis
Beersheba Ch 1981

11...axb5! 12 ♕xa8 ♕xd5!! 13 ♖xd5 ♘xd5

The reason for Black's double sacrifice soon becomes clear.

14 a3 ♗d6 0-1

Not only can the white queen not return to the ranks, but next move it will be dealt a fatal blow by ...♘b6 or ...♘c7, leaving Black a piece ahead.

From the following diagram, Black sacrifices his queen by an unpinning sacrifice that places such a clamp on the white position that Black is able to build up his mating attack at leisure.

18...dxe3!! 19 ♖xd8 ♖fxd8

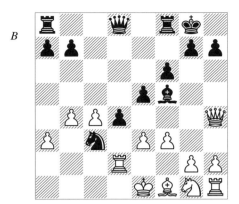

Quinteros – Ribli
Montilla 1974

The threat is mate on d1.

20 ♗e2 ♖d2 21 g4

White could try to return the sacrificed queen by 21 ♔f1 ♘xe2 22 ♘xe2, intending 22...♖d1+ 23 ♕e1 with some chances of survival, but Black can do even better by playing 22...♗d3! 23 ♕e1 ♖d8!, intending 24...♗xc4 and then 25...♖xe2 26 ♕xe2 ♖d1#.

21...♗d3! 22 ♔f1 ♘xe2 23 ♘xe2 ♖xe2 24 ♔g1 ♖d8 0-1

There is no good defence against 25...♗xc4 followed by 26...♖d1+.

The unpinning sacrifices which are most difficult to foresee are those which do not involve a capture. Our final three examples demonstrate some of the forms that they can take. The first (*see following diagram*) is short but very sweet. The white queen pins the d7-knight against the black queen, but is itself unprotected. At the same time, two black minor pieces are standing menacingly over the white king, waiting for a colleague to join them. The finish is simple and elegant:

19...♘de5!! 0-1

White's queen is lost since 20 ♕xe7 allows mate in two by 20...♘xf3+ 21 ♔h1 ♘f2#.

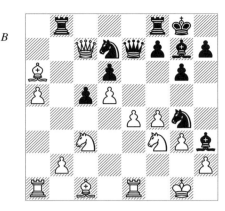

S. Garcia – Pigusov
Moscow 1987

The next example is rare and beautiful, as the piece that is exposed by the unpinning sacrifice can be captured with check.

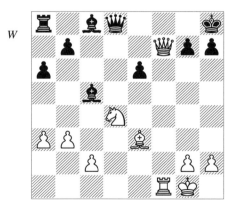

Honfi – Lengyel
Hungarian Ch, Budapest 1961

White is naturally searching for a back-rank mate, but the c5-bishop guards f8, so it must be shifted first. He can uncover an attack on the bishop by 24 ♘f5, but in so doing would block the f-file.

24 ♘c6!!

This move works because after 24...♗xe3+ 25 ♔h1 the black queen is still under attack by the knight, most moves to save it allow mate on the back rank, and the offer of the exchange of queens with 25...♕g8 allows a nice mate by 26 ♕xg8+ ♔xg8 27 ♘e7+ ♔h8 28 ♖f8#. Black has no option but to allow his own bishop to be captured, leaving his king defenceless against an assault on g7.

24...bxc6 25 ♗xc5 ♗d7 26 ♗d4 e5 27 ♗xe5 1-0

In our final example, White's unpinning sacrifice drags the black queen away to allow a decisive sacrificial breakthrough.

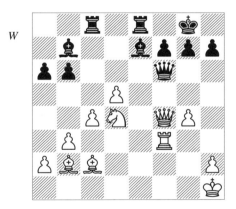

Ornstein – Prodanov
Albena 1978

The white pieces are poised. All that is needed is to lure the queen away from the defence, which is neatly achieved by White's unpinning sacrifice.

25 ♘f5! ♕xb2 26 ♘h6+! ♔h8

Not 26...gxh6 27 ♕xf7+ ♔h8 28 ♕xh7#.

27 ♘xf7+ ♔g8 28 ♗xh7+! ♔f8 *(D)*

White can continue to sacrifice with impunity as 28...♔xh7 allows 29 ♖h3+ ♔g6 (or 29...♔g8 30 ♖h8#) 30 ♕f5#.

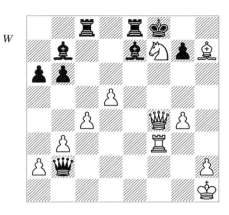

29 ♘h8+ ♗f6

It is too late for the queen to struggle back as 29...♕f6 loses to 30 g5! ♕xf4 31 ♘g6+ ♔f7 32 ♘e5+ ♔f8 33 ♘d7+ ♔f7 34 g6#.

30 ♕d6+ ♖e7 31 ♘g6+ ♔e8 32 ♘xe7 ♕c1+ 33 ♔g2 ♕d2+ 34 ♖f2 ♕g5 35 ♗g6+ ♔f8 1-0

Black lost on time before he was mated by 36 ♘xc8+ ♔g8 37 ♕e6+ ♔h8 38 ♕e8#.

Exercise 51

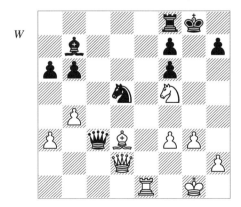

Level 1

White would like to attack on the kingside, but moving his queen away allows ...♕xe1+. What is White's solution to the problem?

Exercise 52

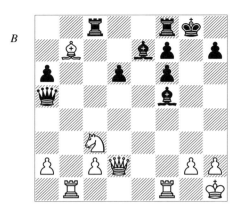

Level 2

After 19...♕xc3 20 ♕xc3 ♖xc3 21 ♖xf5 ♖b8 Black would win a second pawn, but the ending would be tricky to win thanks to the opposite-coloured bishops and Black's ragged pawns. How can he win more quickly?

Exercise 53

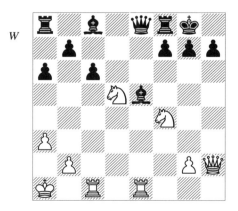

Level 3

White (to move) is three pawns down but he can win material beautifully. How?

The solutions are on page 222.

The Shunning Sacrifice

The theme of passive, unguarding and unpinning sacrifices is to let our opponent do what he intended – to capture the pieces that he attacked or pinned other pieces against. In the case of the **shunning sacrifice**, he has already done it. The capture has been made. The automatic response is to recapture, but many fine games have been resulted when the attacker has left the capturing piece alone and continued with his own designs.

Sometimes this has been called the *intermezzo* or *zwischenzug* ('in-between move'), but both words imply that the sacrificer goes back to make his recapture later. Often, he doesn't recapture at all as his attack is more important to him. Here is an example from Tal.

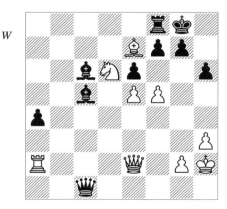

Botterill – Tal
European Team Ch, Bath 1973

A pawn down and with his king rather exposed, George Botterill understandably took the exchange...

42 ♗xf8 ♗e3!!

...only to be stunned when Tal completely ignored his bishop, preferring instead to round on the white king by a shunning sacrifice which threatens 43...♗f4+ 44 g3 ♕h1#. White's reply is forced, but his king is soon hounded to death by a series of simple mate threats.

43 ♔g3 ♗g5 44 ♕c4 ♕e3+ 45 ♔g4 ♗h4! **46 ♗e7**

Taking either piece leads to mate: 46 ♔xh4 ♕g5# or 46 ♕xc6 ♕g3+ 47 ♔h5 ♕g5#.

46...♗xe7 47 ♘xf7 h5+! 48 ♔xh5 ♗e8 49 ♔g4 exf5+ 50 ♔xf5 g6+ 51 ♔g4 ♗d7+ 0-1

While we are with Tal, it is worth pointing out that a shunning sacrifice can have a long-term purpose. The attacker can use the time gained to get his pieces into play or to force weaknesses in his opponent's position. Here is an example where Tal does both.

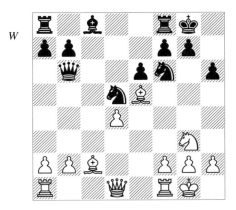

Tal – Flesch
Lvov 1981

Tal lures the black knight forward.

16 ♕d3!? ♘b4 17 ♕d2 ♘xc2 18 ♗xf6!

Now, however, he refuses to recapture the knight, preferring to let his rook go and to use the time to weaken the black king. Tal gives top priority to bringing his pieces over to the kingside and settling his queen and bishop on the long dark-squared diagonal.

18...♘xa1 19 ♘h5 e5 20 dxe5 g5 21 e6! **♕xe6 22 h3 ♕f5 23 ♖xa1**

Only now does Tal take the knight, after which Flesch is unable to withstand the pressure on his king.

23...♗e6 24 ♖e1 ♕g6 25 g4 ♖ac8 26 ♗c3 **♖fd8 27 ♕e3 ♖d3 28 ♕e5 ♖cxc3 29 bxc3** **♔h7 30 ♘f6+ ♔g7 31 ♘d5+ ♔h7 32 ♘e7 1-0**

After the black queen moves away from g6, ♕e4+ will win the rook.

The true *intermezzo* happens when the attacker delays the recapture, but plans to make it once he has made some gain elsewhere. The next example is a personal one in which the gain was not only a pawn but, in the process, the complete breakdown of my opponent's king's position.

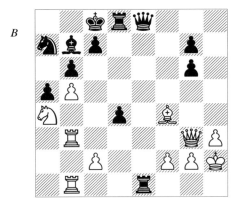

LeMoir – K. Wicker
Hertfordshire vs Kent 1977

Black is a pawn ahead and is looking to pocket the white b-pawn in addition, as it is attacked by his queen and knight and defended by the white rooks. His next move removes a key defender.

25...♖xb1 26 ♗xc7!

A long-prepared shot, shunning the recapture of the rook. The main threat is 27 ♘xb6#, but after he has seen to that, Black will lose both rooks. For instance, 26...♗e4 27 ♘xb6+ ♚b7 28 ♖xb1 and the other black rook has no safe square. Black tries to gain a move in order to clear a square for his king.

26...♖h1+ 27 ♚xh1 ♗xg2+ 28 ♚xg2 ♕e4+ 29 ♚h2 ♖f8 30 ♗xb6

White threatens mate again, and Black must let another piece go.

30...♖f7 31 ♗a7 ♕xc2 32 ♕b8+ ♚d7 33 ♘c5+ ♚e7 34 ♕c7+ ♚f6 35 ♘d7+ 1-0

In the next example, Black plays an *intermezzo* ignoring his opponent's queen sacrifice.

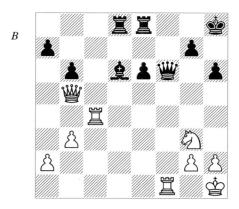

Schlosser – Anon
Stettin 1940

Schlosser's position is in a bad way, as his unnamed opponent immediately demonstrates.

1...♗xg3!

The bishop eliminates the defence of the white rook, which cannot capture the black queen because the d8-rook would reply with mate on the back rank. Schlosser's remedy is to divert the rook to e8.

2 ♕xe8+!

After 2...♖xe8 3 ♖xf6 gxf6 4 hxg3 White has some drawing chances, but Black's stunning reply leaves him helpless.

2...♚h7!!

Nothing has changed. The black queen still threatens mate on f1, the white rook still cannot capture it, and 3 ♚g1 ♗f2+! 4 ♖xf2 ♖d1+ leads to mate. So White must play something like 3 ♖fc1, when 3...♖xe8 is now possible. White resigned and, almost uniquely in chess literature, 'Anon' had won.

In the next diagram, White has gobbled the exchange and a pawn, and is happy to offer a knight in return. However, Black (Nezhmetdinov) has no intention of capturing the knight, preferring to by-pass it completely in order to create a mating-net.

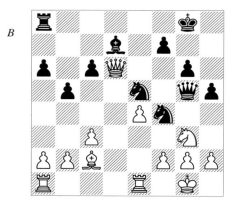

Kalinkin – Nezhmetdinov
Vologda 1962

22...h4

If the white knight moves, it is mate on g2. White has foreseen the move and takes steps to create queenside counterplay.

23 a4 h3!!

Nezhmetdinov's pawn continues forward, not bothering to pocket the knight on the way. The point is that the white king's apparently safe fortress suffers from weak squares at g2, h3 and f3. Nezhmetdinov needs his brave pawn in order to expose them, and White can do nothing sensible to stop Black developing a deadly attack.

24 axb5 cxb5 25 ♖xa6 ♖xa6 26 ♕xa6 hxg2 27 ♗d1 ♗g4 28 ♕a1 ♗f3 29 ♕a8+ ♔h7 30 ♕c8 ♗xd1 0-1

The theme from that game – of ignoring the opportunity to redress a material disadvantage – is continued in the next example. White sacrifices his queen and could capture a rook and bishop on successive moves as compensation. What does he do? He sacrifices a knight.

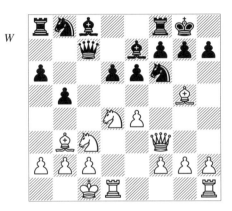

Jurković – Cappellani
Lecce 1987

White starts his combination.

11 e5! ♗b7

There have been several other games with this opening line. A recent example is 11...dxe5 12 ♘dxb5 axb5 13 ♕xa8 b4 14 ♘b5 ♕b6 15 ♕a7 ♕xb5 16 ♕xe7, which led to a win for White in Jurković-Vajda, Budapest 2001.

12 exf6 ♗xf3 13 fxe7 ♗xd1

On the standard table of values (which Deadly Tacticians often ignore) knight and bishop (6 points) for queen and rook (14 points) is an eight-point deficit, which will soon zoom down to one point when the

adventurous e-pawn captures the rook with check and the rook captures the bishop next move.

14 ♘xe6!!

White prefers to throw in a knight (cheaply, of course, because he gets two pawns for it). In Yudasin-Novikov, Kuibyshev 1986, White played 14 exf8♕+ ♔xf8 15 ♖xd1 and the game was later drawn! After the text-move, however, 14...fxe6 15 ♗xe6+ ♖f7 16 e8♕# is mate, and Black's best is 14...♕xe7 15 ♗xe7 ♖e8 16 ♗xd6 fxe6 17 ♖xd1, which gives him a lost endgame. Accordingly, he resigned.

Refusing to recapture can lead to some very attractive play. Here is a combination by Paul Keres which is testimony to his fine imagination and analytical ability.

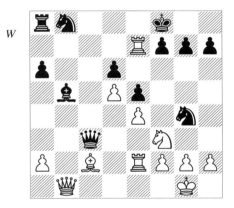

Keres – Raud
Pärnu 1937

Black has given up the exchange, but he now has both of White's rooks under attack. Raud fully expected White's next move, but not the one after that.

22 ♖b7 ♗xe2 23 ♕b6!!

Black was expecting 23 ♖xb8+ ♖xb8 24 ♕xb8+ ♔e7, when White will lose a pawn on f3. However, Keres's amazing queen invasion shuns the chance to regain the piece at once, but it does threaten mate. Now 23...g6 would allow mate in five moves by 24 ♕d8+ ♔g7 25 ♖xf7+ ♔xf7 26 ♘g5+ ♔g7 27 ♘e6+ ♔h6 (or 27...♔f7 28 ♕f8#) 28 ♕g5#.

23...♘c6

Black becomes too adventurous. His best defence is 23...♕c8, leaving him with only a small disadvantage.

24 ♕c7!

24 dxc6 is also good for White, but Keres has a specific idea in mind and again shuns the immediate chance to regain a piece.

24...♘h6 25 ♕xd6+ ♔g8 26 dxc6 ♔h8 27 ♖b8+ ♖xb8 28 ♕xb8+ ♘g8 29 c7! ♗b5

29...♕xc2 threatens mate, but loses to 30 h4 ♕c1+ 31 ♔h2 ♕f4+ 32 g3 ♕xf3 33 ♕xg8+ ♔xg8 34 c8♕#.

30 ♕d8! ♕xc2 31 ♔h1! f6 32 c8♕ ♕b1+ 33 ♘g1 ♕xa2 34 ♕f8 1-0

In the final example, White plays a passive rook sacrifice. He could get a bishop for it, but instead he constructs a surprising mating-net.

W

Sideif-Zade – Gofshtein
USSR Ch semi-final, Aktiubinsk 1985

White has sacrificed a pawn, but his attack appears to have faltered as Black threatens the exchange of queens and the obvious piece sacrifice on e6 loses the exchange. Nonetheless, White goes ahead.

20 ♗xe6! ♕xb3 21 ♗xb3 ♗xh1 22 ♗a4+ ♔e7

The black king has been displaced, and one's first impression is that White must play 23 ♖xh1, with some compensation for the exchange.

23 f5!!

White has seen the chance for mate and goes for it.

23...♖d8

23...f6 allows 24 ♖d7+ ♔e8 25 ♗c7!, when the threat of mate forces Black to return more than the sacrificed rook. Black challenges the white rook, hoping that it will agree that it is time to recapture the bishop.

24 ♖e1!

A stubborn rook. Suddenly it is clear that the game is up, as White threatens to mate by moving his bishop away from the e-file. Black's reply intends to stave off mate by returning some material, but White refuses to be denied.

24...♗d5 25 ♗xg7+ 1-0

The game would end with 25...♔d6 26 ♗e5+ ♔e7 27 ♗c7+ ♗e6 28 f6#.

Exercise 54

B

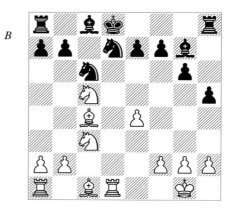

Level 1

After **14...♗xc3**, how does White force a quick win?

Exercise 55

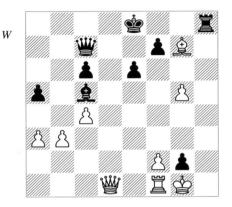

Level 2

After **24 ♗xh8**, how does Black force a quick win?

Exercise 56

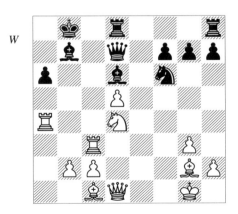

Level 3

How does White (to play) win quickly?
The solutions start on page 222.

Ambush!

Prophylaxis is a powerful concept. We anticipate our opponent's plans and prevent them, hoping to frustrate him into submission. In fact, we can get so bound up with the idea of preventing his ideas that we may even try to prevent him from carrying out bad ones. The Deadly Tactician has another weapon up his sleeve: the **ambush**. He lets the opponent go ahead with his plan; when it is on the verge of success, he springs an ambush that demonstrates – often dramatically – what is wrong with it.

Here is a simple example from my own recent experience.

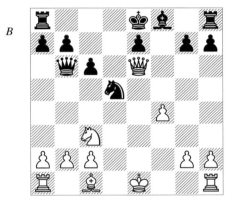

LeMoir – H. Collins
Simultaneous, Norwich 2001

As I came around to the board, I was surprised to find Black playing **13...♘xf4**. The idea is clearly 14 ♗xf4 ♛xb2, attacking rook and knight. I had been caught out by a little tactical trick, as must happen to many 'masters' playing simultaneous exhibitions. I stopped for a moment and soon realized that Black is helping to develop my game, and that if I let him go ahead with his idea I can develop an easy mating attack.

14 ♗xf4! ♕xb2 15 0-0! ♕xc3 16 ♖ad1 ♖d8 17 ♖xd8+ ♔xd8 18 ♖d1+ ♔e8 19 ♗c7!

Decisive. Black can only prevent the threatened mate by giving up his queen.

19...♕c5+ 20 ♔h1 ♕d5 21 ♖xd5 cxd5 22 ♕xd5 g6 23 ♗e5 1-0

The next example has a similar start – Alekhine allows his opponent to capture a pawn on b2 with an apparently lethal double attack – but the result is infinitely more spectacular.

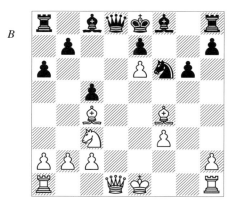

Alekhine – Levenfish
St Petersburg 1912

13...♕b6

After this double attack on the white e- and b-pawns, Alekhine decides to defend the e-pawn.

14 ♕e2! ♕xb2

Black is winning at least a piece, but Alekhine has prepared an amazing double sacrifice.

15 ♘b5!!

Black has the choice of taking both rooks or just the one knight.

15...♕xa1+

Levenfish chose to capture the rooks, which at least ensured, at this early stage of his chess

career, that his name would live forever in the anthologies.

After 15...axb5 16 ♗xb5+ he must give back the piece, whereupon his king will not be able to survive the assault. A typical line is 16...♔d8 17 ♖d1+ ♗d7 18 ♗e5 ♕xa2 19 ♗xf6 exf6 20 e7+ ♗xe7 21 ♖xd7+ ♔c8 22 ♖xe7 with an extra piece and a strong attack.

16 ♔f2 ♕xh1 17 ♘c7+ ♔d8 18 ♕d2+ ♗d7 19 exd7 1-0

Black didn't bother to take it any further as White threatens 20 ♘e6# and both 19...e5 20 ♘e6+ ♔e7 21 d8♕+ and 19...♘xd7 20 ♗e6 lead to mate.

In these first two examples, Black's ideas were faulty and White gladly fell in with them. Sometimes a player sees a bad plan coming, but needs to allow it to happen without making his opponent suspicious. A 'nothing move' is called for.

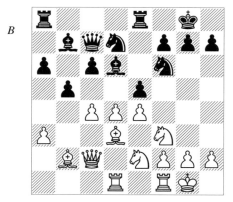

Malich – Kort
IBM tournament, Amsterdam 1971

15...♖ad8

White sees that Black intends to win the white e-pawn in safety. Looking more deeply into the position, he realizes that winning the e-pawn is in fact not so safe. His next move does nothing radical to change the position, and sensibly avoids a possible back-rank mate in the future.

16 h3

For his part, Black has seen some traps and, having worked out how to avoid them, goes ahead with the pawn win.

16...exd4 17 ♘exd4 bxc4 18 ♗xc4 ♘xe4

Black avoids the loss of the exchange by 18...♖xe4 19 ♗xf7+ ♔xf7 20 ♘g5+.

19 ♘f5 ♘df6

Now Black sidesteps 19...♘f8 20 ♗xf7+! ♔xf7 21 ♕c4+, when White wins material or mates.

20 ♘xd6 ♖xd6 *(D)*

This is the point of 15...♖ad8. After the alternative 20...♘xd6 White can choose between weakening the king's fortress by 21 ♗xf6 or retrieving his lost pawn by 21 ♘g5 ♘fe4! 22 ♘xe4 ♘xe4 23 ♖xd8 ♕xd8 24 ♗xf7+ ♔xf7 25 ♕b3+.

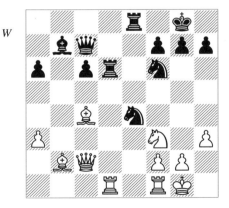

Apparently, Black has picked his way through all potential troubles and pocketed the pawn in safety. In reality, his troubles are only just beginning. From behind the bushes comes the ambush.

21 ♗e5!

This silent sacrifice aims to deflect the black rook from the back rank.

21...♖xe5 22 ♘xe5 ♖xd1 23 ♖xd1 ♕xe5 24 ♖d8+ ♘e8 25 ♕b2!

A second silent sacrifice, and the point of White's play. The black queen is under attack but, on pain of mate, must maintain the defence of the e8-knight.

25...♕e7 26 ♕xb7! 1-0

The repeat dose is more than Black can stand.

These ambushes resulted from plans that were seriously at fault. On the other hand, our opponents sometimes develop plans that are perfectly reasonable in themselves, but we can make them wrong by taking appropriate measures in time.

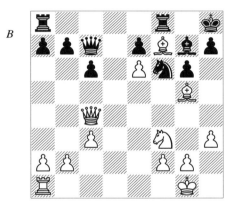

Tal – Kolarov
European Team Ch, Kapfenberg 1970

Black has the exchange for a pawn, but the f7-bishop is a thorn in his side. He works out a plan to give back his extra material in order to remove it.

22...♕a5

He intends 23...♕d5 followed by 24...♖xf7 25 exf7 ♕xf7. Tal understands the idea fully, and works out a remarkable ambush. He will let Black go ahead, but needs to defend his e-pawn and place his queen on the h-file. His method is very crafty. By defending the e-pawn first, he apparently allows the black queen to gain time by forcing the white queen to move.

23 ♖e1! ♕d5 24 ♕h4! ♖xf7 25 ♘e5!!

A startling idea, shunning the rook but intending to meet 25...♖ff8 with 26 ♘xg6+ ♔g8 27 ♘xe7+, winning the black queen. Tal's 23 ♖e1 ensured that Black could not now play 25...♕xe6, as he would lose his queen to the discovery 26 ♘xg6+.

The game is now effectively over as Tal will capture the rook, remaining a pawn ahead and retaining the attack.

25...♘h5 26 ♘xf7+ ♔g8 27 ♗xe7 ♖e8 28 ♘d6 ♗f6 29 ♗xf6 ♕xd6 30 ♗g5 ♖xe6 31 ♕c4 ♘g7 32 ♕b3 ♔f8 33 ♖d1 ♕e5 34 ♗h6 ♖d6 35 ♖xd6 1-0

The ambush played by Ljubojević in the next example is less spectacular, but just as deadly.

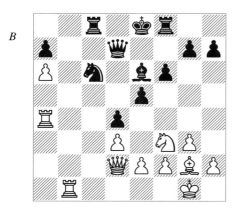

Trois – Ljubojević
Buenos Aires 1979

White's a-pawn supports an outpost on b7, and he clearly intends to place a rook there. Ljubojević could prevent its arrival by 20...♖b8, but prefers to plan a reception committee.

First, he clears his back rank so that the f8-rook can enter play.

20...♔f7 21 ♖b7 ♖c7 22 ♕b2 ♖b8!!

Here is the ambush. The idea is simply to win a pawn. If White now plays 23 ♖xc7 ♖xb2 24 ♖xd7+ ♗xd7, his e-pawn is under attack and saving it by 25 ♗f1 gives Black time for 25...♘b8 26 ♖a1 ♗b5, which annexes the a-pawn.

23 ♖xb8 ♘xb8

By recapturing, the knight attacks the a-pawn and discovers an attack by the black queen on the a4-rook. After the rook moves, the queen will move to c8, also attacking the a-pawn, but it will also double major pieces along the c-file, allowing Black to force an exchange of rooks and finally win the a-pawn. It all hangs together beautifully.

24 ♖a1 ♕c8 25 ♕a3 ♖c3 26 ♕a5 ♖c5 27 ♕a3 ♖c3 28 ♕a5 ♖c1+ 29 ♘e1 ♖xa1 30 ♕xa1 ♕xa6 31 ♕c1 ♕b6 32 ♘c2 ♘d7 33 ♘a3 ♕c5 34 ♕b2 a5 35 h4 ♕b4 0-1

Ambushes can have long-term purposes. For instance, maybe we see that our opponent threatens a sequence that will win the exchange for a pawn. If we are likely to get good positional compensation for it, we can consider letting it happen. In the next example, Dvoretsky deliberately allows his queen to be pinned, as his long-term compensation will be substantial (*see following diagram*).

White has already displaced the black king, and now seeks to exploit its new position.

15 ♗d2

The threat is 16 ♗a5. Dvoretsky comes to the remarkable decision to let White proceed with his plan.

15...♗xd3!! 16 ♗a5 ♗xc2 17 ♖f1 f5 18 ♗xb6+ axb6

The two bishops and flexible pawn-chain represent good compensation for the queen. Most important of all, Dvoretsky is now playing like a man inspired, while Kapengut is unable to cope with the drastic change in the

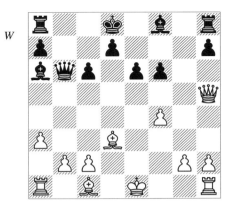

Kapengut – Dvoretsky
USSR Cup, Ordzhonikidze 1978

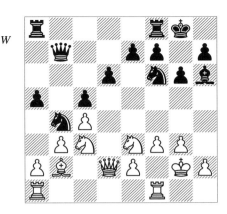

Rubinstein – Nimzowitsch
Marienbad 1925

position. White soon returns all of his extra material without drawing the dynamism from the black position.

19 ♖f3 ♔c7 20 ♖g3 ♖a4 21 ♕f3 ♖c4 22 ♖c1? ♗d6 23 ♕e2 ♖e4 24 ♖xc2 ♗xf4 25 ♖g7 ♗xh2 26 ♕xe4 fxe4 27 ♖d2 ♗d6 28 ♖d4 c5 29 ♖xe4 ♔c6

For the exchange, Black has two connected passed pawns. This advantage proves decisive.

30 b3 h5 31 ♖h4 b5 32 ♔e2 ♗e5 33 ♖g5 ♗d4 34 ♖hxh5 ♖a8 35 ♖h3 ♖xa3 36 ♖g8 e5 37 g4 ♖a2+ 38 ♔f3 ♖f2+ 39 ♔g3 ♖b2 40 g5 ♖xb3+ 41 ♔g4 ♖xh3 42 ♔xh3 ♖d5 43 g6 e4 44 ♖b8 b4 45 ♔g4 ♔c4 46 ♔f4 0-1

Our final example of an ambush is one of the most famous (*see following diagram*). Nimzowitsch wrote much about prophylaxis, and was proud of his ability to use mysterious-looking manoeuvres to turn his opponents' positive plans into ruinous adventures.

17 ♘cd1

The threat is to damage the black pawn-structure by capturing on f6, leaving the d-pawn backward and vulnerable. Nimzowitsch takes specific steps to make this plan bad. His first mysterious idea is to open the b-file.

17...a4! 18 bxa4 ♖fe8!!

Ensuring that that the rook will be on the e-file when Rubinstein opens it with ♗xf6.

19 ♗xf6 exf6 20 ♔f2

This is necessary, to defend the e3-knight.

It would be natural now for Black to play something like 20...♕c6, when White achieves a comfortable position by 21 f4 ♖xa4 22 ♘c3, with a grip on d5. Nimzowitsch's idea is to let the pawn go, using the time gained to bring the bishop to d4, with a big pin on the e3-knight.

20...f5!! 21 ♕xd6 ♗g7 22 ♖b1 ♗d4

Suddenly Black is threatening 23...♘d3+!, discovering an attack on the b1-rook, something that would not have been possible without the move 17...a4!.

23 ♔g2

White can put up fierce resistance by 23 ♖b3!, but his king comes under attack through 23...♖e6 24 ♕f4 ♕e7. A typical line is 25 ♔g2 ♖e8 26 a3! ♘c2! 27 ♘d5! ♖xe2+ 28 ♔h1 ♖xh2+! 29 ♔xh2 ♕e2+, when Black retrieves the rook with a winning attack. Instead, Rubinstein gave up the knight and Nimzowitsch won with his extra piece.

23...♗xe3 24 ♘xe3 ♖xe3 25 ♕xc5 ♖e2+ 26 ♖f2 ♖xf2+ 27 ♕xf2 ♖xa4 28 a3 ♖xa3 29

♕e2 ♖a8 30 c5 ♕a6 31 ♕xa6 ♘xa6 32 ♖a1
♘c7 33 ♖xa8+ ♘xa8 34 ♔f2 ♔f8 35 ♔e3
♔e7 36 ♔d4 ♔e6 37 f4 f6 38 ♔c4 ♘c7 0-1

Exercise 57

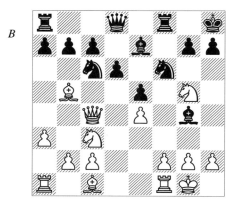

B

Level 1

White is threatening to win a pawn on c6, and he also has the threat of 12 h3 or 12 f3 with ♘e6 or ♘f7+ to follow, depending on where Black's bishop retreats. Black not only avoids material loss, but even finds a way to establish a significant positional advantage. How?

Exercise 58

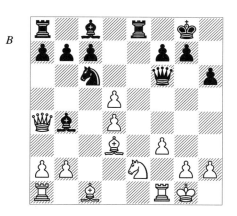

B

Level 2

Black (to play) starts a vicious attack with **13...♗f5 14 ♗xf5 ♖xe2**. White now has to work out what is going on. Should he take the knight or not? Work out what Black intended and find the neat ambush that White springs to make the attack fall to pieces.

Exercise 59

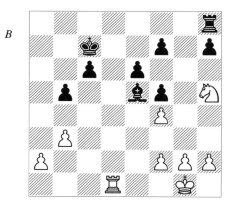

B

Level 3

This is a trap based on an ambush. Black's slight endgame advantage is based on the remote position of the white knight and the vulnerability of the white a-pawn. If Black (to move) can force the white rook away from the d-file, then his own rook can occupy the file and it is worth playing on. If not, then it's an easy draw. Black's next two moves exploit White's reluctance to desert the d-file and they invite an obvious trick to put the a-pawn out of danger. How did Black win?

The solutions start on page 223.

11 Tail-Lights

The sacrifices that we have met to date have either achieved success on their own or have been followed by further sacrifices or some other vigorous attacking gestures. Even silent or passive sacrifices are played with some force in mind, albeit a subtler and less visible force than your classic flash-bang-wallop sacrifices.

However, we should not allow ourselves to be blinded by the bright headlights of a sacrificial vehicle. Occasionally, it is necessary to lengthen our focus and look beyond the dazzling main beam to the dimmer interior of the vehicle, or even to its tail-lights beyond.

The Quiet Follow-Up

The Deadly Tactician does not need to apply a lot of brute force. Not for him the universal use of checks and captures in his sacrifices. He is able to see and appreciate more subtle sacrificial forms. Crucially, he can also foresee quiet moves that sometimes follow his initial sacrifices and that help to make them work.

These quiet follow-ups seem to threaten very little, and so are very difficult for the defender to anticipate. Our opponent may see the possibility of an initial sacrifice, but he is likely to overlook the apparently non-threatening move that follows it. It is one of the great joys of the sacrificer when he sees his opponent gleefully accept the offered material only to go red in the face at the sight of the unforeseen piece of subtlety that follows it.

Here is a beautifully neat, but little-known, Fischer finish.

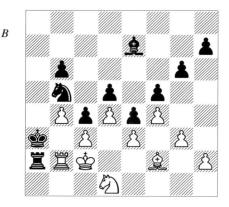

Acevedo – Fischer
Olympiad, Siegen 1970

The sacrifice **47...♘xc3!** seems completely pointless. Clearly 48 ♘xc3 fails to 48...♖xb2+, but **48 ♔xc3** appears to leave Black with nothing for his piece. However, Fischer played the quiet **48...♖a1!!** and his opponent resigned!

White's knight has no escape-square, and White loses material if he protects it. 49 ♔c2 loses back the piece to 49...♖xd1! 50 ♔xd1 ♔xb2, when the black c-pawn will march, while 49 ♖d2 allows mate by 49...♖c1+ 50 ♖c2 ♗xb4#.

It is sometimes the case, as in the above example, that the quiet follow-up wins at once. However, the purpose of the quiet follow-up is often to help the momentum of the attack without causing an immediate defensive collapse. In our next example, one of the great combinative attacks of recent years is crucially aided by a surprise quiet move.

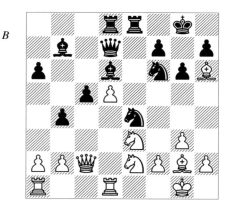

Cifuentes – Zviagintsev
Wijk aan Zee 1995

Black drags the white king into an awkward position with a couple of brutal sacrifices.
24...♘xf2! 25 ♔xf2 ♖xe3! 26 ♔xe3 ♘g4+ 27 ♔f3 ♘xh2+ 28 ♔f2 ♘g4+ 29 ♔f3 *(D)*

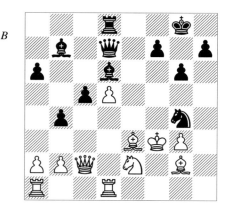

It appears that Black may have to settle for perpetual check, but he has seen that he can strengthen his assault by combining an attack along the e-file with threats to the d-pawn.
29...♕e6!!
This attractive quiet move exploits the pin on the d-pawn to bring the black queen into a

threatening position. Now the d-pawn must go, as 30 ♕e4 ♕xe4+ 31 ♔xe4 ♖e8+ costs White the bishop and 30 ♕d2 ♖e8 threatens both the bishop and 31...♕e4#.

White may play 30 ♗c1 but by delaying the capture of the pawn Black can bring his dark-squared bishop into play by 30...c4!. The benefit can be seen in the variation 31 ♖d4 ♗xd5+ 32 ♖xd5 ♕xd5+ 33 ♕e4 (or 33 ♔xg4 ♕h5#) 33...♘e5+ 34 ♔f2 ♗c5+, when White must lose material because a king retreat to the first rank allows mate on d1.

30 ♗f4 ♖e8

Black is winning anyway with 30...♗xf4 or 30...f5, but this move leads to a spectacular finish.

31 ♕c4 ♕e3+! 32 ♗xe3 ♖xe3+ 33 ♔xg4 ♗c8+ 34 ♔g5 h6+! 35 ♔xh6 ♖e5! 0-1

The final quiet move brings an end to the king-hunt by forcing mate next move through either 36...♖h5# or 36...♗f8#.

The next example features a rare self-pin that wins a crucial tempo for the attack.

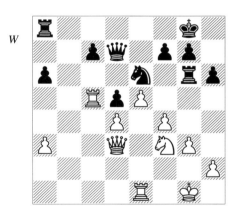

Aagaard – J. Cobb
Hampstead 1998

The attack opens with a passive exchange sacrifice to get White's pawns moving.

26 f5! ♘xc5 27 dxc5 ♖g4! 28 e6 ♕c6?

This is an error, but it takes a remarkable move to prove it. Black should be able to save the game by continuing 28...fxe6 29 ♘e5 ♕a4!.

29 exf7+ ♔f8 30 ♘e5 ♕xc5+ *(D)*

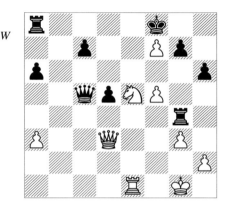

Black anticipates the natural 31 ♔g2?, when 31...♕d4! evades the threat of 32 ♘d7+ while attacking the white queen. The white knight protects the queen, so it would have no time to capture the g4-rook.

31 ♖e3!!

This unexpected self-pin protects White's queen. Now White's threat of 32 ♘d7+ cannot be sidestepped by 31...♕d4, as that allows 32 ♘xg4 without losing the white queen. Black must use a tempo to extricate himself from the immediate threats, and that allows White time to whip up a mating attack.

31...♕c1+ 32 ♔g2 ♕b2+ 33 ♔h3 ♖d4 34 ♘g6+ ♔xf7 35 ♖e7+ ♔f6

After 35...♔g8 White can choose between 36 f6! gxf6 37 ♕f5 ♕b6 38 ♘f4, mating, or 36 ♕xa6!, which is also decisive.

36 ♕e3 ♖e4 37 ♖xe4 dxe4 38 ♕xe4 ♕b5 39 ♕e7+ ♔xf5 40 ♘h4# (1-0)

In that example, the quiet follow-up came several moves after the initial sacrifice. In the next example, Nigel Short follows his sacrifice with a very crafty quiet move on the very next turn.

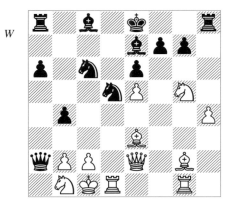

W

Short – Ljubojević
Belgrade 1989

With the black queen far out of play, the sacrifice on f7 seems reasonable.

20 ♘xf7! ♔xf7

Now we might expect something like 21 ♗xd5 exd5 22 ♕g2 hitting both the d- and g-pawns, but Short comes up with a brilliant quiet alternative.

21 ♗e4!!

The threat is 22 ♗g6+. It appears that Black can defend by 21...♘xe5, which guards the g6-square and liberates the f6-square for his bishop, but White has 22 ♕g2!, which not only threatens to capture the g-pawn with a blistering attack on the king, but also menaces 23 ♖xd5!, since 23...exd5 loses the black queen to 24 ♗xd5+.

Understandably, Black runs his king to the queenside, but Short hounds it relentlessly to its death.

21...♔e8 22 ♖xg7 ♗d7 23 ♕g4! ♔d8

He may have better survival chances after 23...♘xe3 24 ♖g8+ ♗f8 (not 24...♖xg8 25 ♕xg8+ ♗f8 26 ♗g6+ ♔d8 27 ♕xf8+ ♔c7 28 ♖xd7+! ♔xd7 29 ♕d6+ ♔c8 30 ♕xc6+

♔b8 31 ♕b6+ ♔c8 32 ♕xe3 with a winning material advantage for White) 25 ♕g7 ♕xb2+! 26 ♔xb2 ♘xd1+, although the white queen can soon pick up more material.

24 ♗xd5 exd5 25 e6 ♗e8 26 ♗b6+ ♔c8 27 ♕f4! ♖a7 28 ♗xa7 ♖xh4 29 ♕g3 ♕c4 30 ♖xe7! 1-0

Mate follows by 30...♘xe7 31 ♕b8#.

In the next example, the quiet move that follows up the initial sacrifice is itself a passive sacrifice. Even Alekhine at the height of his powers could be shocked by such an unexpected turn of events, and he immediately committed an error.

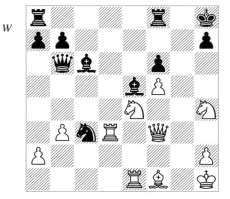

W

Nimzowitsch – Alekhine
Semmering 1926

Nimzowitsch has invited Alekhine's last move 32...♘d5x♗c3, which has the point 33 ♖xc3? ♗xc3 34 ♕xc3 ♕f2 35 ♘g2 ♗xe4 36 ♖xe4 ♕xf1#, because White can decline the offer in a surprising way.

33 ♘g6+!! hxg6

Now we might expect 34 fxg6, but after 34...♔g7 35 ♕h3 ♖h8 36 ♖d7+ ♗xd7 37 ♕xd7+ ♔xg6 Black has time to defend thanks to his own threat of 38...♖xh2#. It appears that Nimzowitsch's sacrifice is far too ambitious, as he is now threatened with the loss of the exchange on e4.

34 ♕g4!!

There is no need to worry about captures on e4, as White threatens to mate by 35 ♖h3+.

34...♖f7?

Under the shock of Nimzowitsch's audacious sacrifice and unexpected follow-up, Alekhine falters at once.

Black's most effective defence is 34...♖g8!, giving his king an escape route. White can achieve a draw, but no more. A typical line is 35 fxg6 ♔g7 36 ♖d7+ ♗xd7 37 ♕xd7+ ♔xg6 38 ♗d3! ♔h6 39 ♕h3+ ♔g7 40 ♖g1+ ♕xg1+ 41 ♔xg1 ♘xe4 42 ♗xe4.

35 ♖h3+ ♔g7 36 ♗c4! ♗d5 37 fxg6

I imagine that time-trouble was affecting Nimzowitsch's play hereabouts. Here he could have played 37 ♕xg6+ ♔f8 38 ♖h8+, safely pocketing the a8-rook.

37...♘xe4 38 gxf7+ ♔f8 (D)

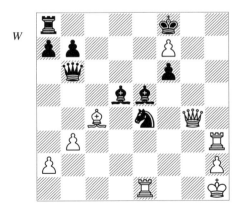

W

39 ♖xe4

Here 39 ♕g8+! is more precise since after 39...♔e7 40 f8♕+ ♖xf8 41 ♖h7+ ♔e8 42 ♕xd5 Black cannot defend his king effectively.

However, the end is not much delayed.

39...♗xe4+ 40 ♕xe4 ♔e7 41 f8♕+! ♖xf8 42 ♕d5 ♕d6 43 ♕xb7+ ♔d8 44 ♖d3 ♗d4 45 ♕e4 ♖e8 46 ♖xd4 1-0

Exercise 60

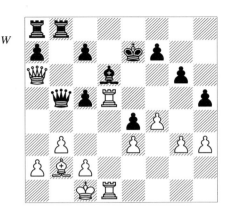

W

Level 1

This is one of mine. I am White, to play. I have just tempted Black to play ...♕d7-b5 in search of a queen exchange. I took advantage of the queen's absence by playing **21 ♖xd6!**. I had in mind a quiet move, a few moves later, which forced instant resignation. What was it?

Exercise 61

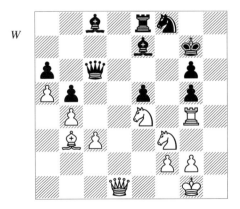

W

Level 2/3

For Level 3, simply try to find White's combination in this position, without reading the next paragraph, and remember that it contains a decisive quiet move. For Level 2, read on.

The white rook is threatened by the c8-bishop, but if it retreats to g3, the e4-knight will be *en prise* to the black queen. White plays a passive sacrifice on move one and a quiet move on his next turn. As a result, he wins a pawn and simplifies to a winning endgame.

The solutions are on page 224.

The Sting in the Tail

Many combinations are only a few moves long, while some are longer and full of sacrifices that gradually tear apart the defender's position. Some, however, appear to have achieved very little but then suddenly comes the move that leaves the defender helpless – the sting in the tail. It takes great imagination and analytical skill to find a decisive move at the end of a long combination, or perhaps it takes extraordinary luck to find that one exists when we get there.

As we saw in Part One, Alekhine had the necessary skill, and it is no accident that some great tacticians feature in the examples that follow, starting with the incomparable Rashid Nezhmetdinov (*see following diagram*).

Nezhmetdinov starts his long combination with a substitution sacrifice (securing d4 for a knight) which ensures that he can open the e-file and draw the black queen to the e6-square.

23 ♘bd4!! exd4 24 ♘xd4 ♕d7 25 ♘xe6 ♕xe6 26 ♖a8+ ♘c8

The first point is that 26...♔f7 loses the queen to 27 ♖xh8 ♗xh8 28 ♗b3, so Black must volunteer to this self-pin.

27 ♗b3 ♕d7

The second point is that 27...♕f5 28 g4 forces the queen back to d7 anyway unless

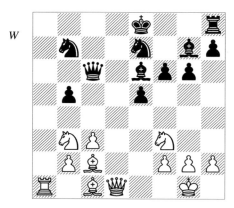

Nezhmetdinov – A. Zaitsev
Russian Ch, Kazan 1964

Black plays 28...♕c5, in which case White regains the piece at once by continuing 29 ♗e6.

28 ♕e2+ ♔d8 29 ♗e6 ♖e8 (D)

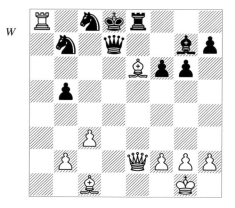

Nezhmetdinov often played combinations like this. He has apparently miscalculated, as Black's last move pinned the bishop that was causing all the trouble. However, he has seen in advance that the pin can be broken, and the black queen's life taken.

30 ♖xc8+!

The sting in the tail. Now after 30...♔xc8 the king would find itself on a square where the capture of the queen is check.

30...♕xc8

Now a queen check breaks the pin.

31 ♕d1+ ♔e7 32 ♗xc8 ♖xc8 33 ♕e2+ 1-0

Alexei Shirov is one of the great modern tacticians. He showed the position below to a number of strong players, and most of them took a long time to find the combination. Then he showed it to Tal's old trainer, Shirov's fellow Latvian Alexander Koblencs, and he found it at once!

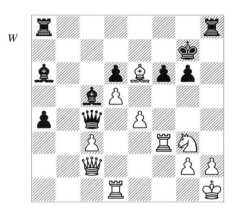

Shirov – King
Troll Masters, Gausdal 1990

Black appears to have good compensation for his pawn, but in reality his king is about to be mown down.

32 e5! dxe5 33 ♘f5+! gxf5 34 ♖g3+ ♔f8 35 ♕xf5 ♕f4 36 ♕g6 ♖a7

Shirov has foreseen a way through Black's apparently impervious defence.

37 ♖h3! ♖xh3 38 ♕g8+ ♔e7 39 d6+! 1-0

Black will be mated after 39...♗xd6 40 ♕f7+ ♔d8 41 ♖xd6+. It is worth pointing out that Shirov could have changed the order of moves by playing 37 d6! (threatening 38

♕g8+! with mate on the following move) 37...♗xd6 (forced) 38 ♖h3!, etc., which, depending on your taste, you may consider to be even prettier.

It is in the nature of some tail-borne stings that they look impossible at the start of a combination but suddenly become possible as the combination changes the way the elements of the position work. The next example is a striking demonstration.

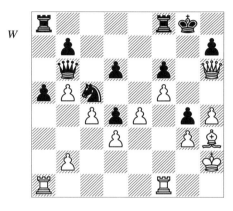

Seirawan – Vukić
Niš 1979

You wouldn't expect White's pawn thrust b4 to have any effect in the future play, would you? Even if the a8-rook were to be unprotected (so that the b-pawn could not be captured) Black could simply move his knight away. Well, that is all about to change!

Black has just played his pawn from g5 to g4 to avoid the opening of his king's position, expecting after 24 ♗xg4 to create counterplay by 24...♘xd3. Seirawan works out a combination that enables him to get at the black king at once, even at the cost of a passive sacrifice of the attacked bishop.

24 ♖f4!! gxh3 25 ♖g4+ ♔f7 26 ♖g7+ ♔e8 27 ♕xh7

27 ♖xh7 also wins, since the threat of 28 ♕g7 is decisive.

27...♔d8 *(D)*

27...♖c8 avoids White's next move, but 28 ♖e7+ ♔d8 29 ♕g7 ♖e8 30 ♖xe8+ ♔xe8 31 ♕g8+ ♔d7 32 ♕f7+ wins the f-pawn with check followed by the d-pawn, and White will eventually have five pawns for the piece, three of which are connected and passed.

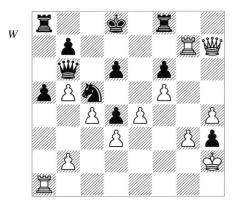

Black can hardly move a muscle, since ...♘xd3 allows ♖xb7, which threatens mate on d7 as well as the queen. The a8-rook is undefended, so the a-pawn is pinned. The preconditions for an effective b4 are satisfied...

28 b4! ♔c8 29 bxc5 dxc5 30 h5 1-0

White is a pawn ahead, and the advance of the h-pawn will be decisive.

The next combination is shorter, but another unexpected pawn thrust turns the game on its head *(see following diagram)*.

The position appears harmless, but Korchnoi plays a version of the ♘d5 sacrifice.

24...♘d4! 25 exd4 exd4 26 ♕c2

Both bishop and knight were under attack. The natural continuation now is 26...dxc3 27 ♖xd8+ ♗xd8 28 ♘xc3 with easy equality. Instead, Black delivers a nasty sting in the tail of his apparently harmless little combination.

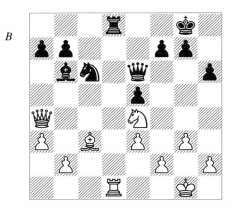

Hartoch – Korchnoi
Biel 1979

26...f5!

Now the obvious knight retreat 27 ♘d2 leads to disaster on f2 after 27...dxc3 followed by 28...♕e2. White's reply is an attempt to maintain material equality, but it walks into a decisive pin on the d-file.

27 ♗xd4 ♕xe4! 28 ♕b3+ ♕d5 29 ♗xb6 ♕xb3 30 ♖xd8+ ♔f7 31 ♗xa7 ♕xb2 32 h4 f4 33 gxf4 ♕c1+ 34 ♔g2 ♕c7 35 ♖d3 b6 36 ♗xb6 ♕xb6 37 ♖e3 ♕g6+ 38 ♔h3 ♕g1 0-1

Jon Levitt annotated the following game *(see diagram on next page)* in *Chess Monthly*. He was very proud to have been party to such a masterpiece, despite the fact that he was the loser. Throughout the course of Adams's combination, Levitt felt that he was safe, and that the best that White could achieve by it was a grovelled draw. As he wrote, "Having got to the position [before the final move below] many players would see the idea, but to conceive of it several moves ago required something special".

White is threatened with mate on the move, so we might expect him to capture the bishop. It is only by looking forward to the end of the game that we can see why he avoids it.

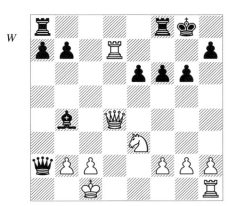

Adams – Levitt
Zonal tournament, Dublin 1993

**23 c3!! ♕a1+ 24 ♔c2 ♕xh1 25 ♕xb4!
♖ad8** *(D)*

The three alternatives all lose quickly:

a) 25...♖f7 26 ♖xf7 ♔xf7 27 ♕xb7+ wins the rook with check.

b) 25...♕xh2 26 ♕e7 ♕h6 27 ♘g4 and the queen can no longer prevent mate.

c) 25...♖ae8 26 ♕h4 ♖f7 27 ♖d1! neatly traps the black queen.

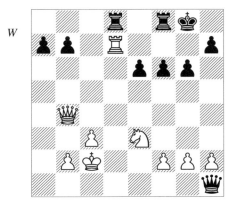

On the other hand, White now seems to have nothing better than 26 ♖xb7 ♕xh2 27

♕e7 ♕h6 28 ♘g4 ♕d2+, when he can draw, but no more. Levitt was stunned to find Adams exchanging rooks, the last thing you would expect him to do when he is on the attack.

26 ♖xd8!! ♖xd8 27 ♕e7!

The sting in the tail. There is no square available for the rook along the d-file, hence the rook must retreat to f8 in order to defend f6 against 28 ♘g4. However, after 27...♖f8 White still plays 28 ♘g4, when Black has no defence against ♘h6+ because the white h-pawn is protected by the knight. Suddenly reduced to helplessness, Levitt resigned.

Now go back to the first diagram and follow the same sequence without the move 23 c3. The line goes 23 ♕xb4 ♖ad8 24 ♖xd8 ♕a1+ 25 ♔d2 ♖xd8+ 26 ♔e2 ♕xh1 27 ♕e7 ♖f8 28 ♘g4, as in the game, and now Black can play 28...♕c1, defending the h6-square because the white king has been forced to e2. Now you can appreciate just how deep was Adams's idea.

Exercise 62

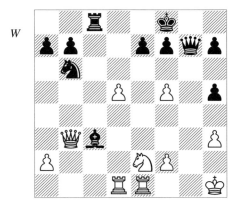

Level 2/3

White is to play. For Level 3, go ahead and work out White's combination without reading the next paragraph, remembering that there is a sting in the tail. For Level 2, read on.

White is the exchange ahead, but after 23 ℤg1 ♕e5 his pawns, especially on the king-side, are a matter for concern. He conceives a back-rank combination to win a piece, but needs to win a tempo at the decisive moment.

The solution is on page 224.

Quiet Stings

The stings in the tail that we have encountered so far have been normal attacking moves, putting enemy pieces or the enemy king under some direct threat. In this section, we consider stings that attack nothing but none-theless force resignation. At the end of a combinative sequence, they can be stunning both in their effect on the defender and in their beauty to the observer. For the first example, let me once more start with a relatively simple example from my own collection.

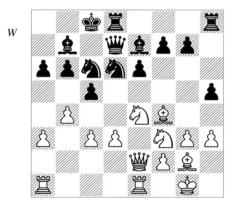

LeMoir – Poolake
Bristol 1968

I wanted to get my queen down to mate on b8, so I played a sacrifice to shift the knight from d6.

18 ♘xc5 bxc5 19 bxc5 ♘b5 20 ♘e5 ♘xe5

I would achieve my wish after 20...♘xc3 21 ♕e3 ♕e8 22 ♘xc6 ♗xc6 23 ♕e5. Mean-while, giving the black king some air by 20...♕e8 loses to 21 a4 (to shift the knight from b5) followed by ♕b2 and a massive at-tack along the b-file.

21 ♕xe5 ♘c7 22 ♗xb7+ ♔xb7 23 ℤab1+ ♔c8 (D)

Moving the king to the a-file is hopeless since White retrieves his piece, but now the position is set up for a quiet sting.

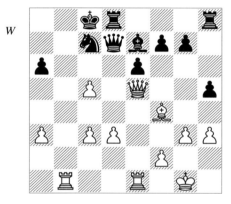

Black threatens to oust the white queen from its powerful position by 24...f6, and to shut the bishop out by a later ...e5. Mean-while, the black knight must stay where it is to prevent mate on b8, the queen must main-tain its protection of the knight (which it can only do from d7 or c6 as things stand), and the king has no breathing space.

24 ℤb6!

My opponent had been looking confident up to now. He was about to reach out to play 24...f6 when he slumped back into his seat. He had just seen 25 ℤeb1 with its threat of mate at b8. He sank back, deep in thought. Every now and again, he would brighten, thinking he had found a defence, but then he would start to frown again. In the end, he reached out his hand in resignation.

My opponent could have made me play on after 24...f6 25 ♖eb1 ♕c6. There are several ways to win (even 26 ♖xc6 is good enough), but most convincing is probably 26 ♕e2 with the likely continuation 26...♕a8 (not 26...♕xc5 27 ♗xc7 exposing Black's king to the white rooks and queen, or 26...♕a4 27 c6, when the queen must give itself up for the pawn) 27 ♗xc7 ♔xc7 28 d4 ♕d5 29 ♕xa6 ♖c8 30 ♕a7+ ♔d8 31 ♖b8 ♕c6 32 ♖xc8+ ♕xc8 33 ♖b8 ♖e8 34 c6 and mate next move.

Here is a quiet sting that completes a spectacular king-hunt by cutting off the enemy king's escape route, ensuring that mate will be delivered by a lowly pawn against huge material odds.

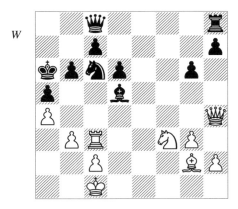

This position allegedly occurred in a game Kasparian-Manvelian, Simultaneous, 1936, with the great endgame composer creating a real-life work of art: **1 ♖xc6! ♗xc6 2 ♕c4+ ♔b7 3 ♕xc6+! ♔xc6 4 ♘e5++ ♔c5 5 ♘d3+ ♔d4 6 ♔d2!! 1-0**.

Black is completely helpless against mate next move by 7 c3#.

However, the exact same finish (starting with 3 ♕xc6+ in this sequence) occurred in a game Blackburne-Gifford, 1874, so I leave it to my readers to decide whether this was an amazing coincidence or whether the later 'game' was in fact a composition.

At the stratospheric levels of a world championship candidates quarter-final match, Polugaevsky managed an analogous feat against the great defender, Viktor Korchnoi.

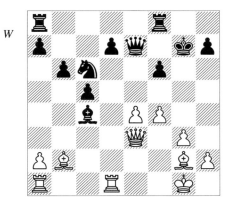

Polugaevsky – Korchnoi
Candidates match (game 12),
Buenos Aires 1980

The combination is prepared by an innocent-looking pawn advance.
23 e5 fxe5 24 ♗xc6! dxc6 25 ♖d7!!
Polugaevsky has cracked open the long diagonal and this silent sacrifice diverts the black queen so that the white queen and bishop can establish themselves on it.
25...♕xd7 26 ♕xe5+ ♔f7 27 ♕f6+ ♔g8 28 ♕g5+ ♔f7
Now the queen check on g7 allows the black king to escape via the e-file. Polugaevsky's solution is easy to see now, but he had to foresee it at the previous diagram unless he was happy with a draw by perpetual check.
29 ♖e1!
Black must give up his queen in order to block the rook's line along the e-file. Even now, there is a lot of work before White can

pocket the point, but Polugaevsky gets there in the end.

29...♕e6 30 ♕g7+ ♚e8 31 ♖xe6+ ♗xe6 32 ♗f6 ♗f7 33 ♗g5

According to Sveshnikov in *Informator*, 33 ♕xh7! is better, when 33...♚d7 34 g4 ♖ae8 35 ♗e5 leads to a winning advantage for White.

33...♚d7 34 ♗h6 c4 35 ♕xh7 c5 36 ♗xf8 ♖xf8

...and Korchnoi fought on for a further 37 moves before resigning.

Here is a sacrificial orgy with a quiet final move that causes a sudden and total collapse.

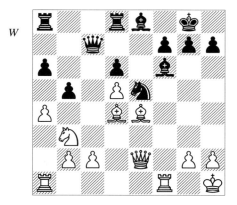

Timoshchenko – Platonov
Cheliabinsk 1975

The combination starts with an exchange sacrifice that wrecks the pawns in front of the black king.

21 ♖xf6! gxf6 22 ♕h5 f5

Running away won't help much; for example, 22...♚f8 23 ♕h6+ ♚e7 24 ♖f1 ♚d7 25 ♖xf6 ♚c8 26 ♗xe5 dxe5 27 d6 with a pawn for the exchange and a continuing attack.

23 ♕g5+ ♚f8 24 ♕f6!!

White plays a passive sacrifice to prevent the rear f-pawn from moving...

24...fxe4 25 ♘c5!

...and then a silent sacrifice to open the d6-square for the d-pawn to advance. Black must decline as 25...dxc5 26 ♗xe5 ♕b7 27 d6 threatens an unstoppable mate, but meanwhile White threatens 26 ♘e6+ forking queen and knight. Black's reply is forced.

25...♚g8 *(D)*

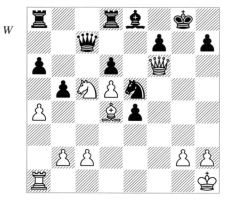

White is a whole rook down. How does he make progress?

26 ♖f1!

Once we realize that White envisages 27 ♘e6! (with the point 27...fxe6 28 ♕f8#), it becomes clear that Black is helpless. The rook also threatens to advance to f5 to deal a direct blow to the king from g5. Black counter-sacrifices to eliminate White's first idea, but he can do nothing about the second.

26...♗c6 27 dxc6 ♖e8 28 ♖f5 ♖ad8 29 ♖g5+ ♚f8 30 ♕g7+ ♚e7 31 ♗xe5 dxe5 32 ♖xe5+ ♚d6 33 ♕f6+ 1-0

In the next diagram we see the wily Korchnoi – the young version, 1960 vintage. Apparently forced onto the defensive, he plays a ridiculous-looking sacrifice that is fully justified by a strange double-purpose sting.

Simagin has sacrificed a piece for two pawns and appears to be winning back at least

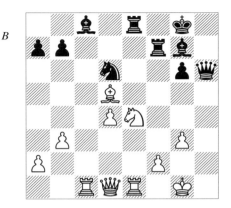

Simagin – Korchnoi
Moscow 1960

an exchange, as 29...♘xe4 30 ♖xe4 ♖xe4 loses to 31 ♖xc8+. With his next move, Korchnoi chooses to give up a whole rook in return for threats against the white king.

29...♗e6!! 30 ♘xd6 ♗xd5 31 ♖xe8+ ♖f8 32 ♖e4 *(D)*

An easy way to prevent the threatened mate but, had he seen what was coming, White might have safeguarded his king by 32 f3 ♖xe8 33 ♘xe8 ♕e3+ 34 ♔g2 ♕xe8 35 ♕d3 ♕e6, although the black bishops would be dangerous.

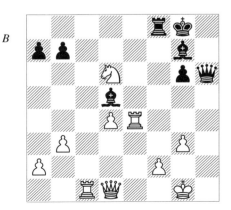

After the move played, White threatens 33 ♖h4, but Korchnoi has an ace up his sleeve.

32...g5!

This unexpected little move prevents 33 ♖h4 and simultaneously discovers an attack on the knight that defends the rook. Curiously, not only must White jettison the knight, but he also finds himself obliged to exchange one of his rooks for the dangerous d5-bishop. He finishes a piece down in a lost position.

33 ♖c7 ♕xd6 34 ♖ee7 ♗f6 35 ♖ed7 ♕e6 36 ♖xd5 ♕xd5 37 ♕h5 ♗g7 38 ♕g6 ♕xd4 39 ♕e6+ ♔h7 40 ♕h3+ ♔g6 41 ♕e6+ ♖f6 42 ♕e2 b5 43 g4 ♔h6 0-1

Here is an example from the mists of antiquity. Staunton sacrifices his queen for a fairly easy-to-see clutch of knight checks that apparently aim at capturing his opponent's queen in return. Having reconciled himself to that, his opponent must have been shocked to see Staunton shun the queen and play a quiet move that simply avoided the exchange of a key attacking piece.

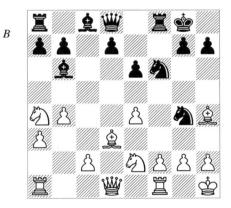

Kennedy – Staunton
Match at odds, London 1845

The opening sacrifice is pretty, but easy to spot.

15...♘xe4!! 16 ♗xd8 ♘exf2+ 17 ♔g1 ♘h3++ 18 ♔h1 ♘gf2+ 19 ♖xf2 ♘xf2+ 20 ♔g1 *(D)*

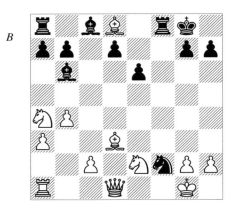

Now we might expect 20...♘xd1+ 21 ♗xb6 axb6 22 ♘xb6 with a material advantage to White. Staunton has seen a sting that maintains his threat to win the queen but introduces the extra menace of mate.

20...♗e3!!

A lovely idea, preserving the bishop from exchange and threatening 21...♘xd1+ winning the queen back for nothing. White is not quite as powerless as he might appear, as both 21 ♕c1 and 21 ♗g5 prevent mate and force the exchange of the lethal bishop, but Black would be the exchange ahead in the resultant endgames.

White prefers a glorious death, and allows checkmate.

21 ♕b1 ♘d1+ 22 ♔h1 ♖f1+ 0-1

In our final example White could follow his sacrifice by a simple winning process, but finds a sting in the tail that both mates more quickly and makes the combination far more pleasing on the eye (*see following diagram*).

1 ♕d8+ ♕f8 2 ♖xh6+! ♗xh6

Now Richter shunned the obvious win by 3 ♕xf8+ ♗xf8 4 ♖h1+ ♗h6 (forced) 5 ♖xh6+

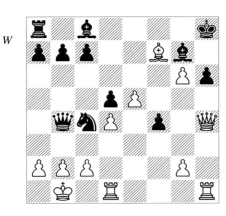

Richter – Anon
Berlin 1935

♔g7 6 ♖h7+ ♔f8 7 ♗xd5, when Black must give up material to delay mate. He produces something quieter, faster... and far more beautiful.

3 ♕f6+ ♕g7 4 ♖h1!!

White allows the exchange of queens. The threat is mate in one.

4...♕xf6 5 exf6 1-0

Black has no defence to the threat of mate next move.

Exercise 63

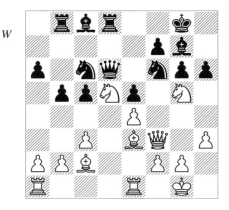

Level 1

White sacrificed a piece by **21 ♘xf6+! ♗xf6 22 ♖ad1 ♕e7 23 ♗xc5! ♖xd1 24 ♖xd1 ♕xc5 25 ♕xf6 hxg5** *(D)*.

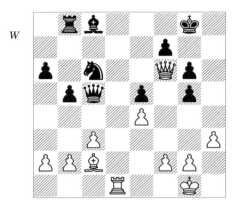

The attack appears to be at an end, but White has prepared a quiet move that causes the complete collapse of the black position. What is it?

Exercise 64

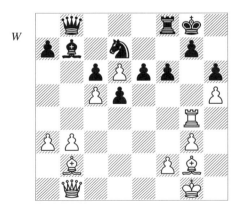

Level 2

White to play. Here I'm going to ask you to analyse a combination that lasts seven moves

before the sting in the tail. The first move is a sacrifice, and you need to make sure that you make the right forcing choice on the fifth move.

Exercise 65

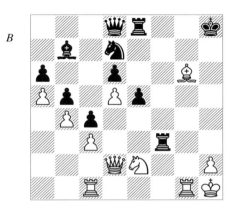

Level 3

The fun starts with **27...♕h4!**, a passive rook sacrifice that defends against the threat of ♕h6+ and intends to create counterplay after 28 ♗xe8 by means of 28...♖d3 followed by 29...♗xd5+. White is able to maintain his big advantage by a combination that features a quiet sting in the tail.

The solutions start on page 224.

Before we end this chapter, I just want to show you one more game. It features so many quiet moves that it could be dubbed 'The Quiet Combination' *(see diagram on following page)*.

Kotov starts with a substitution sacrifice that establishes a knight on f5 in order to remove the important defensive bishop from g7.

21 ♘df5! gxf5 22 ♘xf5 ♕c7

This allows White to play the very strong 23 ♗a5 ♕d7 24 ♗xd8 ♕xd8 25 c5. White

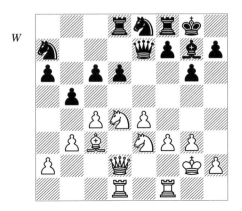

Kotov – Barcza
Interzonal tournament, Saltsjöbaden 1952

presumably had his principal idea prepared against other queen moves, and went ahead regardless.

23 ♘xg7 ♘xg7 24 ♗f6!

This is the first quiet follow-up, settling in on the newly-weakened f6-square. The bishop is only interested in holding down the f-pawn, and has no designs upon the d8-rook.

24...♔h8

24...♘e6 is well met by 25 f4! intending 26 f5 followed by 27 ♕g5#. After the move played, White continues to invade on the dark squares.

25 ♕g5 ♖g8 26 h4

The threat is h5-h6, which Black is able to meet just in the nick of time.

26...♖de8 27 h5 ♖e5 28 ♗xe5 dxe5 29 ♕f6!

Another quiet move, occupying same pinning square.

29...♘c8 30 h6 ♘e7 31 ♖d2! 1-0

There is no need to capture the knight yet. After this final quiet move, the game is up. Doubling rooks followed by ♖d8! ensures that the capture on g7 will be mate. Therefore Black resigned.

12 Pawns Passed and Present

We know how to create and exploit passed pawns in the endgame, but we tend to give very little thought to them in the middlegame. Some of the longer-term thinkers among us create passed pawns in the middlegame, or at least ensure that they can be created when needed, but their focus is on utilizing them in the coming endgame. By contrast, the Deadly Tactician likes to create them in the middlegame in the hope of using them immediately.

Passed pawns could have been invented for Deadly Tacticians, as substantial and surprising sacrifices can be used both to bring passed pawns into being, and to exploit them when they already exist.

Passed Pawn Connections

The sight of two or three connected passed pawns ploughing towards the eighth rank, driving all defenders from their path, is one of the most thrilling on the chessboard. The tradition started long ago, as the romantics of the 19th century realized that connected passed pawns allowed their sacrificial hunger to be satisfied in spectacular fashion (*see diagram on following page*).

Black goes ahead with his intended central expansion even though it loses the exchange.

20...f5!? 21 ♕c4+ ♔h8! 22 ♗a4 ♕h6 23 ♗xe8 fxe4 24 c6 exf3! 25 ♖c2

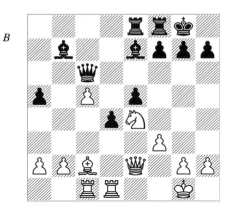

McDonnell – de Labourdonnais
Match 4 (game 16), London 1834

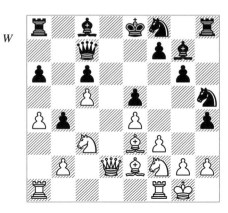

Serper – Nikolaidis
St Petersburg 1993

Black's first intention is to deliver a knock-out blow to the white king, which he would achieve after either 25 cxb7 ♕e3+ 26 ♔h1 fxg2+ 27 ♔xg2 ♖f2+ 28 ♔g1 ♖d2+ 29 ♔h1 ♕f3+ 30 ♔g1 ♕g2# or 25 gxf3 ♕e3+ 26 ♔h1 ♕xf3+ 27 ♔g1 ♖f5 with mate to follow.

25...♕e3+ 26 ♔h1

Strangely, the self-pin 26 ♖f2! is stronger, as 26...fxg2 allows 27 ♕e2!, when the white c-pawn is at least as dangerous as Black's army of passed pawns. In the game, the situation is reversed as the black f-pawn becomes the standard-bearer for the passed pawns, and White's solo passed pawn is no competition.

26...♗c8 27 ♗d7 f2 28 ♖f1 d3 29 ♖c3 ♗xd7 30 cxd7 e4 31 ♕c8 ♗d8 32 ♕c4 ♕e1! 33 ♖c1 d2 34 ♕c5 ♖g8 35 ♖d1 e3 36 ♕c3 ♕xd1! 37 ♖xd1 e2 0-1

The defender in the next example is so horrified at the sight of three advanced connected passed pawns that he instantly gives up a rook for just one of them, only to find himself suffering torture at the hands of the two that remain (*see following diagram*).

First White creates two connected passed pawns...

17 ♘d5! cxd5 18 exd5 f5 19 d6! ♕c6 20 ♗b5!! axb5 21 axb5

...and then there were three.

21...♕xb5

White has sacrificed two pieces to establish a mighty pawn-chain, so Black is justified in using some of his booty in order to break their force. He chooses to give up a rook, but he might do better to invest his queen by 21...♕b7 22 c6 ♖xa1! 23 cxb7 ♖xf1+ 24 ♔xf1 ♗xb7, with chances of survival.

22 ♖xa8 ♕c6 23 ♖fa1!?

White could play the strong move 23 ♖a7, threatening 24 ♖e7+ ♔d8 25 ♕xb4 with a decisive attack. Instead, he deliberately allows his dark-squared bishop to be trapped and the complications rage on.

23...f4 24 ♖1a7! ♘d7

White's passive sacrifices continue after 24...fxe3? with the spectacular line 25 ♕d5!! exf2+ 26 ♔xf2 ♕xd5 27 ♖xc8#. After the move played, White prevents castling and then hammers the black king into submission with the help of a combination that forces the promotion of one of the pawns.

25 ♖xc8+! ♕xc8 26 ♕d5 fxe3 27 ♕e6+ ♔f8 28 ♖xd7 exf2+ 29 ♔f1 ♕e8 30 ♖f7+!!

♕xf7 31 ♕c8+ ♕e8 32 d7 ♔f7 33 dxe8♕+ ♖xe8 34 ♕b7+ ♖e7 35 c6! e4 36 c7 e3

Now Black has two advanced connected passed pawns of his own, but White's remaining passed pawn is the only one that will promote.

37 ♕d5+ ♔f6 38 ♕d6+ ♔f7 39 ♕d5+ ♔f6 40 ♕d6+ ♔f7 41 ♕xe7+! ♔xe7 42 c8♕ ♗h6 43 ♕c5+ ♔e8 44 ♕b5+ ♔d8 45 ♕b6+ ♔d7 46 ♕xg6 e2+ 47 ♔xf2 ♗e3+ 48 ♔e1 1-0

A symphony to the passed pawn.

Those three passed pawns gave Serper great value. One of them was exchanged for a rook while the other two were able to promote. In the next example, White creates two connected passed pawns, but he faces a potentially fierce attack. In the end, he invests a total of a rook to survive the attack and create a third passed pawn connected to the first two, secure in the knowledge that they will be more than good value for it.

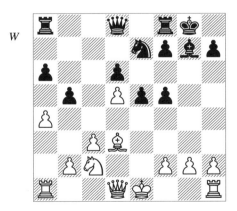

Bednarski – Wirthensohn
Switzerland 1974

White creates his passed pawns while Black prepares an attack.

16 axb5 e4 17 ♗e2 f4 18 ♖xa6 ♖xa6 19 bxa6 ♘f5 20 g3! ♕b6 21 ♘b4 f3 22 ♗xf3!?

It is possible that White could survive the attack after 22 ♗c4 e3, or 22 ♗f1 ♖e8 followed by ...e3, but he makes a sensible pragmatic decision to reduce its force by giving up the bishop.

22...exf3 23 ♕xf3 ♖e8+ 24 ♔f1 ♘d4 25 ♕d3 ♘b3 26 ♔g2 ♘c5 27 ♕c4 ♘e4 28 ♘d3 ♘c5 29 ♘b4 ♘e4

White prefers not to convert his two connected passed pawns into one by exchanging knights on c5. Instead, he sacrifices the exchange to convert them into three.

30 ♖f1!! ♘d2 31 ♕c6! ♕xc6 32 dxc6 ♘xf1 33 ♔xf1 d5 34 ♘xd5 ♗e5 35 f4 1-0

We focus on two connected passed pawns in the next two examples. In the first, the defence appears to be holding, but a further sacrifice and some deadly quiet moves demonstrate the mighty strength of the pawns.

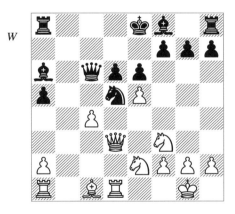

Machulsky – Shneider
USSR 1982

White creates two connected passed pawns while the black bishop munches its way through three of his most important pieces.

16 cxd5!? ♗xd3 17 dxc6 ♗xe2 18 exd6! ♗xd1 19 d7+ ♔d8 20 ♗g5+ f6 21 ♖xd1 ♗c5

Suddenly, we are in the endgame.

Black has no intention of capturing the bishop where it is, as 21...fxg5 22 ♘xg5 leads to a quick win for White. By allowing the bishop to escape, Black hopes to secure the c7-square so that he can blockade the c-pawn and eventually win it. White, for his part, sacrifices his knight to thwart Black's plan, confident that he can prove that his connected passed pawns are more than a match for the extra rook in the endgame.

22 ♗f4 e5 23 ♘xe5! fxe5 24 ♗xe5 ♗b6 *(D)*

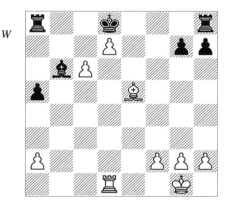

25 ♖b1!?

This is an ambitious move, to which Black must find the right response. However, White should have preferred 25 ♗xg7, when he can maintain an advantage. With his rook still on d1, he could reply to 25...♖g8 26 ♗e5 ♖g6 with 27 ♗g3, with the threat of 28 ♗h4+ ♔c7 29 d8♕+.

25...♖a6

The natural reply 25...♗c7 loses because it blocks the king's escape-square, which means that 26 ♗xg7 simultaneously attacks the h8-rook and threatens 27 ♗f6#. Black's chosen reply tangles up his queenside pieces. The best response is 25...♗a7! intending to reply to ♗xg7 (played at once, or after 26 ♖b7 ♔e7!) with ...♖(h)g8 followed by ...♖g6, when

the pressure on the advanced c-pawn should give Black at least an equal game.

26 ♗xg7 ♖g8 27 ♗f6+ ♔c7 28 ♖c1 ♖f8 29 ♗e5+ ♔d8 30 ♗g3!

White threatens 31 ♖d1 followed by 32 c7+! ♗xc7 33 ♗h4+, mating. Black's best defence is probably 30...♖g8, intending to eliminate the bishop by 31...♖xg3. White should win that endgame, but he can shorten the game by the subtle manoeuvre 31 ♗h4+ ♔c7 32 ♗f1! followed by 33 g4 and 34 ♗g3+, setting up the threat of 35 ♖d1 again with his bishop shielded from capture by the advanced g-pawn.

Black misses his chance to extend the game and White finishes with a little flourish.

30...♖f6 31 ♖d1!

Threatening 32 c7+.

31...♗xf2+

Black tries a final desperate throw.

If the black rook covers the d-pawn's queening square by 31...♖a8, it no longer has the option of capturing the c-pawn. Then 32 ♗h4 will win for White as 32...♗xf2+ 33 ♗xf2 ♖xf2 34 ♔xf2 leaves his connected passed pawns intact.

32 ♗xf2 ♖xf2

Black is hoping for 33 ♔xf2, whereupon 33...♖xc6 keeps the game going. However, White is wide awake, and takes the opportunity to force the promotion of his d-pawn.

33 c7+! 1-0

In the following diagram, Botvinnik creates his first passed pawn neatly and his second one brilliantly, but the deadly quiet finale is worthy of Alekhine or Tal at their best.

27...♖c3!

The acceptance of this silent sacrifice creates a passed pawn deep in enemy territory, and opens two lines – the d-file and the a7-g1 diagonal. The significance of the d-file is immediately apparent as White must lose his d-pawn. The importance of the diagonal becomes clear later.

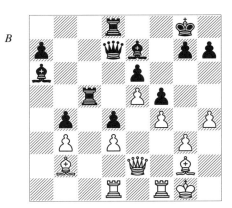

Yurgis – Botvinnik
Leningrad 1931

28 ♗xc3 dxc3 29 ♕e3 ♗xd3 30 ♖f2

30 ♖fe1 avoids the following combination, but White still stands badly.

30...♕d4 31 ♕xd4 ♖xd4 32 ♗f1 c2 33 ♖c1 ♗xf1 34 ♖cxf1 ♖c4!!

Black threatens both to promote the c-pawn and to pin the f2-rook with ...♗c5.

35 bxc4

White captures the rook as now 35...b3 36 ♖xc2! bxc2 37 ♖c1 would be winning for him, but he is in for a shock.

35...♗c5!!

This wonderful quiet move leaves White helpless against the pawns.

36 ♔g2 ♗xf2 37 ♔xf2 b3 0-1

Now we descend further from positions with two connected passed pawns to take a quick look at the solo passed pawn. It is rarely worthwhile creating a single passed pawn with a substantial middlegame sacrifice unless its promotion is inevitable or we can see that it will play a direct role in a mating attack. Those ideas feature in the sections following this one. It takes a player as bold as the young Kasparov to invest a whole piece in order to create a passed pawn whose main purpose is to distract his opponent's pieces from the defence of their king.

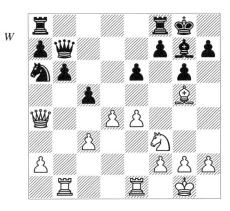

Kasparov – Přibyl
European Team Ch, Skara 1980

Kasparov creates his passed pawn and runs it through to the seventh rank at breakneck speed.

16 d5! ♗xc3 17 ♖ed1 exd5 18 exd5 ♗g7 19 d6 f6 20 d7! fxg5 21 ♕c4+ ♔h8 22 ♘xg5 ♗f6

Black has removed the bishop that covered the queening square, but that has left his king-side weak. The white knight will leap in to the e6-square to renew the queening threats, and to pick up the exchange in return for the bishop that White has sacrificed.

23 ♘e6 ♘c7 24 ♘xf8 ♖xf8 25 ♖d6 ♗e7

Both 25...♕b8 26 ♖bd1 ♕d8 and 25...♗d8 leave Black horribly squeezed behind the d-pawn, but now White is able to sacrifice it to create threats against the black king. He will soon win a piece.

26 d8♕! ♗xd8

26...♖xd8 leads to an amusing finish after 27 ♖xd8+ ♗xd8 28 ♕f7 ♕d5 29 ♕xd5 ♘xd5 30 ♖d1, skewering the knight and bishop.

27 ♕c3+ ♔g8 28 ♖d7 ♗f6 29 ♕c4+ ♔h8 30 ♕f4 ♕a6?

He could make White suffer a long endgame by 30...♗g7 31 ♕xc7 ♕xc7 32 ♖xc7 ♗d4, but there is little doubt that he would lose in the end. Black has allowed his second rank to become deserted and now the axe falls instantly.

31 ♕h6 1-0

Mate is unavoidable.

A sizeable mass of connected pawns tends to squeeze out the opposing forces, even if they do not attempt to advance towards the eighth rank. Many fine sacrifices have had the simple purpose of removing the defender's central pawns so that their opposite numbers can exert a total domination. The Daddy of them all is this effort by Bronstein.

Bronstein – Rojahn
Olympiad, Moscow 1956

1 e4 e5 2 ♘f3 ♘c6 3 ♗c4 ♘f6 4 ♘g5 d5 5 exd5 ♘a5 6 d3 h6 7 ♘f3 e4 *(D)*

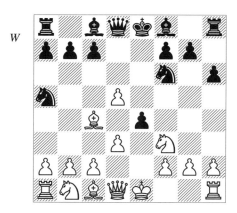

This position had been reached many times before, and the customary continuation 8 ♕e2 ♘xc4 9 dxc4 gives Black plenty of compensation for the pawn. Bronstein plays an unguarding sacrifice in order to establish a huge unopposed pawn-centre.

8 dxe4!? ♘xc4 9 ♕d4 ♘b6 10 c4 c5

Bronstein's idea was soon defused by the idea of returning the extra piece to clarify the position. Here, for instance, 10...c6 (and if 11 c5, then 11...♘bxd5 12 exd5 ♕xd5) is considered very satisfactory for Black. As the game goes, the white pawns gradually creep forward and the black pieces are pressed back to the rear ranks.

11 ♕d3 ♗g4 12 ♘bd2 ♗e7 13 0-0 0-0 14 ♘e5 ♗h5 15 b3 ♘bd7 16 ♗b2 ♘xe5 17 ♗xe5 ♘d7 18 ♗c3 ♗f6 19 ♖ae1 ♗xc3 20 ♕xc3 ♕f6 21 e5 ♕f5 22 f4 ♗g6 23 ♘e4 ♖ab8 24 ♕f3 ♗h7 25 g4 ♕g6 26 f5 ♕b6 27 ♕g3 f6 28 e6 *(D)*

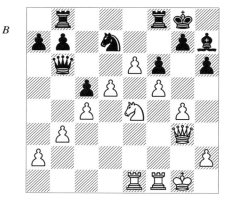

A lovely position, and full justification for Bronstein's piece sacrifice.

28...♘e5 29 h4 ♔h8 30 g5 ♖bc8 31 ♔h1 ♕d8 32 g6 ♗xg6 33 fxg6 b5 34 d6 ♕b6 35 d7

Each breaking of ranks by the pawns leads to a further material gain.

35...♘xd7 36 exd7 ♖cd8 37 ♘xf6 ♕c6+ 38 ♕g2 1-0

Black lost on time.

In our final example, Black discovers that White's central passed pawns leave him with no good squares for his pieces.

Plaskett – Short
Banja Luka 1985

Plaskett starts with an unusual ♘d5 sacrifice.

14 ♘d5! exd5 15 cxd5 ♗b7 16 ♘xd4 ♖fe8 17 ♘f5 ♗f8 18 ♘e3 g6 19 f4 ♖ad8 20 e5

White's advancing pawns have already taken over.

20...♗g7

Short prefers to return the piece rather than exile his knight to h5. In his turn, Plaskett decides to strengthen his centre before making the capture.

21 d4! ♕b8 22 dxc5 bxc5 23 exf6 ♗xf6 24 ♗xf6 ♘xf6 25 ♕d3

After all that, White is a passed pawn ahead and has the makings of a strong attack against Black's weakened king. He presses home his advantage in attractive style.

25...♕a7 26 ♖c4 a5 27 f5! g5 28 h4 h6 29 hxg5 hxg5 30 ♕d2 ♘h7 31 ♘g4 ♕b6 32 f6 ♗c8 33 ♘h6+ ♔f8 34 ♕c2! ♘xf6 35 ♕h7! ♖d7

35...♘xh7 allows an immediate mate by 36 ♖xf7#.

36 ♖xf6 ♕xf6 37 ♕g8+ 1-0

Black loses a piece after 37...♔e7 38 ♖e4+ ♔d6 39 ♖xe8 ♕xh6 40 ♖xc8.

Exercise 66

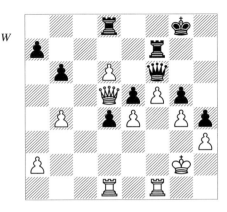

Level 1

How can White sacrifice to launch an armada of passed pawns that will drown the black major pieces?

Exercise 67

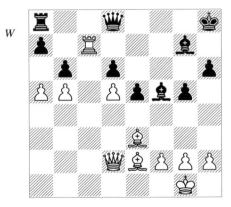

Level 2

White's aim is to obtain two connected passed pawns. How does he create them, and how does he then exploit them?

Exercise 68

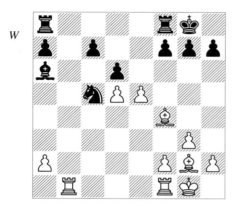

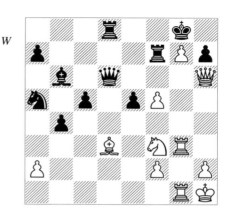

Anderssen – Zukertort
Barmen 1869

Level 3

White (to play) has a fairly obvious combination to establish a passed pawn, but Black has a good defence to which White must find the right reply. How does the game go from here?

The solutions start on page 225.

A protected pawn on g7 or f7 can be so dangerous that heavy sacrifices are often justified to get it there. Once the pawn is in place, the tactician turns his talent to exploiting the resulting mating opportunities. Some glorious and spectacular combinations can then arise.

The Mating Habits of the Passed Pawn

If we can establish a passed pawn near to our opponent's king, the chances are that mating combinations will pop up of their own accord. Here is an old game with a standard, but lovely, mating pattern (*see next diagram*).

By sacrificing queen and bishop, White gains the necessary time to manufacture a rook mate on h8.

29 ♕xh7+! 1-0

The same mate can occur via two routes, starting 29...♔xh7 30 f6+, and now:

a) 30...♕xd3 31 ♖h3+ ♔g8 32 ♖h8#.

b) 30...♔g8 31 ♗h7+! ♔xh7 32 ♖h3+ ♔g8 33 ♖h8#.

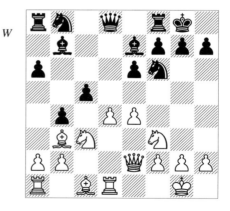

Ki. Georgiev – Dlugy
World Junior Ch, Belfort 1983

12 d5!?

A typical passive sacrifice that sends the pawn dashing to the f7-square.

12...bxc3 13 dxe6 ♕b6 14 e5 ♘e4 15 exf7+ ♔h8 16 e6

The e-pawn ensures the long-term protection of the f7-pawn, and now the air buzzes with potential combinations based on the threat of advancing to e7.

16...♗f6 17 ♘e5!

Already, White is able to exploit the fact that the bishop cannot capture the knight without allowing the pawn to advance to e7. The knight is poised to rip open the black king's position.

17...♕c7 18 ♘g6+! hxg6 19 ♖d3

The threat is mate with ♖h3+, so Black prepares to interpose on h7.

19...♘g5 20 ♗xg5 ♗xg5 21 e7!

The sting in the tail of White's combination. The promotion of the e-pawn is forced as 21...♗xe7 22 ♖h3+ is mate next move.

21...♘c6

Black will emerge with two pieces against a rook, but his position will be hopeless as he is still tied down by the f7-pawn.

22 e8♕ cxb2 23 ♕xb2 ♘d4 24 ♖h3+ ♔h6 25 ♕e3 ♔h7 26 ♕bc1 ♘f5 27 ♕exc5 ♕d8 28 ♕e1 ♕g5 29 ♖g3 ♕f4 30 ♕ce5 ♕h4 31 ♖xg6! ♔xg6 32 ♗e6 ♕g5 33 g3 ♕f6 34 g4 ♕xe5 35 ♕xe5 ♘e7 36 ♗f5+ ♔xf7

At last the pawn is back in the box, but the black king will pay a heavy price.

37 ♕e6+ ♔e8 38 ♗g6+ ♔d8 39 ♖d1+ ♘d5 40 ♕d6+ 1-0

In the next diagram, White sacrifices a piece to establish a solo passed pawn on f6, which makes possible several potential mating combinations. Most of them are hidden in the notes, but the last one sees the light of day.

White has a passed pawn on d6, but by sacrificing two pawns and then a piece he manages to replace it by one on f6.

20 e5!? ♘gxe5 21 ♘c5 ♕xd6 22 f4! ♘d7 23 fxg5! ♘xc5 24 gxf6

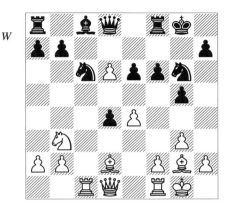

Adorjan – Hulak
Interzonal tournament, Toluca 1982

With this pawn as the advance guard, White is able to bring up the rest of his army with remarkable speed.

24...e5 25 ♕h5 ♖f7 26 ♗h6 ♘e6 27 ♗e4 ♘f8

There is no good defence:

a) 27...♗d7 loses the black queen to 28 ♗xh7+! ♖xh7 29 ♕g6+ ♔h8 30 ♗g7+ ♘xg7 31 fxg7+ ♖xg7 32 ♕xd6.

b) Safeguarding the queen by 27...♕d7 fails to 28 ♗xh7+! ♖xh7 29 ♕g6+ ♔h8 and now the pawn joins in to force mate with 30 f7! ♕d8 31 ♗g7+! ♖xg7 32 ♕h6+ ♖h7 33 f8♕+ ♘xf8 34 ♖xf8+ ♕xf8 35 ♕xf8#.

c) 27...♕d8 loses in a somewhat different fashion to 28 ♗xh7+ ♖xh7 29 f7+ ♔h8 30 ♖xc6! bxc6 31 ♕xe5+ with a quick mate.

The text-move prevents the troublesome 28 ♗xh7+, but allows White to sacrifice his queen for mate.

28 ♕g5+ ♔h8 29 ♕g7+! 1-0

Black is mated by 29...♖xg7 30 fxg7+ ♔g8 31 ♖xf8+ ♕xf8 32 gxf8♕#.

Even a central passed pawn can assist in mating a castled king. In the next example, it supports a back-rank mate.

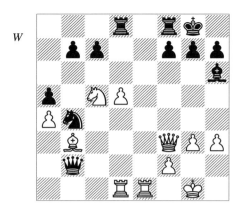

Moreda – F. Garcia
Malaga 2001

The key to White's combination lies in the diagonal from the b3-bishop to the black king on g8. The combination starts with a silent knight sacrifice which combines substitution, to establish the pawn on e6, and a kind of line-grabbing motif, as the recapture potentially opens the line of the bishop lurking behind on b3.

25 ♘e6!! fxe6 26 dxe6!
White throws in his queen as well.

26...♖xf3
Black sees that the attempt to counter by cutting off the protection of the bishop by the white queen with 26...♘d3 loses his own queen to 27 e7+ ♕xb3 28 ♖xd3! ♕xd3 29 exf8♕+ ♖xf8 30 ♕xd3, and he prefers to die a glorious death by accepting the queen.

27 ♖xd8+ 1-0
Black is mated by 27...♖f8 28 e7+ ♕xb3 29 ♖xf8# (or 29 exf8♕#).

The next example is more complex. White cleverly forces Black to create for him a protected passed pawn in the centre. The black queen is the only piece that can blockade it, and when the queen is removed, the pawn is able promote and force mate.

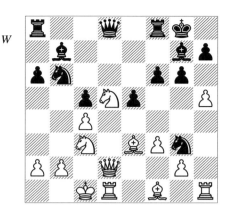

Knaak – J.C. Fernandez
Halle 1978

The first move is played to deny squares to Black's kingside pieces.

19 h6! ♗h8
After 19...♘xh1 20 hxg7 White has plenty for the exchange, and the black knight on h1 will have difficulty getting back into the game. Now White is prepared to give up his rook in the corner in the interests of creating a passed pawn.

20 ♗xc5!! ♘xd5
The variation 20...♗xd5 21 ♗xb6 ♕xb6 22 ♕xd5+ demonstrates one point of the preparatory 19 h6! as Black must play 22...♖f7, allowing 23 ♕xa8+.

21 cxd5 ♘xh1 22 ♗c4
This is a very good square for the bishop as White's passed pawn will run and run.

22...♖c8
Black sensibly tries to rid himself of at least one of the white bishops.

If Black tries to save his knight by 22...♘g3, then White can continue 23 d6+ ♖f7 24 d7! with decisive threats such as 25 ♗b6! or 25 ♗xf7+ followed by 26 ♕c2 and 27 ♕b3+ mating.

23 d6+ ♖f7 24 b4! ♘g3 25 d7 ♖xc5 26 bxc5 ♘f5

Black is still a piece ahead but the axe is about to fall.

27 ♕b2! ♘e3

Black is helpless. He must lose his bishop, as 27...♗a8 allows a silent queen sacrifice that forces the promotion of the pawn and mate: 28 ♕b8! ♕xb8 29 d8♕+ ♕xd8 30 ♖xd8#. After the text-move, White has to be content with a less scenic square for his queen.

28 ♕b6! 1-0

We shall give the final word to Tal, who can be relied upon to find original combinative twists. Here he uses a cross-pin to force mate or the win of Black's queen, not to mention the promotion of his own passed pawn.

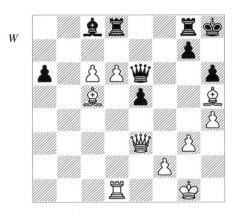

Tal – I. Zaitsev
USSR Ch, Alma-Ata 1968/9

Tal has given up the exchange to create a pair of dangerous connected passed pawns. The unusual play starts with Tal advancing one of his passed pawns.

42 d7!

The purpose appears to be to win Black's bishop, but Tal ignores it in favour of using the sixth rank for his rook.

42...♗xd7 43 ♖d6!

It is all about gaining tempi.

43...♕f5 44 ♗g6! ♕g4

Tal has chosen to regain the exchange in preference to a piece, as he thereby keeps a dangerous passed pawn.

45 ♗b6 ♗e8 46 ♖xd8 ♗xg6 47 c7 ♗f5

Black appears to have stopped the pawn. Now, however, comes the astonishing point of Tal's play.

48 ♕b3!

He takes aim at the black rook with a threat of mate. The reply is forced.

48...♗e6 49 c8♕! 1-0

Tal often used pins in his combinations. This one's a double! Capturing one queen allows mate, while taking the other loses Black his own queen.

Exercise 69

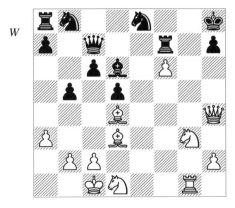

Level 1

The f6-pawn shields the black king from White's d4-bishop. If White is to advance his f-pawn, he must remove the black rook from its path. What is the best way to do so?

Exercise 70

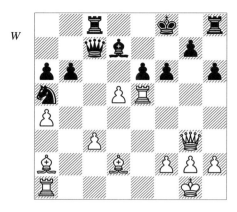

Level 2
Find White's winning combination.

The solutions are on page 226.

The Pawn-Dash

The **pawn-dash** is one of the clearest expressions of what Nimzowitsch called the lowly pawn's 'lust to expand'. It dashes to the seventh rank, often in a roughly diagonal direction, while leaving one or more of its minor or major pieces to be captured. Once it reaches the seventh rank, it can cause mayhem.

We have already seen the pawn-dash on several occasions, in the famous Bogoljubow-Alekhine pawn-promotion combination (page 39), Tal-Hecht (page 27), Leyton-Basman (page 64) and Georgiev-Dlugy (page 170).

The passive sacrifices and the almost manic speed of the advance to the seventh rank give it a unique character, one that clearly attracted Alekhine, since he played another beautiful pawn-dash against Sämisch the year after his encounter with Bogoljubow.

Alekhine's pawn makes the journey from f2 to f7 in successive moves.

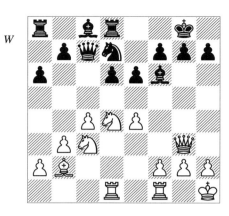

Alekhine – Sämisch
Exhibition game, Berlin 1923

16 f4 b6 17 f5 ♗e5 18 fxe6!! ♗xg3 19 exf7+ ♔h8

How many moves is White away from victory?

20 ♘d5! 1-0!

Just one. This is one of the great 'brilliant resignations'. Sämisch cannot save the game, so instead he saves himself the trouble of playing on. The f7-pawn hamstrings his pieces, and he cannot cope with the white knights that will crawl throughout his position.

A typical line is 20...♕b8 21 ♘c6 ♗e5 22 ♘xb8 ♖xb8 23 ♗xe5 dxe5 24 ♘c7! (threatening 25 ♘e8) 24...♖f8 25 ♘e6 g6 26 b4 followed by c5-c6. In *Mega Database 2001*, Kasparov gives the pretty finish 20...♕b7 21 ♘e6 ♖g8 (or 21...♗e5 22 ♘xd8) 22 fxg8♕+ ♔xg8 23 ♘e7+ ♔h8 24 ♗xg7#.

The pawn-dash seems to suit the tactical style of some players. It takes imagination and vision to foresee what a pawn can do once it reaches the seventh rank, and it takes a certain amount of courage (or foolhardiness) even to consider such an adventure. It may not surprise you to know that Tal was its most prolific practitioner. Besides Tal-Hecht,

I know of at least four other occasions where he played successful pawn-dashes. Here are two beautiful examples.

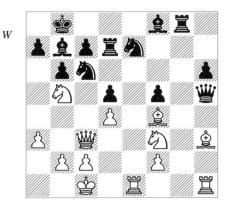

Tal – Padevsky
Alekhine Memorial, Moscow 1963

This was a highly appropriate tournament for Tal to play a dash. The basis for his combination is his pressure on c7. If we replace the d7-rook with a white pawn on the same square, we can readily see that the black king is in trouble (the c7-square is weak) and the pawn threatens to promote thanks to such tricks as ♘xc7 followed by ♘e8+, cutting off the rook from the queening square. Tal kicks off with a move that forces Black to give him a passed pawn but, in return, Black can apparently win the exchange.

24 ♘e5! ♘xe5 25 dxe5! d4 26 e6!!

The harmless-looking pawn that a few moves earlier stood on d4 becomes a monster once it reaches d7.

26...dxc3 27 exd7 ♗g7 28 ♘xc7! 1-0

What is it about pawn-dashes that provokes early resignations? Padevsky was right, of course, as the three main variations show:

a) 28...cxb2+ 29 ♔b1 ♗xh1 (or 29...♕h4 30 ♘e6+ ♕xf4 31 ♘xf4 with a comfortable win) 30 ♘e8+ ♔b7 31 d8♕ ♖xe8 32 ♖xe7+

♖xe7 33 ♕xe7+ ♔c6 34 ♕d6+ ♔b7 35 ♕d7+ ♔a6 36 ♗f1+ ♔a5 37 ♕xa7#.

b) 28...♘c6 29 ♖e8+ ♘d8 30 ♖xg8 ♕h4 31 ♘e6+ and the capture on d8 will win back the queen with a massive material advantage.

c) 28...♕f3 29 ♘d5+ ♔a8 30 ♗g2! ♕xg2 31 ♘c7+ ♔b8 32 ♘e8+ and the pawn promotes next move.

The second Tal example is simply stunning in its audacity and originality, a back-rank combination with a difference.

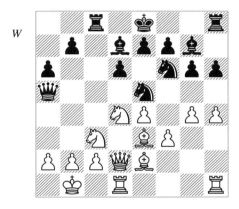

Tal – Anon
Simultaneous, Germany 1969

If we remove the black rook from h8, knight from f6 and bishop from g7, and replace them all with one white pawn on g7, we can see that the pawn is bound to promote – and it will be mate if Black is not careful. A great idea, but Tal must jettison all of his major pieces to bring it about.

14 g5! hxg5 15 hxg5 ♖xh1 16 gxf6!! ♖xd1+ 17 ♘xd1!!

White wins a crucial tempo by discovering an attack on the unguarded black queen.

17...♕xd2 18 fxg7! 1-0

White's threat is to promote with mate, and meanwhile the black queen is attacked.

Ironically, after the spectacular queen and rook sacrifices White will come out well up on material.

Another player of pawn-dashes is my friend George Leyton, whom I introduced in Chapter 7 (You and Me). Besides the game with Basman, I have three other games by him that feature pawn-dashes. The vast majority of players, including me, have played none in their entire chess lives. Clearly, like Alekhine and Tal, Leyton has what it takes. He hasn't yet managed to sacrifice his queen in the process, but his other pieces have shared out the pain between them.

The example below is an unusual one, but typical of his imagination and vision.

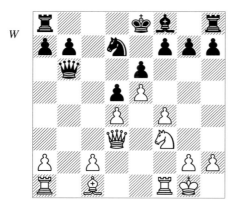

Leyton – A. London
Middlesex League 1983

Two pawns go for little dashes, starting with the f-pawn.

12 f5 h6

Black prevents ♘g5, but the weakness that this move creates at g6 means that he will be best advised to reply to fxe6 with ...♕xe6, to avoid an invasion by the white queen. Leyton immediately exploits that fact.

13 ♖b1!!

This silent sacrifice diverts the queen from guarding the e6-square while decoying it to b1. On that square it will be vulnerable to a bishop move, which will discover an attack by the f1-rook.

13...♕xb1 14 fxe6 0-0-0

After 14...fxe6 Black loses his queen to 15 ♕g6+ ♔d8 16 ♗g5+ hxg5 17 ♖xb1. However, on c8 the king is not immune from checks that force it onto a dark square, as we shall see.

15 exd7+ ♖xd7 16 e6!

The first pawn rush ended in the death of the pawn. The second one, starting from the fifth rank, will end more fortunately.

16...♖c7 (D)

Now that the diagonal from f4 to b8 is opened, 16...fxe6 is met by 17 ♕c3+ ♖c7 18 ♕xc7+! ♔xc7 19 ♗f4+, winning back the queen, leaving White with an extra piece. The variation 16...♖e7 17 ♕c3+ ♔d8 18 ♗a3 ♕b6 19 ♗xe7+ ♗xe7 20 ♘e5 wins comfortably for White.

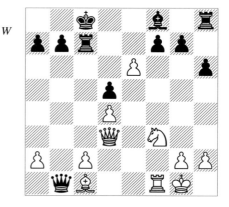

Therefore, Black decided to nudge his rook instead to c7 in expectation of 17 ♗f4 ♕xc2, when the threat to exchange queens puts Black out of danger.

17 ♕f5! ♕xc2

Black also loses after 17...♗d6 18 exf7+ ♔b8 19 ♕xd5 ♕b6 20 ♘e5!, when White has

too many threats. After the move played, there is a simple conclusion to the e-pawn's dash.
18 e7+! ♕xf5 19 e8♕# (1-0)

Generally, the pawn-dash is played with short-to-medium-term tactical chances in mind. It can, of course, be played with the long-term purpose of tying the opponent down with a far-advanced passed pawn, although in this case the amount of material sacrificed must be small, as in the following example.

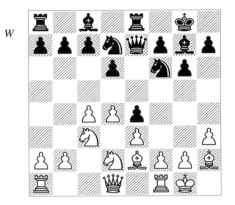

Spassky – Bukić
Bugojno 1978

Spassky sees his chance to batten down the already cramped black queenside.
12 ♘b5! ♕d8 13 c5! a6 14 cxd6! axb5 15 dxc7 ♕e7 16 ♗xb5
White has three pawns for his piece, and all the room he needs on the queenside to increase the pressure gradually. As the game goes, Black eventually feels obliged to counterattack on the kingside, but the weaknesses that he creates in the process contribute to his downfall.
16...♗f8 17 ♘c4 ♕e6 18 ♕c2 ♕d5 19 a4 ♖e6 20 ♖fc1 ♘e8 21 ♕c3 ♘ef6 22 ♘e5 ♘b6 23 ♘c4 ♘fd7 24 ♕b3 ♖f6 25 ♗xd7 ♘xd7 26 ♕b5! ♕f5

Exchanges do not favour Black, as he remains fatally cramped; e.g., 26...♕xb5 27 axb5 ♖xa1 28 ♖xa1 ♖e6 29 ♖a8 ♖e8 30 ♗d6 f5 31 ♖b8 h6 32 ♗xf8 ♔xf8 33 ♘d6 ♘b6 34 ♘xb7 ♗xb7 35 ♖xb7 and the passed pawns will force the win.
27 ♗g3 ♖fa6 28 d5 ♕f6 29 a5 h5 30 b4 h4 31 ♗h2 ♕f5 32 ♖f1 g5 33 f3 ♖g6 34 ♖ad1 exf3 35 ♖xf3 ♕c2 36 ♖d2 ♕c3 37 d6 ♖a6 38 e4 ♕c1+ 39 ♖f1 ♕c3 40 ♕d5 ♘f6 41 ♖xf6! 1-0
41...♕xf6 loses at once to 42 d7, while the alternative 41...♖xf6 42 ♗e5 also proves fatal.

In our final example, Korchnoi's pawns tie down his opponent to such an extent that his pieces would be completely hamstrung if he simplified to an endgame.

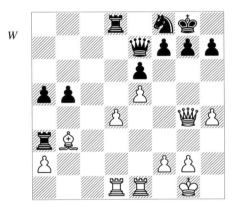

Korchnoi – Najdorf
Wijk aan Zee 1971

Korchnoi lets his bishop go in order that his d-pawn can dash to f7.
25 d5! a4 26 dxe6! axb3 27 exf7+ ♔h8
The pawn is immune thanks to 27...♔xf7 28 ♖xd8 ♕xd8 29 e6+ ♔g8 (or 29...♔e7 30 ♕xg7+ ♔d6 31 e7) 30 e7 winning the black queen.

28 ♖xd8 ♕xd8 29 axb3 ♕e7 30 e6 ♖a6

The f7-pawn is supported by White's e-pawn, but the whole edifice of White's attacking position seems about to collapse as the e-pawn cannot be defended.

31 f4!!

It is not the move itself that deserves the exclamation marks but Korchnoi's whole concept from move 25.

31...h6

Korchnoi had seen that the endgame after 31...♖xe6 32 ♖xe6 ♕xe6 33 ♕xe6 ♘xe6 34 f5 ♘f8 is winning for him because after 35 h5 g6 (or 35...h6 36 g4! g6 37 f6!) 36 h6!! gxf5 37 ♔f2 (D) Black is paralysed.

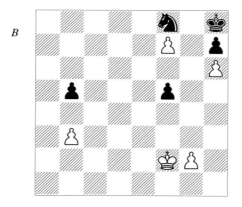

Black can only play his knight back and forth from the f8-square while the white king gobbles up the black b-pawn and promotes his own.

32 f5 ♘h7 33 ♖c1 ♖a8 34 ♕f4 ♘f6 35 ♕c7 ♕b4 36 ♕c8+

It is a shame that time-trouble errors begin to creep in. White's advanced pawns would win comfortably for him after the simple 36 ♕c5!.

36...♔h7 37 ♕xa8?? ♕d4+ 38 ♔f1 ♕f4+??

Black misses his chance to draw by means of 38...♕d3+.

39 ♔e2 ♕e5+ 40 ♔d1 1-0

Exercise 71

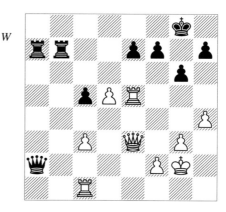

Level 1

Black's queen attacks the d-pawn, and he intends ...f6 to knock the defensive rook away. How does White (to play) allow ...f6 and exploit the resulting kingside weakness?

Exercise 72

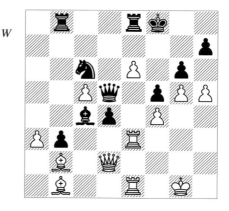

Level 2

White plays a pawn-dash combination. See if you can find the flashiest follow-up if Black accepts your sacrifice.

The solutions are on page 226.

13 Multiplication

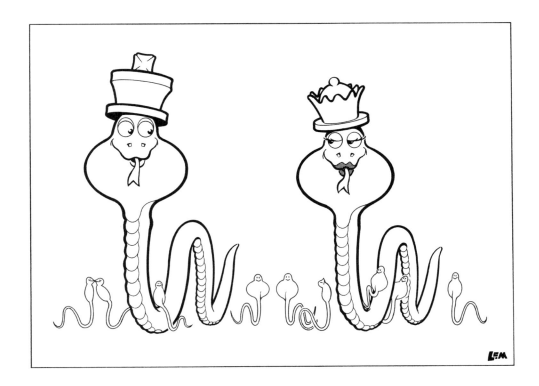

In Chapter 9 (Complex Silent Sacrifices) we saw how the Deadly Tactician combines *motifs* to make his silent sacrifices more deadly and more difficult to anticipate. The same, of course, can happen with the sacrificial *methods* that we have encountered throughout Part Two.

The fusion of different sacrificial methods can cause great combinational power to be generated. As we shall see, some astonishing sacrifices and combinations have been created when two or more methods are used on the same move.

Multiple Methods

The most popular pairing is probably the combination of silent and passive methods in a single sacrifice. One piece is already *en prise* and, not content with that, the attacker leaves it where it is (passive method) and throws another piece onto an empty square which is under opposition control (silent method).

In the diagram on the following page, Anderssen has strong pressure along the f- and g-files. 21...♘h2+ is good, since 22 ♘xh2 ♛xf2# is mate, and after 22 ♚g1 ♖g4 the

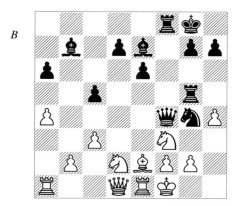

Szen – Anderssen
London 1851

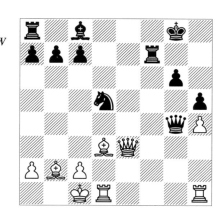

Keres – V. Petrov
USSR Ch, Moscow 1940

g2-square is also very tender thanks to the b7-bishop. However, Anderssen prefers a beautiful idea that leaves the g5-rook *en prise* and throws the queen deep into White's kingside.

21...♕h2!!

Now 22 ♘xh2 loses to 22...♖xf2+ and mate in two more moves, while the alternative capture 22 hxg5 also loses at once, to 22...♕h1+ 23 ♘g1 ♖xf2#. The white king has no alternative but to flee, but Anderssen soon runs it to ground.

22 ♗c4 ♕h1+ 23 ♔e2 ♕xg2 24 ♘xg5 ♗xg5 25 hxg5 ♕xf2+ 26 ♔d3 ♕f5+ 27 ♔e2 ♕e5+ 28 ♔d3 ♘f2+ 29 ♔c2 ♕f5+ 30 ♔b3 ♘xd1 31 ♖axd1 ♕xg5 32 ♗d3 ♖f2 33 ♘e4 c4+ 34 ♔a2 ♗xe4 35 ♗xe4 ♕a5 36 ♖a1 ♕xc3 0-1

In the following example, Keres turns Anderssen's method on its head by sacrificing his queen passively and the lesser piece (a bishop) silently.

Black's kingside weaknesses are obvious – the backward g-pawn, the unguarded back rank and the open a1-h8 diagonal. On the other hand, White's queen is under attack, and if he is not careful Black will be able to

consolidate. His solution to this dilemma is very elegant.

21 ♗c4!!

Neither *en prise* piece can be captured. 21...♘xe3 allows 22 ♖d8+ ♔h7 23 ♖h8#, while 21...♕xc4 also allows mate, by 22 ♕e8+ ♖f8 23 ♕xg6#. Meanwhile, there is no good defence to the threat of capturing on d5.

Black's attempted solution allows a neat finish.

21...c6 22 ♖xd5! ♕xc4

22...cxd5 23 ♕e8+ ♖f8 24 ♗xd5+ leads to mate.

23 ♕e8+ 1-0

In the following diagram, White's rook and queen both appear to be in trouble, but he finds a beautiful snap mate.

White could win with 42 ♕d3 ♖8e3 (or 42...gxf4 43 ♕f3 followed by ♕g4+) 43 ♗h7+ and 44 ♕f5, but he played the infinitely more pleasing **42 ♖e4!!**, leaving his queen *en prise* and placing his rook *en prise* to both black rooks. The queen's line to g5 is cleared so that the queen can deliver mate if the rook is captured, while 42...♖xd2 allows 43 ♖xe8#. Black therefore resigned.

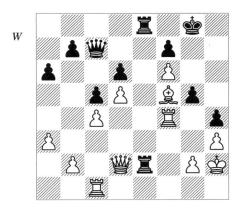

Cuellar – Reshevsky
Interzonal tournament, Sousse 1967

With most double piece sacrifices, only one of the pieces can be captured. That does not apply, of course, if one of the pieces can be captured with check, as Spassky allowed in the next example.

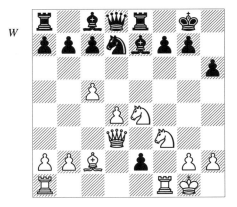

Spassky – Bronstein
USSR Ch, Leningrad 1960

Spassky could play 15 ♖f2 with a comfortable advantage, but his fantasy gets the better of him.

15 ♘d6!!?

A bewildering idea, giving up both the rook (with check) and the knight.

Of course White is threatening mate by ♕h7+ and ♕h8#, so Black must ignore the knight for the time being. If Black captures the rook and then guards h7 with a knight, White finishes gloriously by sacrificing his knight and queen: 15...exf1♕+ 16 ♖xf1 ♘f6 (16...♘f8 17 ♘xf7! transposes to the game continuation, while 16...♛xd6! 17 ♕h7+ ♚f8 18 cxd6 transposes into the line in the next paragraph) 17 ♘xf7! ♚xf7 18 ♘e5+ ♚g8 19 ♕h7+! ♘xh7 20 ♗b3+ ♚h8 21 ♘g6#!

It is possible to weather the attack, but to do so Black must appreciate that his only defence is 15...♛xd6! 16 ♕h7+ ♚f8 17 cxd6 exf1♕+ 18 ♖xf1 cxd6 19 ♕h8+ ♚e7 20 ♖e1+ ♘e5 21 ♕xg7 ♖g8! 22 ♕xh6 ♕b6! 23 ♔h1 ♗e6 24 dxe5 d5, which various analysts have assessed as roughly equal.

Bronstein could not cope with the complications and slid rapidly downhill.

15...♘f8?! 16 ♘xf7! exf1♕+ 17 ♖xf1 ♗f5

17...♚xf7 is mated by, e.g., 18 ♘e5++ ♚g8 19 ♕h7+ ♘xh7 20 ♗b3+ ♚h8 21 ♘g6#.

17...♕d5 18 ♗b3! ♕xf7! is best, although White retains the attack.

18 ♕xf5 ♕d7 19 ♕f4 ♗f6 20 ♘3e5 ♕e7 21 ♗b3 ♗xe5 22 ♘xe5+ ♔h7 23 ♕e4+ 1-0

Bronstein resigned because 23...♚h8 loses to 24 ♖xf8+! with mate in three more moves.

The silent and passive sacrificial methods make the most natural pairing, but there are several others. I have found several sacrifices that combine the passive and shunning methods. In other words, the attacker makes a move that both leaves an already attacked piece *en prise* and also declines to recapture a piece that has captured another of his pieces. It is two 'brilliant blunders' in one, and shows that the attacker has only one priority – attack. Here is one from Benko in which he feels obliged to use his beleaguered king as an attacking piece.

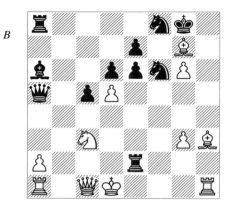

Kovacs – Benko
Debrecen 1975

Two pieces are attacked, the white bishop on g7 and the black rook on e2. Benko neither captures the one nor safeguards the other. The white knight on c3 is the only piece between Black and victory, as it takes the a4-square from his queen, so he concentrates his efforts on that.

22...♘e4!!

One threat is instant mate on f2, and there are two further mating ideas based on diverting the white knight: 23 ♘xe4 ♕a4+ 24 ♕c2 ♕xc2# and 23 ♘xe2 ♘f2+ 24 ♔c2 ♘d3+ 25 ♔b2 ♖b8#.

In the most crucial line, White exploits the vulnerable state of the black king by sending it for a long walk up the board. It looks extremely encouraging for White as 23 ♗xe6+ ♘xe6 24 ♖h8+ ♔xg7 25 ♕h6+ ♔f6 26 g7+ ♔e5 27 ♕xe6+ forces the king onto its fifth rank, but suddenly the king skips out of reach and after 27...♔d4 28 ♕e4+ (or 28 ♘xe2+ ♗xe2+ 29 ♔xe2 ♕d2+ mating) 28...♖xe4 29 ♘xe4 ♔xe4 30 ♖xa8, it delivers the *coup de grâce* by 30...♔d3!.

Kovacs cleverly attempts to close the d4-square so that ♕xe6+ (move 27 in the above sequence) will be mate.

23 ♗d4!? ♘xc3+

This simple reply wins a piece. In time-trouble, White allows mate.

24 ♕xc3 ♕a4+ 25 ♔c1 ♕xd4 26 ♕f3? ♕xa1# (0-1)

We might expect Alekhine to come up with an unusual pairing of sacrificial methods, and he does not let us down. In his game against Isakov, he combines unpinning with a silent sacrifice merely in order to exchange some pieces and force the win of the black h-pawn.

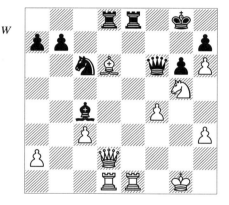

Alekhine – Isakov
Moscow 1919

24 ♗e7!

This silent unpinning move seeks to exploit Black's weak back rank through the ideas 24...♘xe7 25 ♕xd8! and 24...♕xe7 25 ♖xe7 ♖xd2 26 ♖xe8#. The first inkling of the vulnerability of the black h-pawn comes in the line 24...♖xe7 25 ♕xd8+! ♘xd8 26 ♖xd8+ ♕f8 27 ♖xf8+ ♔xf8 28 ♖xe7 ♔xe7 and now 29 a3! forces 29...♗g8, when the bishop will be fatally tied down in the endgame.

24...♖xd2

Black chooses to keep a few more pieces on the board in order to retain some counter-chances.

25 ♗xf6 ♖xe1+ 26 ♖xe1

The threat is 27 ♖e8#. Now 26...♖e2 loses to 27 ♖d1 ♗e6 28 ♘xe6 ♖xe6 29 ♗g5 followed by the rook manoeuvre ♖d7 (forcing Black to move his b-pawn to leave the knight unguarded) and ♖c7 followed by ♖c8+ and ♖h8, winning the h-pawn. The black rook cannot leave its third rank as that would allow White to play ♖g7+ followed, if the black king retreats to h8, by ♗f6.

26...♗f7

Black decides to keep his rook active, but Alekhine works his way towards the crucial h-pawn by creating mating threats.

27 ♘e4! ♖xa2 28 ♗g7! ♗b3 29 ♘f6+ ♔f7 30 ♘xh7 1-0

Black resigned since 31 ♘g5+ followed by 32 ♗f6 will leave him helpless against the advance of the white h-pawn.

Just occasionally, we come across sacrifices that combine three or more methods. In our first example, White shuns the recapture of a knight, leaves a rook *en prise*, unguards a threatened bishop and silently sacrifices his queen, all in one move (*see top diagram in next column*).

1 ♕e7!!

Simple, really. It is mate in three more moves at most:

a) 1...♖xe7 2 ♖xf8#.

b) 1...♘xf2 2 ♕xg7#.

c) 1...♘xh6 2 ♖xf8+ ♖xf8 3 ♖xf8#.

1...♘f5 2 ♖xf5! 1-0

The mates still stand.

In the next example, Black plays a pawn sacrifice to open the position. White has two alternative ways of accepting the pawn. His chosen way allows Black to play a neat silent knight sacrifice. However, the alternative way would allow Black to play the same knight

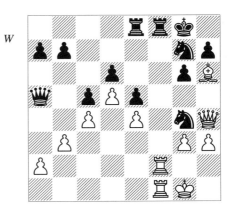

Gavashelishvili – Vdovin
USSR 1978

sacrifice, and to follow up with a crushing triple-method sacrifice which is well worth studying.

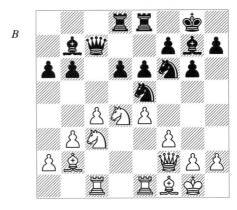

R. Byrne – Andersson
IBM tournament, Amsterdam 1979

Black's combination starts with a standard break-out move in a Hedgehog position.

17...d5! 18 exd5

It is after the other capture 18 cxd5 that we see the best variations. Black plays the silent

18...♘fg4!, which cannot be captured as after 19 fxg4 ♘xg4 the d4-knight can be captured with check. To defend against the latent threat to mate on h2, White must play 19 ♕g3 (D).

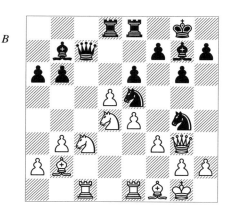

B

The unprotected white knight on d4 again provides the clue for Black's idea, which is 19...♘d3!!, allowing White the choice of capturing the queen or either knight (unpinning, silent and passive methods combined). All three captures result in a rapid victory for Black:

a) 20 ♗xd3 ♗xd4+ 21 ♔f1 ♘xh2+ costs White his queen.

b) 20 fxg4 ♗xd4+ 21 ♔h1 ♘f2+ 22 ♔g1 ♘xe4+ also wins the queen.

c) 20 ♕xc7 allows a pretty mate by the bishop and knights with 20...♗xd4+ 21 ♔h1 ♘gf2+ 22 ♔g1 ♘h3++ 23 ♔h1 ♘df2#.

18...♘fg4!

The same sacrifice, but it is followed up in a different way.

19 ♕g3 ♘xf3+!

This time, 19...♘d3 doesn't work so well because 20 ♕xg4 protects the d4-knight.

20 gxf3

20 ♘xf3 allows 20...♕c5+ 21 ♔h1 ♘f2+ 22 ♔g1 ♘e4+ winning the queen, so White must give back the pawn and one more for luck.

20...♗xd4+ 21 ♔h1 ♕xg3 22 hxg3 ♘e3 23 ♗d3 exd5 24 cxd5 ♘xd5

Black won on move 41.

Exercise 73

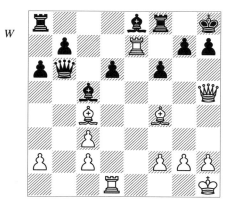

W

Level 1

White's queen is attacked by the e8-bishop, but he responds by ignoring it and playing a silent sacrifice that threatens mate. However, your work is not over when you find it. You must identify the three feasible defences, and find a quick checkmate in reply to each.

Exercise 74

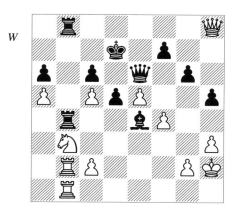

W

Level 2

White is a pawn ahead but his queen appears out of play on h8 and is under attack. He finds a remarkable move that leads to a simple knight versus bishop ending where his extra pawn and positional advantage are decisive.

Exercise 75

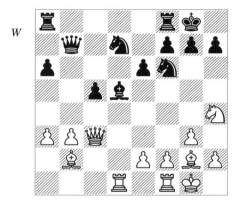

Level 3

It is White to play and win.

The solutions start on page 226.

Shirov's Multiple Sacrifices

The spirit of Mikhail Tal is alive and well, and is living in Alexei Shirov. He too is a native of Latvia, and he too is capable of the most wonderfully original flights of sacrificial fancy. His sacrifices are often long-term in their purpose, and he seems to play games in which sacrificial themes are lurking around every corner. His games can be so tactically rich and complex that commentators sometimes describe them as being on 'Planet Shirov'. I wish to share with you just one of his games here, but it serves as a summary of much that

we have seen so far since the play features no fewer than seven sacrifices on a variety of themes, and there are seven further sacrifices in the notes.

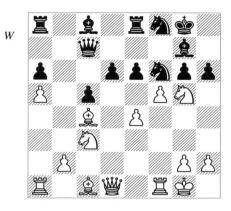

Shirov – Hauchard
Paris Ch 1990

17 e5!

Number one. Shirov shares with Kasparov the tendency to open his sacrificial assault with a pawn sacrifice. This one opens the e4-square for his pieces, and also opens the diagonal to g6.

17...dxe5 18 fxg6!

Number two, a passive knight sacrifice that brings his unmoved dark-squared bishop into the attack and, by deflecting the black h-pawn, opens the h-file for the white queen.

18...hxg5

He would like to remove the g-pawn, but 18...♘xg6 loses comparatively simply to 19 ♖xf6! ♗xf6 20 ♕h5 ♕g7 21 ♘ge4 ♗g5 22 ♘xg5 hxg5 23 ♗d3, when the fact that both of Black's rooks are unprotected proves his undoing. His knight is pinned against one and 23...♔f7 allows 24 ♗xg6+ ♕xg6 25 ♕f3+, forking the other.

19 ♗xg5 ♘8d7 20 ♕f3! ♖a7 21 ♖ad1 ♕b7 22 ♕h3 ♕c6 *(D)*

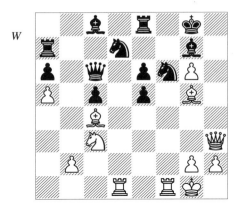

W

23 ♘d5!

Number three, a silent knight sacrifice with the intention of grabbing the a2-g8 diagonal for the bishop.

23...exd5 24 ♖xd5!

Number four. This substitution of the sacrificed knight by the rook is an exchange sacrifice that must be declined as acceptance diverts the knight from guarding h7 and deflects it from the f-file so that 24...♘xd5 25 ♕h7# is mate. The sacrifice is better than 24 ♗xd5+ ♕xd5 25 ♖xd5 ♘f8, when there is still some resistance left in Black's position.

24...♔f8

The alternative defence, 24...♘b6, would allow Shirov to show off his sacrificial versatility with three further blows: 25 ♖d7+! (passive) 25...♘xc4 26 ♖xf6! (direct) 26...♕xf6 27 ♕h7+ ♔f8 28 ♖xa7! (shunning the capture of the queen) and White will checkmate.

25 ♕h7 ♖e6! 26 ♗h6 ♔e8 27 ♕xg7!

Number five, a passive sacrifice of the exchange that brings the white queen deep into the black position.

27...♘xd5 28 ♕h8+ ♔e7 29 g7!

Number six, unpinning so that his bishop can be captured.

29...♖xh6 (D)

After 29...♖g6 comes a pawn-promotion sacrifice... 30 ♕f8+! ♘xf8 31 gxf8♕+ ♔e6 ...followed by the silent sacrifice 32 ♗g5!. The threat is 33 ♕f5+ winning the rook, while 32...♖xg5 loses the black queen to 33 ♖f6+ and 32...♖ag7 loses the other rook to 33 ♖f6+! ♖xf6 34 ♕xf6+ ♔d7 35 ♕xg7+.

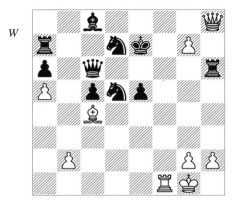

W

30 ♖f7+!!

Number seven, which not only gives up the rook directly but also shuns the immediate promotion (which would fail to the capture of the old queen by the black rook). It ensures that White promotes with check, which means that both queens will survive and therefore mate is but a few moves away.

30...♔xf7 31 g8♕+ ♔e7 32 ♕d8+ 1-0

This *tour de force* brings to an end our survey of hard-to-see sacrificial methods. If you feel suitably inspired, we can move on to some practical considerations relating to calculating sacrifices and combinations.

Part Three: Calculation

14 Preparing to Sacrifice

Most of the examples in Part Two featured the attacker diving straight into his sacrificial scheme. In the case of quiet-move follow-ups and stings in the tail, we saw him visualizing some difficult moves that would occur on the board well into the future.

In this chapter, we shall briefly take a practical point of view. Many sacrifices need to be prepared before they can be effective, and many need to be thought through deeply before they can be played. We shall look at the preparation and delving that goes on, with a view to ensuring that, in our games, we focus not only on present sacrificial opportunities but also on ones that may arise in the near future.

The Sacrifice in Order to Sacrifice

There are many ways to prepare a sacrifice. We may need to get one or two of our pieces onto the right squares, and maybe we need one of the opponent's pieces to move away from its current position, or to a specific square which allows our sacrifice to go ahead. A simple example comes from Alekhine.

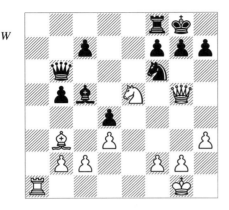

Alekhine – Duras
St Petersburg 1913

Alekhine wants to increase the pressure against f7, which he could attempt to do with 22 ♕f5 followed by 23 g4, intending 24 g5. In reply, 22...♗d6, intending to exchange bishop for knight, would fail because 23 ♘xf7! ♖xf7 24 ♕e6 wins the rook. However, Black could play 22...♗e7, keeping open the black queen's line along the third rank and thus avoiding White's sacrifice on f7 followed by ♕e6. Then if White plays 23 g4, Black can organize an efficient defence with 23...g6. Then:

a) 24 ♕f4 ♕d6 25 g5 ♘d7 26 ♗xf7+? ♔g7 and White cannot save his bishop.

b) 24 ♘xg6!? hxg6 25 ♕xg6+ ♔h8 26 ♗xf7 ♘h7 is unclear.

Alekhine's solution is to hide his intentions for the moment.

22 g4! ♗d6?

It is natural to aim to eliminate the dangerous knight, but it slips away, leaving the bishop blocking the black queen's defence of the third rank.

23 ♘xf7! ♖xf7 24 ♕f5!

There is no defence to the twin threats of 25 g5 and 25 ♕e6. The game ends quickly.

24...g6 25 ♕e6 ♔g7 26 ♕xf7+ ♔h6 27 ♗e6 1-0

Alekhine's sly switch in move-order not only ensured that he was well prepared for his knight sacrifice, but it also tempted Black to block his own queen. Of course, Black must guard against ♕e6 by keeping his own queen's line open, so 22...♗e7 would have been far better than 22...♗d6?.

The most pleasing way to prepare a sacrifice is by another sacrifice. Here is a personal example where a small preliminary sacrifice aims to divert a defending piece from guarding the square on which I wished to sacrifice. Totally unaware of the danger, my opponent fell into the trap, allowing me to play a lovely little triple-method sacrifice to end the game at once.

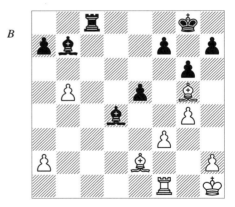

R. Williams – LeMoir
Gloucestershire vs Dorset 1969

Black can win a pawn by 23...♖c2, but I had seen a lovely finish that required a little cooperation from my opponent.

23...e4!? 24 fxe4

The first preparatory move opened the long diagonal, but now I paused in my attack. As we shall see, I need to lure the g5-bishop away from the c1-h6 diagonal.

24...f6

I was trusting that my opponent would assume that I had made a silly miscalculation. After 25 ♗xf6 ♗xe4+ 26 ♗f3 I cannot win a piece by simple means as both of my bishops are *en prise*. It turned out to be just sufficient distraction to prevent him from looking for a deeper reason for my pawn sacrifice.

25 ♗xf6?

25 ♗h6 is safe. After the move played, there comes a very pretty finish.

25...♗xe4+ 26 ♗f3 ♖c1!!

This is a silent sacrifice of a rook combined with a passive sacrifice of each bishop. All of Black's pieces are *en prise*, but White must lose at least a piece.

27 ♗xd4 ♖xf1+ 28 ♔g2 ♖xf3 29 ♗xa7 ♖a3+ 0-1

In the next game, White has a spectacular queen sacrifice in mind, but he must retain a bishop that is threatened with exchange and bring two further pieces to positions that will ensure the success of the sacrifice. Meanwhile, he will tempt Black with the opportunity to win some material, which ensures that he misses White's intentions (*see following diagram*).

White has seen a combination starting with ♕xh7+. There are three requirements to make it work. Firstly, he needs to follow up with a rook check on the h-file, and secondly he needs to be able to reply to ...♗h6 (after the h-file check) with ♖xh6+ ♔g7, f6+ ♔f8, ♖h8#. Unfortunately, if he uses his f1-rook for the h-file check (without further preparation) then the pawn check at f6 will be ineffective as the pawn can be captured. The solution is to play ♗g5 before sacrificing in order to guard the f6-square. Finally, the combination does not work if White allows his

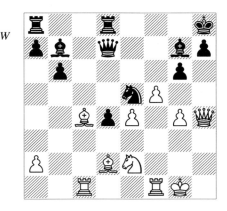

W

J. Lauridsen – J.T. Hansen
Stavanger 1991

light-squared bishop, currently attacked by the e5-knight, to be exchanged, as that gives the black king free use of g8 and f7.

So the bad news is that a lot of preparation is required, but the good news is that Black has a ready-made attacking scheme of his own that will distract him. The advance of his hungry d-pawn looks very dangerous, and White has worked out that he can afford to let it eat his knight.

After all that discussion, the moves are easy to understand.

25 ♗e6! ♕d6 26 ♗g5!! d3 27 ♖f2!! dxe2?

Black ploughs blindly onwards. 27...gxf5 28 gxf5 ♖g8 keeps Black in the game.

28 ♕xh7+! ♔xh7 29 ♖h2+ ♗h6 30 ♖xh6+ 1-0

It is not always necessary to mislead our opponent into allowing us to prepare the right conditions for our sacrifice. In the position below, Black simply sacrifices the exchange to ensure that the conditions for the big breakthrough are fully satisfied (*see diagram on following page*).

Black's idea is ...♖xf5 followed by ...♖h5+, drawing the white king into the open. In the

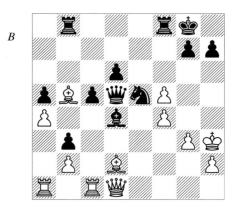

Primshtein – An. Bykhovsky
Moscow 1979

current position, 28...♖xf5 carries no threat, as the white queen guards the h5-square and there is no black piece protecting it. To make the threat work, the black knight must move out of the way so that the black queen will protect the rook when it arrives at h5.

28...♘d3 would be ideal, as the threat of 29...♘f2+ wins the tempo that allows the rook to make the planned capture on f5. However, 28...♘d3 is prevented by the white bishop on b5, so Black's course of action is clear: remove the bishop and then everything will fall into place.

28...♖xb5! 29 axb5 ♘d3 30 ♗e1 ♖xf5!! 31 ♕xd3

After the defence 31 g4, Black reveals another reason for wanting to have his knight available on d3 by mating with 31...♘xf4+ 32 ♔h4 g5+ 33 ♔g3 ♕g2#.

31...♖h5+ 32 ♔g4 ♖xh2

The threat is 33...♕h5#.

33 f5 h5+ 34 ♔f4 g5+

Black could mate more quickly by means of 34...♕e5+! 35 ♔f3 g5! 36 fxg6 ♕f6+ 37 ♔e4 ♕e6+ 38 ♔f3 ♕g4#, but even after the text-move the white king cannot survive out in the open.

35 ♔xg5 ♕e5 36 ♕c4+ d5 37 ♕xd4 ♕xd4 38 ♖xa5 ♕g7+ 39 ♔f4 ♖e2 0-1

Here is a short but extremely sweet example of the *sacrifice in order to sacrifice*. White is happy to sacrifice most of his army to be left with the bishop and knight he needs for mate.

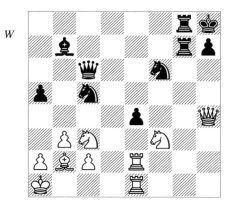

Tietz – May
Vienna 1912

Remove the two knights from the a1-h8 diagonal and place a white knight on f7. It's mate, isn't it? That forms the idea behind a glorious combination. White plays to draw the black queen onto the e4-square, when the f3-knight will be able to play ♘g5, and the threats of mate at h7 or f7 will win the queen. Getting the queen to e4, however, will cost a lot of material.

1 ♘xe4! ♘cxe4 2 ♖xe4! ♘xe4 3 ♖xe4 ♕xe4 4 ♘g5!!

This is an object lesson in the calculation of combinations. White's analysis at move one might have stopped when he noticed that his own queen is now under attack from the black queen. White was not fazed because he knows that his objective is mate at f7, and that his queen is not directly involved in the mating pattern.

4...♕xh4 loses to 5 ♘f7#, so White's analysis can continue. Black's best option is now 4...♖e8, but White can exchange his bishop and knight for the black queen and one rook with an easily winning endgame. Black's actual choice allows a spectacular finish.

4...♕g6 5 ♕xh7+!! ♕xh7 6 ♘f7# (1-0)

Now for the obligatory Tal example. His preparatory sacrifices are passive, as he needs time both to set up the decisive strike and to play his quiet follow-up. The result is a remarkable position in which Black is a rook ahead but in the grip of a deadly pin.

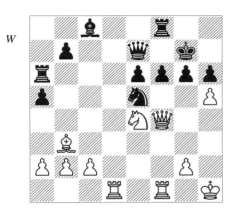

Tal – Bilek
Asztalos Memorial, Miskolc 1963

Tal's idea is to sacrifice on f6, and then to pin the recapturing piece with ♕xe5. The position of the black rook on a6 means that it will struggle to get around to defend f6, so a later ♖f1 by White will win back the sacrificed material. For now, however, 26 ♘xf6 meets the reply 26...♕xf6, so Tal retreats his queen to ensure that it is the black rook that must recapture on f6.

26 ♕g3! a4

Here is White's problem. The b3-bishop is lost, but Tal has calculated that he will get back all of the sacrificed material, remaining with a positional advantage in the endgame. As we have seen before, the prospect of a better ending is all that Tal needed to tempt him into playing a combination.

27 ♖xf6! ♖xf6 28 ♕xe5 axb3

He must accept the extra piece because 28...b6 loses to 29 ♘xf6 ♕xf6 30 ♕c7+ ♕f7 31 ♕xc8 and 28...gxh5 lets the bishop out so that White wins comfortably with 29 ♗c4 ♖c6 30 ♗b5 ♖xc2 31 ♖f1.

Even now, Tal remains calm, as Black can be prevented from mounting any counterplay.

29 axb3! b6

29...gxh5 is best, as 30 ♖f1? ♖a5 is equal. White does better to play 30 ♘xf6 ♕xf6 31 ♕c7+, winning back all of the sacrificed material; he would have the better ending thanks to Black's shattered pawn-structure.

Bilek's chosen move protects the a5-square so that he can answer 30 ♖f1 with 30...♖a5, but Tal's stunning quiet reply leaves him helpless against the threat of ♖f1.

30 b4!! 1-0

The unpinning 30...♔f7 loses to 31 ♘xf6 ♕xf6 32 ♕c7+, winning the c8-bishop.

Birth of a Combination

Where do the ideas for sacrifices come from? Obviously, many combinations come from combinational patterns stored in our memories, but the ability to see sacrifices several moves ahead often requires something less tangible.

Here is an example that I witnessed first-hand. It seems to me that the brilliant sacrificial sequence played by White was the result of a logical flow of thought (*see diagram on following page*).

Derek Wise's grandiose idea may have been conceived through a wish to trap the black knight at b4. Let's put ourselves in his shoes and imagine how it developed:

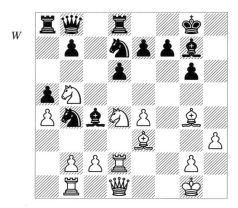

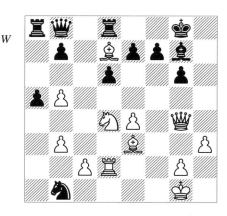

D.M. Wise – L. Burnett
West of England Ch,
Weston-super-Mare 1976

"Black's knight has no retreat after 23 b3 ♗xb5 (forced) 24 axb5, and there is an immediate threat to win it by 25 c3. My problem is that the immediate reply 24...♘a2 threatens 25...♘c3, forking rook and queen, and the defence 25 ♖d3 is met by 25...♘b4 with a likely repetition.

"Can I allow 25...♘c3? If so, what useful move can I make in the meantime? For instance, where can the white queen go, before or after ...♘c3? The g4-square looks pretty good for the queen and after 25 ♗xd7 ♘c3 26 ♕g4, it protects my bishop and there are ideas of ♘f5 or ♖f2 followed by ♖xf7 in the air.

"On the other hand, 26...♘xb1 *(D)* now attacks the other rook."

White is only the exchange behind in this position, so it is possible that Wise stopped here in his analysis, thinking that 27 ♖f2 should give him good attacking chances. But it is possible that the position reminded him of a combination that he had seen before, and the idea of 27 ♗e6!! came into his mind even this far into his calculations.

Whatever the case, he saw something he liked, because he went ahead.

23 b3!? ♗xb5 24 axb5! ♘a2
Black should play 24...♘f6! 25 c3!? ♘xe4 26 cxb4 axb4, but that c3-square, and the line-up of the white pieces, is just too tempting.

25 ♗xd7! ♘c3 26 ♕g4! ♘xb1 27 ♗e6!!
White combines a silent sacrifice of the light-squared bishop with a passive sacrifice of the d2-rook.

27...fxe6
The alternatives also lead to mate:

a) 27...♘xd2 28 ♕xg6 ♖f8 29 ♘f5 is mate next move.

b) 27...♖f8 loses to 28 ♕xg6 intending ♘f5.

c) 27...♗xd4 allows 28 ♕xg6+ ♗g7 29 ♗d4.

28 ♕xg6 ♖f8
28...d5 29 ♘xe6 ♕e5 30 ♗d4 is hopeless for Black.

29 ♘xe6 ♖f7 30 ♖f2! ♕f8
Black offers his queen since 30...♕e8 31 ♗h6 ♘c3 32 ♘g5 e6 33 ♖xf7 is clearly fatal for him. White is in the happy position of being able to ignore the offer.

31 ♘g5! b6 32 ♕h7# (1-0)

The winning idea in the next game probably suggested itself from a survey of White's kingside problems.

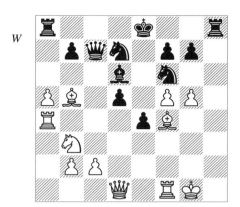

Mesing – Marjanović
Yugoslavia 1978

White's king appears to be in some danger. His obvious continuation is 21 gxf6, but after 21...♗xf4 22 ♗xd7+ ♔d8!! 23 ♖xf4 (not 23 ♕e2 ♗e3+! 24 ♕xe3 ♕h2#) 23...♕xf4 24 ♕e2 ♕g3+ 25 ♕g2 ♕e1+ 26 ♕f1 ♖h1+! Black is winning. White also experiences a few kingside problems after the sober 21 ♗xd6 ♕xd6 22 ♕d2 ♕g3+ 23 ♕g2 ♕e3+ 24 ♖f2 ♘h7 25 g6 ♘g5.

White can instead play 21 ♕d2 in reasonable safety, but the above variations probably led White to seek a way to remove Black's dangerous dark-squared bishop. The idea of 21 ♖c4 suggests itself, as 21...dxc4 22 ♗xd6 replaces Black's dangerous bishop with its hyperactive white counterpart. Analysing on, White could see that the rook can be useful even if its life is spared.

21 ♖c4!! dxc4

21...♕b8 22 gxf6 ♗xf4 23 ♗xd7+ ♔d8 (not 23...♔xd7 24 ♕xd5+) seems to be the same as in the analysis of 21 gxf6 above, but the presence of the rook on c4 means that 24 ♖c8+ can be played, winning the black queen. Therefore Black is forced to accept the rook offer.

22 ♗xd6 ♕c8

22...♕d8 allows 23 ♕d4! (intending 24 ♕e5+) 23...♘d5 24 ♕xg7!, mating or winning the black queen.

23 gxf6 cxb3 24 ♕d5 ♔d8

24...♕xc2 allows mate by 25 ♕e5+ ♔d8 26 ♕e7+ ♔c8 27 ♕xd7#.

25 ♕xf7 ♖e8 26 fxg7 1-0

Finally, the pawn promotes.

Ideas can arise quite by accident from lateral thinking. Here is a personal example in which thoughts about King's Gambits led me to play a powerful long-term sacrifice.

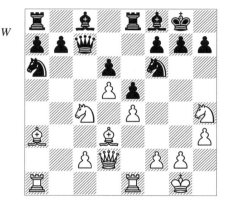

LeMoir – O. Hindle
Norfolk Ch, Norwich 2001

My pawn sacrifice in the opening had not been particularly rewarding. I wanted to play 16 f4, but it is clear that it loses material to the reply 16...b5. After 17 ♘a5 exf4 White cannot recapture the pawn as that leaves the knight unprotected on a5, and 17 ♘b2 loses a piece to 17...b4! 18 ♗xb4 ♕b6+. This means that 17 ♘e3 is forced, when 17...exf4 18 ♘ef5 g5 allows Black to secure a second pawn.

I was not too worried about this, as I liked the looseness of the black kingside, and I started to think about the position after 19 ♗b2 ♘d7.

The position after 20 ♘f3 f6 21 h4 interested me. It is just like a King's Gambit, but my bishop is very threatening on that long diagonal (although it can be blocked by ...♘e5). In fact, I thought, I could leave the knight on h4, and if Black decides to take it I can play ♕xf4 with attacking chances, quite similar to the King's Gambit lines where White allows the black g-pawn to capture a knight on f3.

Then it came to me. If I play 20 g3 Black cannot capture the pawn because 21 ♕xg5+ is mate next move. If he captures the h4-knight, then I recapture, not on h4 but on f4, and not with the queen but with the pawn. The g-file is open and the e5-square is a less hospitable place for the black knight. It is no longer anything like a King's Gambit, but it doesn't need to be!

A little more analysis and I went ahead with this line.

16 f4!? b5 17 ♘e3! exf4 18 ♘ef5 g5 19 ♗b2 ♘d7 20 g3!! gxh4 21 gxf4 f6 22 ♕g2+ ♔h8 23 ♔h2 ♘e5 24 ♖g1 ♕f7

24...♘g6!? 25 ♗xf6+ ♔g8 is a better defence, but White's attack would still be very strong.

25 fxe5 ♖xe5

White wins after 25...dxe5 26 ♗xb5 ♗xf5 27 ♗xe8 ♖xe8 28 ♖xa6 ♗g6 29 ♕f2, so Black gives up the exchange. I am now clearly winning, but with time-trouble affecting both sides, I managed to grab defeat from the jaws of victory:

26 ♗xe5 dxe5 27 ♗xb5 ♗xf5 28 exf5 ♘c5 29 ♗c6 ♖d8 30 ♖xa7! ♗e7 31 c4

31 d6! ♖xd6 32 ♖xe7! is better, when Black can only resign.

31...e4! 32 d6??

The preliminary 32 ♔h1 wins. I failed to ask myself why Black moved his e-pawn on his last move. I found out at once.

32...♗xd6+ 33 ♔h1 ♕xa7 34 ♗d5 ♗g3 35 ♕b2 ♕e7 36 ♖a1 e3 37 ♖a7 ♖d7 38 ♖a8+ ♔g7 39 ♖g8+ ♔h6 0-1

White lost on time.

When preparing a sacrifice, it is important that we look for the best moves for the defender. When we find them, we should not necessarily be afraid of them. If a sacrifice looks right to us, then we may well be able to find an idea that will defeat even the cleverest defence.

Here is an example of an apparently strong defence that would have stopped many of us in our tracks.

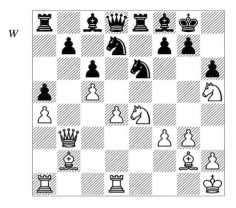

W

King – A.D. Martin
British League (4NCL) 1995/6

In *Chess Monthly*, Howell reported that King thought for ages before playing 24 ♕c3, leaving himself with only a few minutes to get to the time-control. He analysed the long-diagonal breakthrough 24...♘c7 25 d5! ♘xd5 26 ♖xd5! cxd5 27 ♘xg7, but he could not find a way around 27...♖e5, leaving White a whole exchange down and with two knights *en prise*. He suspected that there might be a way around it, so he went ahead, but he took the precaution of accompanying his next move with a draw offer!

Luckily for him, Martin not only refused the offer, but also thought for long enough for King to be able find what he had been missing – the idea to defeat 27...♖e5.

24 ♕c3! ♘c7 25 d5! ♘xd5 26 ♖xd5! cxd5 27 ♘xg7 ♖e5! 28 ♘h5!!

It's a passive sacrifice of the e4-knight with a silent sacrifice of the other knight. The threat is 29 ♘ef6+ and 28...♖xh5 allows 29 ♕h8#, so Black must take on e4.

28...dxe4 29 f4!

The long diagonal remains a potent weapon and soon leads to the win of a piece.

29...♕c7 30 fxe5 ♕xc5 31 ♕e1! f5 32 e6 ♘e5 33 ♖c1 ♕d6 34 ♕c3 ♗xe6 35 ♕xe5 ♕xe5 36 ♗xe5

White won after 20 further moves.

Exercise 76

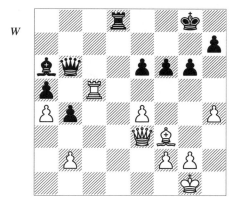

Level 1

White is very keen to play 28 ♖c8, as it discovers an attack by his queen on its opposite number, and 28...♕xe3 allows 29 ♖xd8+ followed by recapturing the queen, leaving White with an extra rook. Unfortunately, after 28 ♖c8 there is a way to protect the rook with the queen. What is it, and what preparatory move did White play in an attempt to prevent it? In the game, White's move led to a very quick win as Black fell in with his plans, but even with best play Black would have been forced to accept a severe positional disadvantage.

Exercise 77

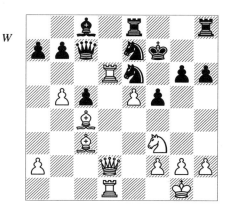

Level 2

White wants to play ♘g5#. How does he bring it about with a 'sacrifice in order to sacrifice'?

Exercise 78

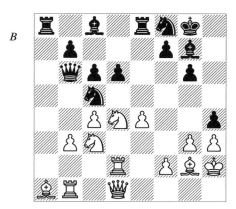

Level 3

Here Bronstein played **20...♖xa1**. Before committing himself to it, he had to look beyond the first wave of the combination. Can you do the same?

The solutions start on page 227.

15 How Not to Calculate Combinations

Calculation for Athletes

The ability to calculate accurately, economically and quickly is one of the main differences between masters and the rest of us, yet until comparatively recently there had been very little written on the subject.

In 1971, Kotov's *Think Like a Grandmaster* was published in English. It contained the first attempt to recommend a system that players could use to improve their calculating abilities. In the 1990s, Mark Dvoretsky's chess training books set out Kotov's views in conjunction with his own, and also presented the views of other writers.

The main targets of their advice are strong or ambitious players – the competitive athletes of the chess world – who have the time and motivation to commit both to thinking about the subject, and to undertaking specific training. I have aimed this book at a wide range of playing strengths and attitudes, including strong and ambitious players, so I shall summarize some of the main points below. Club players can select which points to act upon and which to set aside.

Select candidate moves: When it is our turn to move, Kotov's advice is to list in our minds all moves that we could play in the position in front of us (the **candidate moves**). That way, we should miss nothing. We have probably all gone back over a game and found that we played a bad move without even considering any other possibilities in the position, and we have all had positions in which we didn't even consider a move that was clearly superior to the one that we played.

Kotov goes on to recommend that, as we analyse, we should list in our minds all of our opponent's possible replies to each of our candidate moves, and then list all possible replies that we could make to each of them, and so on. Each line should stop when we feel that we can make a clear assessment of a resulting position or, presumably, when we cannot visualize any further, in which case we should make any assessment that we can.

For most of us, and even for masters if the position is complex, such a process would be impractical, and Dvoretsky presents the opinion of Krasenkov that we should first define the aims of our analysis (e.g., to gain a decisive material advantage, or to increase our positional advantage), then look for ideas that might help to achieve the aim. Only then should we mentally create a short-list of candidate moves that could achieve the aim.

Perform a quick assessment of each candidate move: Even then, there is no need to dive into deep analysis of each candidate move. A quick preliminary assessment of each candidate move should enable us to decide the order in which we will analyse them (normally in order of likelihood of success). Some moves are likely to eliminate themselves completely, and occasionally it will be clear that one move is so strong that the rest can be ignored.

Terminate each variation with a definite conclusion: Our conclusion may not necessarily be that we have a clear advantage or that our aim is achieved. For instance, we might draw the conclusion that the position is unclear and that further analysis will be needed later on as the specific position comes closer. To commit to the variation in advance, we need to be reasonably sure that nothing better exists or that the attendant risks are worth taking.

Don't try to analyse too deeply: The deeper we analyse, the more likely it is that we have overlooked something on the way. We need to use our judgement to cut down on analysis time.

The advice of Dvoretsky et al. doesn't specifically cover the analysis of a combination, which is the main subject that interests us here. In *Paul Keres Chess Master Class*, Neishtadt makes the observation that the aim of a combination is normally to transform an unclear position into a clear one. It follows from this that if we are playing a combination, we should analyse as far as is necessary to enable us to draw a clear conclusion. This means that we have less need for long lines of analysis with long-term sacrifices.

Go through each line once, and once only: Anyone who keeps repeating lines of analysis is likely to waste a lot of time, but this advice should not mean that we bar ourselves from re-visiting a line that we have already been through. For instance, an idea might come up in our analysis of another line that may be worth trying in a line that we have rejected earlier.

Create stepping-stone diagrams: This is not covered by the Dvoretsky books, but is a concept described by Jonathan Tisdall, and referred to by Jesper Hall in *Chess Training for Budding Champions*. The idea is that, at a critical point in our analysis (for instance, where there are several alternative candidate moves that need to be considered) we should create a clear picture of the position in our mind's eye. This should enable us to return to the position without forgetting the squares where the critical pieces are situated.

Calculation for Joggers

Learning to calculate is like learning to walk. As children, once we get used to the feeling of walking we make rapid progress and are soon running, jumping and performing all sorts of athletic feats that seemed forever beyond us when we were at the crawling stage.

We make progress without the intervention of others. Sports teachers encourage us to run, but there is no need for them to show us how to do it better. However, the best runners become ambitious; they want to approach perfection, so they work with highly qualified athletics coaches who show them how to 'run properly', and who ensure that all the right muscles are exercised in the right ways. The same preparation for ordinary people, even casual sportsmen, would be a waste of time at best.

So it may be with calculating at chess. We learn chess, and we soon start to calculate on our own. With practice (just playing chess) comes rapid progress in our ability to calculate. It can be argued that learning how to 'calculate properly' is for those who wish to approach perfection, and that specialized preparation is not appropriate for the rest of us.

On the other hand, even a small expansion in the number of candidate moves that we consider might help us to improve our play. It is worthwhile having some ideas about how to look for them. Here are the ideas that are most likely to be useful in helping us find and calculate combinations.

Ask what is the drawback of our opponent's last move: If that move was surprising, we should not meekly assume that it was right. The search for the weakness in a move can suggest candidate moves that we might not otherwise have considered.

Ask what our opponent is trying to do: In most positions, we consider moves that prevent the more dangerous of our opponent's intentions. That is prophylaxis. For combinative

play, however, we might let him go ahead if we can see a way to take advantage. For instance, can he try to win material, and if so can we profitably let him succeed? This was the subject of the section 'Ambush!' in Chapter 10 (pages 141-6).

Look for tactical weaknesses in the opponent's position: Has he left a piece unprotected, are two pieces in a position where they could possibly be forked, skewered or subjected to a pin? Are there any weaknesses in the way he has arranged for his king's defence? Once we see the weakness, we can work out whether there is a way to exploit it.

Look for forcing lines: Most masters look first at moves that force the opponent's reply. The rest of us often miss golden opportunities to win quickly and easily because we habitually ignore this simple little discipline.

Ask what might be possible if we were allowed several moves in a row: Jesper Hall suggests this method to help us to identify our opponents' weaknesses, and to uncover potential combinative themes. If we find that a combination would be possible after a few preparatory moves, we can start playing them now. In the meantime, if our opponent tries something active or threatening, we can work out whether it is worth letting him go ahead, using passive sacrifices if necessary, if it allows us to play our combination. It is a matter of judging whose threats are the more dangerous.

Look for moves that lose material: Kotov described how Chekhover, a master from Leningrad, would begin his analysis by working out which pieces he could put *en prise*. Only when he could see no advantageous way of losing material did he start to look at quieter moves. It is clear that Tal, too, was constantly on the lookout for sacrifices, both in the position in front of him and in the lines along which his analysis took him.

Have we more pieces available for an attack on the king than our opponent has for its defence? If we do, then we should look for attacking moves. If a sacrifice would bring about a situation in which we have the greater number of pieces available for the attack, then we should consider that sacrifice.

Besides not being too fussy about the number of candidate moves that we aim to consider, there is another small compromise to the discipline of the ambitious player that we might wish to consider. The advice to go through each line of our analysis "once and once only" is clearly sensible when we can clearly visualize the final position and the moves that lead up to it. I frequently find myself getting to a point in my analysis where either I cannot see the position sufficiently clearly in my mind's eye to enable me to identify the candidate moves available, or the ones that I have listed are unacceptable to me.

I need to create a stepping-stone diagram. Although it uses up clock time, I find that if I go back to the beginning of the line and quickly repeat the moves in my head, I can normally improve the clarity with which I can visualize the position in question. Sometimes I even spot a better move on the way.

This is only worth doing when we feel that it is worth the extra clock time – for instance if we sense that we are close to an answer to the problems of the position but it is tantalizingly out of reach.

Intuition versus Calculation

Intuition is a wonderful thing. It enables people to draw conclusions in life without gathering all the information that is available and without analysing it fully. In chess, it can be a blessing and a curse. It helps us to gain a quick grasp of the essence of a position, to shorten the list of candidate moves, and to shorten the length of the lines that we will calculate because we feel confident in our ability to assess positions which are not completely clear. It helps us to make intellectual 'leaps in the dark' which lead us to consider ideas that appear to defy logical analysis.

On the other hand, intuition can make us lazy and superficial. We get used to being able to make quick decisions on limited information, so we don't bother to analyse in sufficient depth or to choose a wide enough range of candidate moves to enable us to reach the truth about a position. Worse, what happens if our intuition is faulty? We assume that intuitive people have good intuition – that is not necessarily so, and even a small amount of logical reasoning might lead to better results.

When I say 'we' in the paragraphs above, I do mean 'we'. I am intuitive. Luckily for me, my intuition can be pretty good. I often play moves, with little consideration, that astonish my more analytical opponents. However, I am often appalled by how much more deeply my lower-graded opponents have seen into a position than I have managed. On the other hand, I often find this out when analysing with them at the end of a game that I have won. My decisions were superior, however I happened to arrive at them.

Intuition and logic (or calculation) both have crucial roles to play in achieving success in chess. Dvoretsky tries to ensure that his students develop a balance between intuition and calculation, as part of his policy of improving their areas of weakness. As with the Olympic athlete, this is right for ambitious players aiming at the top.

For club players, it may be that the opposite approach is better. In other words, intuitives may be more likely to succeed at club level if they try to exploit their intuition, and improve its quality, than if they make the conscious effort to become analytical. By the same token, analytical players might also benefit most from sticking to, and trying to improve, what they do best.

This is my opinion, and I leave it to the individual to decide.

Tactical Trackwork

We can train our ability to calculate and to visualize positions by solving published chess puzzles without using the board and pieces, and by following games from chess books and magazines in the same way. We should be able to gauge our progress by how many moves we can play in our minds from the start of a game before losing sight of what is going on, although most of us would be doing well to reach beyond the opening stage.

In my youth, I played blindfold consultation chess, which absolutely forces the players to keep a picture of the position in their heads. The advantage of playing in pairs is that two heads are better than one when it comes to remembering every detail of a position.

There is no doubt that blindfold chess helps develop visualizing skills, and Jesper Hall also suggests playing 'move-after' chess. White announces his first move but doesn't make it on the board, and Black follows suit. Then White announces his second move but only makes his first move on the board. The players must keep in their minds a position that is once removed from the one that is on the board. I would also suggest that, as their confidence increases, they could move on to 'two-moves-after' chess, and so on.

If you would like to improve your general intuitive or logical/analytical skills, then here is a summary of Dvoretsky's advice in *Attack and Defence*:

To improve intuition: Intensively study chess games and positions. When analysing a position, try not to analyse it right to the end. Using a limited amount of analysis, try to come to a definite conclusion about the position as quickly as possible. Then compare your own conclusion with the 'correct' answer.

To improve logic and analytical skills: Solve strategic problems, such as devising the concrete plan that should be followed in the transition from the opening to the middlegame. Do exercises in the calculation of complex variations that demand concentrated, painstaking attention.

In this book my aim is to help my readers to improve both their intuition and their analytical skills in the playing of sacrifices and combinations.

Any exposure to chess games and analysis tends to enhance our intuition as it increases the store of our experience (even if it is indirect). One of my aims is to feed the imagination, through exposing my readers to a large amount of material on the subject of each type of sacrifice and through doing and repeating the exercises. Feeding the imagination should in turn feed the intuition.

For those who want to improve their analytical skills, most of the exercises demand at least some analysis, and at Level 3 it can be very complex and demanding.

That brings us neatly to the part of the book where you do all of the work...

16 Have You Been Paying Attention?

In this chapter, there is a set of twelve exercises for each of the three levels from Level 1 (least difficult) to Level 3 (most difficult). While Level 1 exercises continue to include helpful hints, at Level 2 there is very little help, and at Level 3 none at all. The exercises do not follow the order of the sacrificial types covered in the rest of the book – the order is random. All that you can be sure of is that somewhere in each exercise there is at least one sacrifice or quiet move of the type discussed in Part Two.

As recommended in the Introduction, my advice to you is to try the Level 1 exercises first, trying to see and calculate the solution without using a board and pieces. If you cannot work it out that way, then use a board. When you have tried the Level 1 test, move on to the higher levels. It is quite likely that most readers will need a board and pieces to tackle the Level 3 exercises.

A month or so after first completing the tests, read through the book again, and repeat the text exercises and the tests. You should be able to complete a larger proportion of them from the diagrams alone. If you repeat the process on at least one further occasion, you should find your tactical confidence and ability increasing.

Ready? Then off you go...

Level 1 Test

Test 1.1

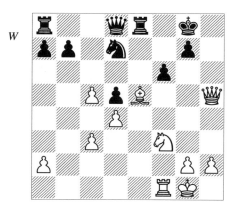

White to play. Black will be forced to decline the sacrifice, but he cannot prevent mate in a few further moves.

Test 1.2

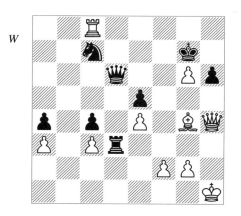

White's sacrifice here combines diversion with decoy. It must be declined, but even so White wins material.

Test 1.3

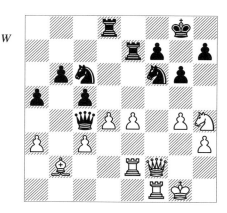

White's first move is a sacrifice and his second is a quiet follow-up that forces mate or the win of the black queen.

Test 1.4

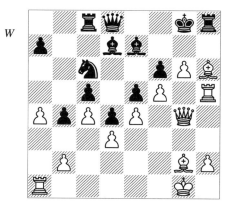

White plays his move and Black resigns at once as he faces a very quick mate.

Test 1.5

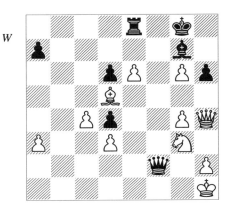

White finds a way to force the promotion of his passed e-pawn.

Test 1.6

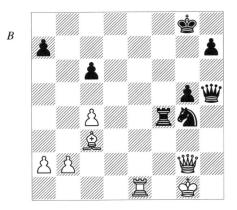

Black is already winning, but he finishes the game off quickly by winning the white queen very neatly.

Test 1.7

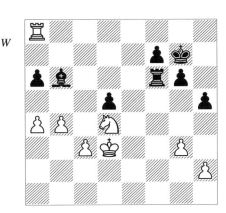

Black has just played his rook from d6 to f6. Why did he do that, and what should White's reply be?

Test 1.8

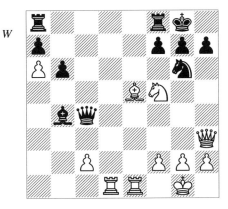

White to play and mate in a few moves.

Test 1.9

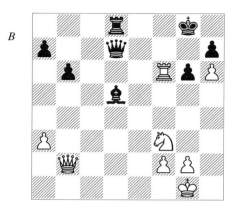

Black played **30...♗xf3** in this position. What was White's reply?

Test 1.11

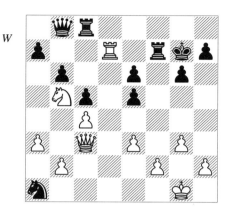

White is a rook down, so he is looking for a draw in this position. How does he force perpetual check?

Test 1.10

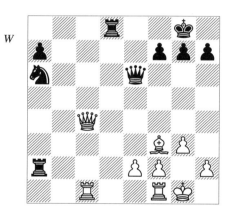

White wins with a combination that exploits Black's weak back rank. Make sure you play the right way, as there is a feasible combination that only draws.

Test 1.12

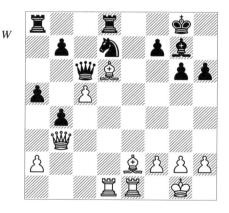

You have a chance to start a king-hunt with **1 ♕xf7+**. Do you go for it?

The solutions start on page 228.

Level 2 Test

Test 2.1

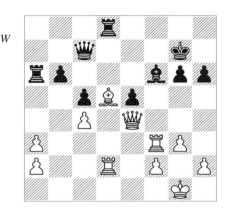

White to play and win quickly.

Test 2.3

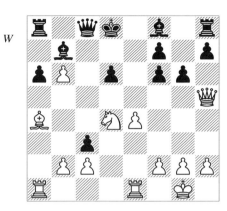

White to play and win quickly.

Test 2.2

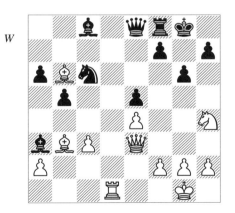

White played **25 ♘xg6** and followed it up with two fairly quiet moves that left Black in deep trouble. What were they?

Test 2.4

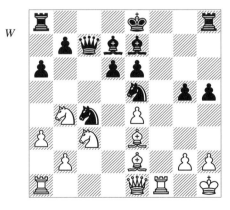

It is White to play, and his sacrifice gains at least a significant positional advantage.

Test 2.5

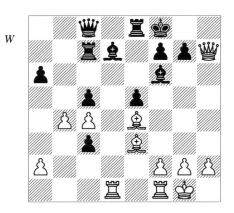

What is the quickest (and prettiest) way for White to win?

Test 2.6

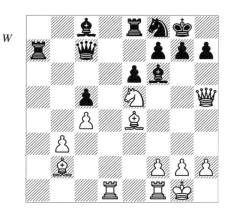

White to play and win.

Test 2.7

White is the exchange and a pawn ahead and threatens mate. What can Black (to play) do?

Test 2.8

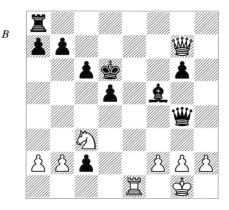

Black to play and win.

Test 2.9

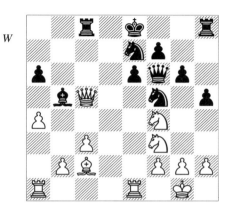

White to play and win quickly.

Test 2.11

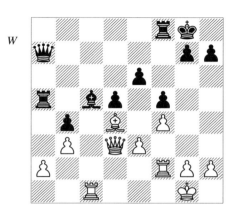

White to play and win.

Test 2.10

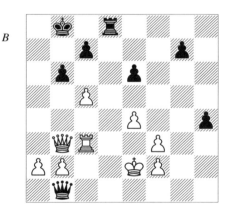

Black to play and win.

Test 2.12

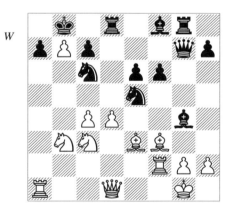

White to play and win quickly.

The solutions start on page 230.

Level 3 Test

Test 3.1

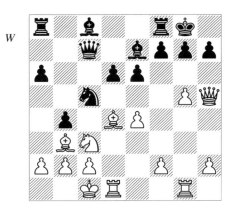

White can play three good silent sacrifices in this position. What are they, and which one is best?

Test 3.2

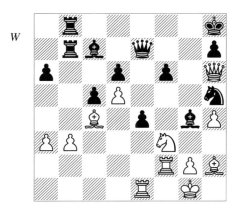

White to play and win.

Test 3.3

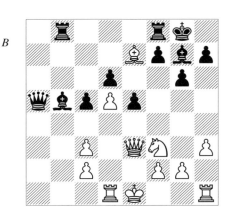

Black to play and gain the advantage. The acceptance of his sacrifice allows a clear win for Black.

Test 3.4

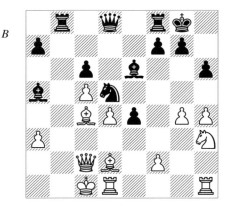

Black could gain a comfortable pawn advantage by 23...♗xg4, but prefers to sacrifice for a more certain win.

Test 3.5

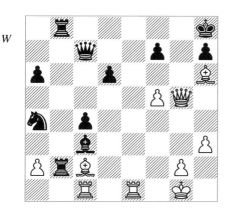

White can win a piece by the simple 1 ♗xa4, but his beauty compulsion kicks in, and he finds a lovely way to finish the game quickly.

Test 3.6

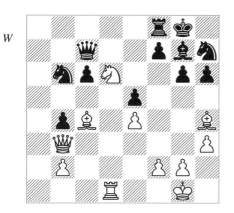

White to play and win. Try to find the most effective line.

Test 3.7

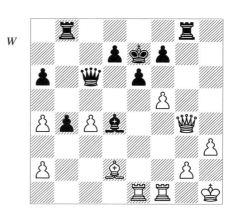

White to play and win quickly.

Test 3.8

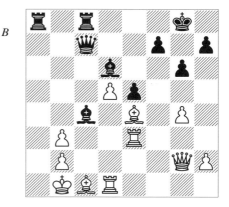

Black to play and win.

Test 3.9

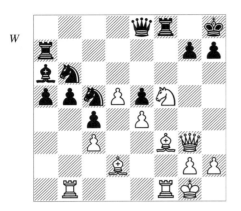

White, to play, has in mind a sacrifice that requires some preparation.

Test 3.10

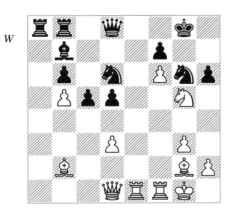

White to play and win.

Test 3.11

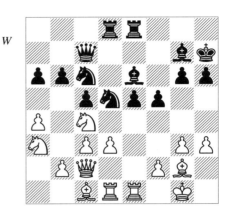

White plays **24 ♕b3** with the point 24...♖b8 (to protect the b-pawn) 25 f4 exf4 26 ♖xe6 ♖xe6 27 ♗xd5. What does Black do about it?

Test 3.12

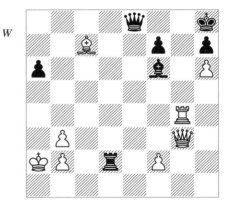

White to play and win.

The solutions start on page 232.

17 Solutions

If you are looking for some help with the solutions and haven't made a real effort to solve the exercises, shame on you – this is not cheats' corner. Turn back to the exercises now! If not, read on.

Solutions to Text Exercises

In order to help you navigate between the exercises and their solutions, immediately before each group of solutions, we give the title of the chapter and section in which the relevant exercises appear.

Chapter 1: The Old Romantics

1)

Nathan – Anderssen
Berlin 1850

22...♘d3!! discovers an attack by the d6-bishop on White's f4-knight, and also an attack by the queen on the e1-rook. It covers the f2- and f4-squares so that 23 ♖xe8 ♗xf4# is mate. White can also capture a second piece, the knight itself, but 23 ♕xd3 loses to 23...♕xe1+ 24 ♔h2 ♗xf4#. Black therefore resigned.

2)

Anderssen – Mayet
Berlin 1865

31 ♘f8!
This move serves a quadruple purpose:
a) It clears the h7-square so that White is threatening mate by 32 ♕h7+ ♔xf8 33 ♕h8#.

b) It seeks to divert the king from guarding the h8-square so that 31...♔xf8 32 ♕h8# is mate.

c) It enables White to reply to 31...f6 with 32 ♘g6, threatening 33 ♕h8+ followed by 34 ♕f8# or 34 ♖e7#.

Finally, as the game shows, it gives White a winning answer to Black's obvious defence.
31...♘f6 32 ♘d7! ♗e6
Agreeing to divert the knight from guarding the h7-square by 32...♘xd7 loses to 33 ♕h7+ and mate on h8. Meanwhile, White was threatening to exchange knights followed by ♕h7+ and mate next move.

With the text-move, Black blocks the e-file in the hope that his king can escape via e7.
33 ♖xe6! 1-0
33...fxe6 allows 34 ♗xe6#.

3)

Mayet – Anderssen
Berlin 1862

18...♘h5!
18...♖xe5!? 19 fxe5 ♘g4 20 ♘c3 ♕g6!, threatening both 21...♕h5 and 21...♘f2+, is also very good for Black.
19 bxc5
19 ♕xh5 allows 19...♕xg2#. The nicest line is 19 ♘c3 ♕xf4!! (19...♕xg2+ is good but less decisive) 20 ♖xf4 ♘xf4 21 ♕c2 ♗xg2+ 22 ♕xg2 (not 22 ♔g1 e2+ and mate next move) 22...♘xg2 23 bxc5 ♖xe5 24 ♔xg2 e2 winning a piece with an easily winning endgame.
19...♘xf4 20 ♖xf4 ♖d1+! 21 ♖f1 ♕xg2+ 22 ♕xg2 ♖xf1# (0-1)

Chapter 2: The Birth of Dynamism

4)

Alekhine – Anon
Simultaneous, Trinidad 1939

1 ♖c8! ♖xc8
The line 1...♕xd7 2 ♕f8+! demonstrates why the king's position is important – this idea would fail with the king on g8.
2 ♕e7!! ♕xe7
2...h6 allows 3 ♕xe6 fxe6 4 dxc8♕+.
3 dxc8♕+ 1-0
It is mate next move.

5)

Alekhine – Kimura
Simultaneous, Tokyo 1933

20 ♘e4!!
Deeper than it appears.
Answer to first question: After **20...♖xe7 21 ♘xf6+!** Black cannot recapture the knight as 21...gxf6 allows mate by 22 ♕g4+ ♔f8 23 ♕g7+ ♔e8 24 ♕g8#. Following **21...♔h8 22 ♘xe7 ♕xe7**, Black simultaneously threatens back-rank mate, rook and knight.

Answer to second question: Alekhine had prepared the surprising **23 ♕e4!**, threatening 24 ♕xh7#, and so forcing **23...♕xe4 24 ♘xe4**, when White remains a pawn up. This, together with his dominant rook and knight, gives him an easily winning endgame. Black resigned on move 38.

6)

Alekhine – Van Mindeno
Simultaneous, Holland 1933

14 ♖h5 ♕e6
Answer to first question: Alekhine played **15 ♖dh1 f5** (not 15...f6 16 g6 with mate to follow) **16 ♘e5!! dxe5** (or 16...♕xe5 17 g6! mating) **17 g6!** and Black resigned as after 17...♕xg6 18 ♕c4+ there is no d-pawn to

interpose so the game will end 18...♖f7 19 ♖h8#.

Answer to second question: 14...f6 would force White to proceed more slowly with 15 g6 ♕e8 16 ♘h4! ♖d8 (there is nothing constructive to do; e.g., 16...f5 17 ♖h1 ♘f6 18 ♘xf5!, or 16...♘g5 17 ♘f5! threatening 18 ♘e7+! ♕xe7 19 ♕h4) 17 ♖h1 ♖d7 18 ♕d1! ♘g5 19 ♖h8+! ♔xh8 20 ♕h5+ ♔g8 21 ♘f5 and mate on h8.

Chapter 3: The New Romantics

7)

Spassky – Tal
Tallinn 1973

26...♗b7!!
White cannot reply 27 ♕b8+? ♔h7 28 ♕xb7 because of 28...♗xf2+!, when 29 ♖xf2 allows 29...♖xc1+ and mate next move, while 29 ♔h1 loses the c2-rook. Now that his bishop is activated, Tal finishes off brilliantly.
27 ♕f3 ♕g5 28 ♕b3 ♖c7 29 g3 ♗xf2+! 30 ♔xf2 ♕f6+
30...♕f5+! 31 ♔g1 ♕e4 is the same position that Tal achieves on move 35.
31 ♔e1 ♕e5+ 32 ♔f1 ♗a6+ 33 ♔g1 ♕d4+ 34 ♔g2 ♕e4+ 35 ♔g1 ♗b7! 36 h4 ♕h1+ 37 ♔f2 ♖f7+ 38 ♔e2 ♕e4+ 0-1

8)

Thorbergsson – Tal
Reykjavik 1964

35...♗xh3+! 36 ♔xf3
36 ♔xh3 ♕h4+ 37 ♔g2 ♘e1+ costs White his queen.
36...♕g1!!
This deadly quiet move threatens to mate by 37...♗g4+ 38 ♔e4 f5#.
37 ♗xg6
37 ♗h6 allows 37...♗g4+ 38 ♔f4 ♗h5!, threatening mates on e3 and g4.
37...♕g4+ 38 ♔f2 ♕xf4+ 39 ♔g1 hxg6 0-1

9)

Tal – Beliavsky
Aker Brygge 1989

Tal invites Beliavsky to win the exchange.
15 ♕f3!? ♗g4 16 ♕g3 ♗xd1 17 ♘f5 ♗g4 18 ♘xe7+ ♔h7 19 ♕h4
It is a good idea because now Black can do nothing sensible to prevent the 'sacrifice' of the bishop on h6, after which Tal will have a pawn for the exchange and an attack against the weakened black king.
19...♘b6 20 ♗xh6! gxh6 21 ♕xf6 ♘d7 22 ♕h4 ♗e6 23 ♘cd5 ♖ae8 24 ♖d1 ♕a5 25 ♘f6+ ♘xf6 26 ♕xf6
The threat is 27 ♗xe6 fxe6 28 ♕g6+ ♔h8 29 ♕xh6#.
26...d5
26...♗xb3 allows mate after 27 ♘f5!.
27 exd5 ♗c8 28 c3 1-0

Chapter 4: The Dynamic Romantics

10)

Kasparov – Ligterink
Olympiad, Malta 1980

22 ♘c8!
The knight is immune from capture because 22...♖xc8 can be met by 23 ♕f5, threatening mate and the rook.
22...♘c6
22...♖c7 allows 23 ♖xb8 ♗f8 24 ♖fb1, unpinning the knight while it is still immune from capture.
23 ♘xa7 ♘xa7 24 ♗d5 1-0
After 24...♖f8 (or 24...♗f6 25 ♖b7 attacking the knight and f7) 25 ♖b7 ♘c8 Black is the exchange down and remains paralysed.

11)

Winants – Kasparov
Brussels 1987

47...♕xf3!!

Kasparov's idea is to exchange queens without losing time.

48 ♕xa7 ♕h1+ 49 ♔g4 h5+

49...hxg5!, threatening 50...♕h5#, leads to an even quicker win, but Kasparov's idea is very amusing.

50 ♔f4 ♕f1+ 51 ♔e5 ♕f5+ 52 ♔d6 ♕e6+ 53 ♔c7 ♕e7+ 54 ♔b6 ♕xa7+ 55 ♔xa7 c2! 0-1

It turns out that Kasparov's purpose in sacrificing his rook was to exchange queens. Now the rook is helpless against the pawn, since it can reach neither the first rank (thanks to the c-pawn itself) nor the c-file (thanks to the d-pawn).

12)

Kasparov – Van Wely
Wijk aan Zee 2000

20 ♘xe6! fxe6 21 ♖xe6+ ♔f7

21...♗e7 fails to 22 ♖xe7+, when 22...♔f8 23 ♖xd7 ♕xa4 24 ♖xb7 and 22...♘xe7 23 ♕xd7+ ♔f8 24 ♕xe7+ ♔g8 25 ♖d7 both win for White.

22 ♕d3!!

White leaves two pieces *en prise* with one move.

22...♗g7

Both Black's main alternatives lose rapidly:

a) 22...♔g8 23 ♕g6+ ♔h8 (or 23...♗g7 24 ♗xd5 ♗xd5 25 ♖e7 ♖h7 26 ♗h6 ♔f8 27 ♖de1) 24 ♖e2! ♕xa4 (or 24...♘e7 25 ♗xe7 ♗g7 26 ♖xd7 ♕xa4 27 ♗xb7) 25 ♗xd5! ♖xe2 (25...♗xd5 26 ♖xh2+) 26 ♕g8#.

b) 22...♔xe6 23 ♗xd5+ (23 ♕g6+ is also good) 23...♗xd5 24 ♕g6+ ♘f6 25 ♕xf6+ ♔d7 26 ♖xd5+ ♖xd5 27 ♘b6+ winning the queen.

23 ♕f5+ ♔g8 24 ♖xd5! ♕xa4

24...♗xd5 loses to 25 ♕xd5! ♕xd5 26 ♗xd5, attacking the rook and threatening a big discovered check.

25 ♖e7 1-0

Chapter 6: Material Matters

The Expendable Pawn

13)

D. Fridman – Shabalov
Europe vs Americas, Mermaid Beach 1998

10...d5! 11 cxb5 axb5 12 ♕xb5 ♕c7

Black dominates the centre...

13 ♕e2 ♘c6 14 ♖fc1 ♗a6 15 ♕d1 e5 16 d4 e4 17 ♘e5 ♘xe5 18 dxe5 ♕xe5 19 ♘a4 ♕f5 20 ♘xc5 ♗g4 21 ♕d2 ♗c8 22 ♖c2 h5!

...and here comes the big attack.

23 b4 h4 24 a4 hxg3 25 fxg3 ♕h5 26 h3 ♘e5 27 g4 ♗xg4! 28 hxg4 ♘xg4 29 ♗f1 ♖ad8 30 ♕d1 ♗d6 31 ♗d4 ♗h2+ 32 ♔h1 ♗g3+ 33 ♔g1 ♖d6!

Under cover of the pawns, the pieces gradually feed themselves into the attack.

34 ♖aa2 ♖h6 35 ♗g2 ♗h2+ 0-1

A deadly knight check follows on either king move, discovering an attack on the white queen.

14)

Panchenko – Chiburdanidze
USSR Ch First League, Tashkent 1980

23 f5! ♗xc4

23...gxf5 24 exf5 ♗xf5 25 ♗xb7 ♘xb7 26 ♘d5 leaves White ahead on material.

24 ♗e2! ♗xe2 25 ♕xe2

Now White has ownership of the key d5-square, which he uses to mount a brilliant attack.

25...f6 26 b4 ♘d7 27 ♘d5 ♕a8 28 ♘e7+! ♔f7 29 ♕c4+! ♔xe7 30 ♕e6+ ♔d8 31 ♖xd6 ♕a7

31...♔c8 loses to 32 ♖c1+ ♔b8 33 ♖xd7 ♖xd7 34 ♕xd7 ♕xe4 35 ♗xb6 ♕b7 36 ♕d6+ ♔a8 37 ♖c7, winning the queen.

32 ♖xd7+! 1-0

White wins the black queen after 32...♖xd7 33 ♗xb6+.

15)
Anand – Timman
Tal Memorial, Riga 1995

18 h4!?

White surprisingly opens lines in front of his own king. Anand decides that the black king is the one in danger, and his main attacking ideas, most importantly the organization of his king and rooks, can be seen from the game continuation.

18...♗xf5 19 gxf5 d5 20 ♔h1!? ♗xh4 21 ♖g1 ♗f6 22 ♘h2 g6 23 ♕f3 dxe4 24 dxe4 ♘d7 25 ♕h3 ♕e7 26 ♗e3 ♗g7 27 ♘g4 ♘f6 28 ♘xf6+ ♕xf6 29 ♖g3 ♘e7 30 ♖h2! c4 31 ♖h1 h6 32 ♗xh6 ♗xh6 33 ♕xh6 ♖ad8 34 ♔g2 ♕g7 35 ♕e3 ♖d6 36 b3 ♖c8 37 bxc4 bxc4 38 ♖hh3! ♔f8 39 ♕c1!? ♔g8 40 ♖f3 ♖cd8 41 ♖hg3 f6 42 fxg6 ♕d2 43 ♕b1 ♕f8 44 ♕h1 ♕g7 45 ♖xf6! 1-0

The Out-Gunned Rook

16)
Tal – Zaichik
Tbilisi 1988

The white bishop on c3 cannot move without exposing the e1-rook to capture.

25 ♗xf6! ♗xe1 26 ♕h5!

Tal is able to develop a rapid attack.

26...gxf6

The black king is in dire peril after 26...h6 27 ♕g4 g6 28 ♗xg6!.

27 ♕xh7+ ♔f8 28 ♕h8+ ♔e7 29 ♕xa8

A pawn ahead, Tal won the endgame.

17)
Beliavsky – Kasparov
World Cup, Barcelona 1989

32...♖xd4! eliminates the knight that was guarding the f5-square.

Until now, Black was threatened with action on the h-file. Now that Black has f5 available for his knight, he can play ...♔g7 without facing ♕h6+ in reply, and Black can himself use the h-file for attacking purposes. The knight will also support the potential advance of the passed e-pawn.

33 ♗xd4 ♘f5 34 ♕h3 ♔g7! 35 ♕c3 a5 36 c5 ♘xd4 37 ♖xd4 ♗xc5 38 ♖c4 ♖h8+ 39 ♗h3 e3+ 40 ♔h2 ♗c6 41 ♕c2 ♗a6 42 ♔g3 ♗xc4 43 ♕xc4 ♕d7 44 ♗g4 ♕d2 45 ♗e2 ♖d8

Black won the endgame using his extra pawn.

18)
Lautier – Karpov
Linares 1995

Karpov wants to mobilize his pawn-centre. 15...bxc5 loses the b7-bishop, so he dangles the temptation of winning the exchange under Lautier's nose.

15...♗a8! 16 ♗a6 ♖c7 17 ♗g3 bxc5! 18 ♗xc7 ♕xc7 19 ♕c3

Black's threat was 19...♕a5+, and 19 0-0 would allow Black to win another pawn for the exchange by 19...c4 20 ♕a4 ♗c6 21 ♗b5 ♗xb5 22 ♕xb5 ♖b8, so White allows the following clever expansion of the black central pawns.

19...e5! 20 ♗d3

There are three ways to go wrong:

a) 20 dxe5? d4 21 ♕d2 ♘xe5.

b) 20 dxc5 d4.

c) 20 0-0 exd4 21 ♘xd4 ♕b6.

20...exd4 21 ♘xd4 ♖e8+ 22 ♔f1

22 ♘e2? loses to 22...d4 23 ♕d2 c4 24 ♖c1 ♘e5.

22...♕b6 23 ♘f5 d4

Karpov's exchange sacrifice has given him a pawn, a dominant centre and an open diagonal for his bishop. He soon turns on the white king with decisive effect.

24 ♕d2 ♘e5 25 ♖e1 ♖e6! 26 ♗b1 ♗b7 27 ♔f2 d3 28 ♖hf1 c4+ 29 ♔g3 ♘h5+ 30 ♔h3 ♘g6! 31 g3 ♗c8 32 ♖e4 ♕c5 33 g4 ♘gf4+!

34 ♖xf4 ♖e2! 35 ♕c1 ♘xf4+ 36 ♕xf4 ♗xf5 37 gxf5 ♖xb2 38 ♖e1? ♕f2 39 ♕g3 ♕xg3+ 40 hxg3 ♖xb1! 0-1

The All-Powerful Queen?

19)
Reeh – Lau
Bundesliga 1993/4

20 ♕xc7 ♖xc7 21 ♖xc7
White has rook and bishop for the queen, so the deficit is only a pawn on the usual scale of material values. The rook is very well placed on the seventh rank and Black will be hard-pressed to reduce its influence. Finally, the white bishops are very strong, and there is no way for Black to prevent the dark-squared bishop from reaching e5, when Black will be almost completely hamstrung and his king will be in great danger.

All that is well illustrated in the game continuation.
21...♗c8 22 ♗e7 ♕f7 23 ♗b5 ♗d7 24 ♗d6 ♖d8 25 ♗e5 ♕e8 26 ♗a6 ♖a8 27 ♗b7 ♖b8 28 ♗a6 ♖a8 29 ♘b3 ♘c4 30 ♗xc4 dxc4 31 ♘c5 ♖d8 32 ♗f6 ♖b8 33 ♖xb8 ♕xb8 34 ♖b7! ♕f8 35 ♘xd7 ♕a3 36 ♘e5 ♕f8 37 ♖g7+ 1-0

20)
Toran – Tal
European Team Ch, Oberhausen 1961

16...♖xe3!!
Now 17 ♕xe3? ♗xd4 wins at once for Black, but Toran aims for perpetual check.
17 ♗d5+ ♔h8 18 ♘f7+ ♕xf7! 19 ♗xf7 ♖d3
Tal's compensation for the queen is two bishops and a pawn (the d-pawn goes with check next move). He is winning because the white king and queen are both going to be knocked about by the bishops and the rook.
20 ♕e2

One attractive line is 20 ♕g2 ♗xd4+ 21 ♔h1 ♘e5 22 ♗d5 c6 23 ♗e4 ♗d2!!, winning back the queen.
20...♗xd4+ 21 ♔g2 ♘e5 22 ♖d1 ♖e3 23 ♕f1 ♗e4+ 24 ♔h3 ♖f3 25 ♕e2 ♗f5+ 0-1

21)
Speelman – Azmaiparashvili
Spanish Team Ch, Cala Galdana 1994

25 ♕xh5! gxh5
25...♖xe4 loses to 26 ♗xe4 gxh5 27 ♗xe5+ ♔f8 28 ♖df1+ ♔e8 29 ♖g8+ ♔d7 30 ♗f5+ ♔c7 31 ♖g7, winning back the queen.
26 ♗xf4+ ♘g6
The alternatives all lose:
a) 26...♘g4 27 h3.
b) 26...♔h8 27 ♗g5.
c) 26...♔f8 27 ♗g5 ♕c7 28 ♖df1+ ♔e8 (or 28...♘f7 29 ♗h6+ ♔e7 30 ♖xf7+ ♔xf7 31 ♖g7+) 29 ♘f6+ ♔d8 30 ♘xh5+ ♔d7 31 ♖f7+!! ♘xf7 32 ♗f5+ ♔e8 33 ♘g7+ ♔f8 34 ♘e6+.
27 ♗g5! ♕e5
27...♕g7 loses to 28 ♘f6+ ♔h8 29 ♘xh5 ♕f7 30 ♖df1 ♕e8 31 ♗f6+ ♔g8 32 ♗c3.
28 ♘f6+ ♔h8 29 ♗xg6
29 ♘xh7! ♔xh7 30 ♗xg6+ is marginally better, but the move played leads to a terrific finish.
29...hxg6 30 ♖de1 ♕xh2 31 ♖e7!!
A rare motif – White leaves a rook to be taken with check.
31...♕xg1+ 32 ♔c2 ♕f2+ 33 ♔b3 ♕f3+ 34 ♔a2 ♕xf6 35 ♗xf6+ ♔g8 36 ♖xb7 b5 37 ♖g7+ ♔f8 38 ♖h7 bxa4 39 ♗c3 ♖e8 40 ♖h8+ ♔f7 41 ♖xe8 ♔xe8 42 ♗f6! 1-0

Chapter 8: Simple Silent Sacrifices

Inside the Silent Sacrifice

22)
In Kuijf-Hodgson, the first silent sacrifice was played with the intention of occupying

the b3-square with the knight (giving checkmate), so it was a *substitution* sacrifice. The second sacrifice lured the bishop away from the b1-h7 diagonal, so it was a *deflection* sacrifice.

23)
Alekhine – Hallegua
Paris 1914

22 ♘h7! ♚xh7 23 fxe5 ♕xf1+
23...♕g7 allows 24 ♖xf8 ♕xf8 25 ♕xh5+ ♚g8 26 ♕h8+ ♚f7 27 ♗xg6+, winning the queen, so Black prefers to give it up immediately. He was eventually mated on move 44.

When the king captured on h7, its position allowed White, in the above line, to play 25 ♕xh5+ because the g-pawn was pinned by the white bishop on d3. So 22 ♘h7 is a *decoy* sacrifice.

Square Clearance

24)
Zagorskis – Sadler
Olympiad, Elista 1998

"Somewhere else" is e4.
28...♖e4!!
After all the previous sacrifices, this move ensured that the game was widely acclaimed as the best in the Elista Olympiad.
29 ♖c3
29 fxe4 loses to 29...♗e3+ 30 ♕f2 ♕g3+!, winning the queen for nothing.
29...♖h4
This is why the black rook retreated to the e4-square.
30 f4
30 ♕xh4 is hopeless as the white pawns are vulnerable.
30...♕h1+ 31 ♚f2 ♖h2+ 32 ♚e3 ♕e4+ 0-1
After 33 ♚d2 ♗xf4+ 34 ♖e3 ♕xe3+ 35 ♚c2 ♖xe2+ Black wins everything.

Line Clearance

25)
Keres – Boleslavsky
USSR Ch, Moscow 1957

The black knight blocks the king's escape from the back rank, so with the white knight gone, ♖d8+ would force mate next move.
30 ♘b5! 1-0
The knight is immune thanks to the mate threat, so this attack on the rook wins the exchange. 30...♘f5 31 ♘xc7 ♘xd6 does not help because 32 exd6 protects the knight.

Deflection

26)
Tate – Campbell
Sutton 1987

30...♗h4!
Black deflects the white queen in order to open the a7-g1 diagonal for his own queen.
31 ♕xh4 ♘xe4+ 32 ♖f2
32 ♚h1 allows 32...♘g3+, when the queen must give up its life for the knight.
32...♘xf2 33 ♖b7
33 ♕xf2 loses to 33...♕xf2+ 34 ♚xf2 ♗xb1 (I told you that the bishop was on the same diagonal as the rook).
33...♘xh3++ 34 ♚f1 ♗d3+ 0-1
White is mated by 35 ♚e1 ♕g1+ 36 ♘f1 ♕xf1#.

27)
Schüssler – Rantanen
Stockholm 1977/8

25 ♖d7!!
This move attacks the black queen, with the point 25...♕xd7 26 ♕xd7 ♖xd7 (or 26...♖xe1 27 ♕xf7) 27 ♖xe8#. 25...♘e5 doesn't help Black, thanks to the reply 26 ♖xe5!, when the threat to the queen remains.

25...♘h6

This looks good as it threatens 26...♘xg4+ and prevents mate (...♘g8 will block a back-rank check).

26 ♕xg7+! ♔xg7

26...♖xg7 loses to 27 ♖xe8+ ♘g8 28 ♖xb7 ♖xb7 29 ♗xf6+, winning more material. Now White emerges a pawn ahead.

27 ♖xb7 ♖xb7 28 ♖xe8 c4 29 ♖e6 ♘g8 30 ♖xa6 ♖c7 31 ♗d4 1-0

28)

Ivkov – Gheorghiu
Buenos Aires 1979

31 ♖1e6!

White aims to open the seventh rank.

31...fxe6

31...♘f5 avoids mate but 32 ♕xb8 ♖xb8 33 ♖e8+ ♖xe8 34 ♖xe8+ ♔g7 35 ♖c8 brings about an easily winning endgame for White.

32 ♕f6 1-0

Mate is inevitable.

29)

Plachetka – Zinn
Děčín 1974

12 ♕h5!!

In *Informator*, Plachetka indicated that Zinn resigned here, but *Mega Database 2001* gives some further moves:

12...♘f6

12...gxh5 opens the g-file for 13 ♖g3+ ♔h8 14 ♘xf7#.

13 ♘g4!! gxh5

13...♘xg4 is met by 14 ♕xh7#, while if 13...♘xh5 then 14 ♘h6#.

14 ♘xf6+ ♔h8

It is mate after 14...♔g7 15 ♘e8++ ♔h6 16 ♗g7+ ♔g6 17 ♖g3+ ♔f5 18 ♖g5+ ♔e4 19 ♘c3#.

15 ♖xh5 h6 16 ♘xd5+ 1-0

After 16...♔h7 17 ♘xc7 ♗xc7 18 ♖xc5, White has three extra pawns.

Diversion

30)

J. Polgar – Svidler
Haifa rapidplay 1998

28 ♖d1!

The black queen cannot maintain the defence of the e-pawn. Svidler gives up his queen, as the material position is acceptable for him, but he is facing a mating attack.

28...f6 29 ♖xd4 exd4 30 ♗e6 d3 31 cxd3 ♖xd3+ 32 ♔b2 ♖d4 33 ♘c8 ♖xb4+ 34 ♔a1 1-0

31)

Yudasin – Brynell
Leningrad 1989

White could mate by ♕xh6, ♕g7 or ♕g8 if only he could divert the knight or the queen from protecting those squares. A double diversion is required, and **21 ♘d6!!** does the trick. Black resigned after **21...♗e6 22 ♘xf5**.

32)

Horowitz – Kevitz
New York 1931

The mating sequence starts with **22 ♕g5!**, threatening mate on g7. As 22...♕xg5 allows 23 ♖xe8#, **22...g6** is forced. Now comes a cascade of sacrifices that must be accepted: **23 ♕h6! gxf5 24 ♖g4+! fxg4 25 ♗xh7+ ♔h8 26 ♗g6+ ♔g8 27 ♕h7+ ♔f8 28 ♕xf7# (1-0)**.

Decoy

33)

Fischer – Shocron
Mar del Plata 1959

After **39 ♖xe6! ♕c8**, Fischer's **40 ♗d7!!** forced resignation since 40...♕xd7 41 ♖xg6+ wins the black queen.

34)

Wagner – Rellstab
Swinemünde 1930

20 ♖e8!!

The intention is to decoy the black queen to e8, where it will be lost to a knight fork after 20...♕xe8 21 ♘h5+ ♔h7 22 ♘f6+.

The sacrifice is a diversion as well as a decoy, as the queen was originally covering the f6-square.

20...♕g5 21 ♕e3(?)

White misses a lovely mate by 21 h4!! ♕xg3 22 ♖e7+ ♔f6 23 ♖f7#, but even after the text-move Black's king remains in a helpless state.

21...h5 22 ♕e5+ 1-0

35)

Keres – Alexander
Hastings 1954/5

16 ♘e5!! ♘xe5 17 ♗f5!

Keres decoys the black queen to the f5-square.

17...♕xf5 18 ♖xe5 ♕d3

Protecting the bishop by 18...♕d7 allows White a very strong attack with 19 ♕xa7 ♕e8 (or 19...♕d6 20 ♖e3 ♕a6 21 ♕xa6 bxa6 22 ♖xe7 with an extra pawn) 20 ♖ae1 ♘e4 21 ♕a8+ ♔d7 22 ♕xb7 and now both options leave White well ahead:

a) 22...♘d6 allows 23 ♖xe7+ ♕xe7 24 ♖xe7+ ♔xe7 25 ♕xc7+ with a queen and three pawns against two rooks.

b) 22...f6 loses Black's queen to 23 ♖xd5+ ♘d6 24 ♗xd6.

Therefore, Black must allow his bishop to be captured. 18...♕g6! is the best way, when 19 ♖xe7 ♖d7 20 ♖xd7 ♘xd7 21 ♕xa7 leaves White a pawn ahead. Alexander's choice loses quickly, as Black cannot avoid loss of material.

19 ♖xe7 ♖d7 20 ♖e3! ♕a6 21 ♕xa6 bxa6 22 ♗e5 1-0

Interference

36)

Fuchs – Korchnoi
Erevan 1965

25...♗d3!!

The bishop cuts the communication between White's rooks and bishop. Now 26 ♖(either)xd3 interferes with the line of the bishop to f1 so that 26...♖e1+ is mate next move. White must lose the exchange.

26 ♗xd3 ♕xd6 27 ♗f1 ♕c5 0-1

37)

H. Johner – P. Johner
Frankfurt 1905

There are two potential mates: 1 h3+ ♔g3 2 ♖f3, covered by the b7-bishop, and 1 h3+ ♔g3 2 ♗e1, covered by the e8-rook. The solution is to interfere with the two lines: **1 ♗e4!! 1-0**. 1 h3+ ♔g3 2 ♗e4!! is the same, but the move played is a little more artistic.

38)

Rusakov – Verlinsky
Moscow 1947

7...♘e4 may well be best, but it is Black who is winning after **7...dxc3 8 exf6?** (8 ♘xc3 is much better), since **8...cxb2 9 ♕e2+ ♕e7!!** forces White to block the e-file himself. The game concluded **10 fxe7 ♗g7! 0-1**. Black wins back a whole rook and queen, emerging the exchange ahead.

Substitution

39)

P.H. Nielsen – Larsen
Danish Ch, Esbjerg 1997

The sequence 23...♕h1+ 24 ♔f2 ♘e4+ leaves the white king with no squares, but the e4-square is guarded by the white f-pawn. A substitution sacrifice overcomes that problem.

23...♗e4!! 24 fxe4

24 ♕d2 loses two exchanges to 24...♗xb1 25 ♖xb1 ♕h1+, although Black might prefer to keep attacking with 24...e5!?.

24...♕h1+ 25 ♔f2 ♘xe4+

White must give up his queen in return for the knight.

26 ♕xe4 ♕xe4 27 ♗f3 ♕h4+ 28 ♔g2 a4 29 b4 ♖ac8 30 ♖bc1 d5 31 cxd5 exd5 32 ♖c5 ♕e7 33 ♗f2 b6 34 ♖b5 ♖c4 35 ♔f1 ♕d6 36 ♖xd5 ♕xb4 37 ♖d7 ♕a3 38 ♗d5 ♕h3+ 0-1

Line-Grabbing

40)
Ranneforth – Dobell
Berlin 1903

22 ♖e7! ♕d8 23 ♕e5!! 1-0

23...♗xe5 allows 24 ♗xe5#, and 23...♕f8 is no defence because 24 ♖e8 forces mate in any case.

41)
Bednarski – Minev
Berne 1975

17 ♖d5!! exd5

17...♕b4 18 ♗d4! exd5 19 ♗xd5+ is very similar. Now the white bishop changes direction by grabbing the a2-g8 diagonal. The black king is battered by White's rampant pieces.

18 ♗xd5+ ♔e8 19 ♗d2 ♗b4

19...♕b6 is better but White has a strong attack after 20 ♖e1+ ♗e7 21 ♕a3.

20 ♕h5+! g6 21 ♕e2+ ♔d8 22 ♗g5+ ♔c7 23 ♗f4+ ♔b6 24 ♕e3+ ♕c5 25 ♗xb8 ♕xe3+ 26 fxe3 ♗b7 27 ♗e5! ♖e8 28 ♗d4+ ♔c7 29 ♗xb7 ♔xb7

Black has emerged two pawns down and he resigned on move 49.

Chapter 9: Complex Silent Sacrifices

♘d5 and All That

42)
D. Shaw – P. Peck
Smith & Williamson, Witley 2000

The first point of **18 ♘d5** is that acceptance of the sacrifice loses a pawn for Black because 18...exd5 19 exd5 attacks the queen with the pawn and discovers an attack on the e7-bishop. The presence of the knight on d7 means that the queen cannot get back to protect the bishop.

The second point is that declining the offer by **18...♖e8?** allows the exchange of Black's dark-squared bishop, whereupon White can win the d-pawn, which is what happened in the game: **19 ♘xe7+ ♖xe7 20 ♕d2 h6 21 ♕xd6 ♕xd6 22 ♖xd6** and White won on move 36.

Black should retreat his bishop by 18...♗f8, when he has nothing immediate to fear.

43)
R. Fridman – K. Kneip
Recklinghausen 2000

After **15 ♘d5 exd5 16 cxd5 ♘db8 17 ♘d4 ♕d7 18 dxc6 ♘xc6**, White played a well-calculated attack:

19 ♘f5! f6 20 ♗c4+ ♔h8 21 ♕g5! g6

21...fxg5 allows 22 ♗xg7#, while 21...♖g8 simply loses the exchange to 22 ♕g4.

22 ♖xd6! ♕c7

22...♗xd6 loses to 23 ♗xf6+ (or 23 ♕xf6+), mating.

23 ♘xe7! ♕xd6 24 ♘xg6+! ♔g7

24...hxg6 allows 25 ♕h6#.

25 ♘xf8+ ♔xf8 26 ♕g8+ 1-0

44)
Nunn – Marin
Interzonal tournament, Szirak 1987

After **14 ♘d5 ♘xd3+ 15 ♕xd3 exd5 16 exd5 ♗e7**, Nunn played **17 ♘c6! ♗xc6 18 dxc6**.

Now Black should give back the piece by 18...0-0 19 cxd7 ♕xd7, although the isolated black d-pawn gives White the advantage. His chosen defence allowed a decisive double sacrifice.

18...♘f6? 19 ♗b6!

This line-clearance and diversion sacrifice leads to a second sacrifice.

19...♕xb6 20 ♖xe7+! ♚f8

20...♚xe7 allows 21 ♕xd6+ ♚e8 22 ♖e1+, winning. Now White gains a second pawn for the piece and keeps a powerful attack.

21 ♕xd6 ♚g8 22 g5 hxg5 23 fxg5 ♖c8 24 c7! ♕xd6 25 ♖xd6 ♘g4 26 ♖d8+ ♚h7 27 ♖ed7! 1-0

Multiple Motifs

45)

LeMoir – A.D. Martin
Hertfordshire vs Essex 1977

White played **29 ♗f7!**, blocking the queen's defence of h7 and so threatening mate by the queen on h7. 29...♖xf7 allows another mate by 30 ♖xe8+ ♚g7 31 ♕xh7+ ♚f6 32 ♖e6#. Black gave up a rook by **29...h5** and resigned four moves later.

46)

Horwitz – Popert
Hamburg 1844

White is obliged to defend against mate on h2. The fact that the black king is surrounded by its own pieces provides a clue to White's combination. The move ♗xa6 is mate for White if the black b-pawn can be removed. The pawn can be removed by White playing ♕xc6+, but the rook must move from d5 first, and meanwhile the black queen is guarding the c6-square. It is extremely convenient for

White that the same move that defends against the mate can be used to clear the queen's line and divert the black queen.

1 ♖h5!! ♕xh5 2 ♕xc6+! bxc6 3 ♗xa6# (1-0)

47)

Tal – Grigorian
Erevan 1982

25 ♗f5!

Tal combines clearance of the e-file with deflection (25...gxf5 26 ♕g5+) and diversion (25...♖xe1+ 26 ♖xe1 ♗xf5 27 ♖e8#). Grigorian now covers the critical e1-square.

25...♕c3

The remainder of Tal's combination revolves around regaining the e1-square.

26 ♖xe8+ ♗xe8 27 ♖c1 ♕e5 28 ♕d8! gxf5 29 ♚f1! 1-0

The alternative 29 ♗d2 carries the same threat, but 29...♘c6! 30 ♕xa8 ♘d4! gives Black chances to survive. After the move played, Black cannot prevent ♖e1. Tal gave the line 29...♘d7 30 ♕xa8 ♘f8 31 ♖e1! ♗b5+ 32 ♚g2 ♕xe1 33 ♕xf8#.

Chapter 10: Brilliant Blunders

Passive Sacrifices

48)

Mkpadi – Alboni
Richmond rapidplay 1998

24...d4!!

This passive queen sacrifice leaves White amusingly helpless against a rook invasion on h2 and subsequent checkmate.

25 ♘xc6 ♗xc6 26 ♖e1 ♖xh2+ 27 ♚g1 ♖xg2+ 28 ♚f1 ♖h1+ 29 ♗g1 ♖hxg1# (0-1)

49)

S. Finn – R. Heasman
England 1993

The white king is badly placed, but Black needs to strike before White is able to cover the d-file with ♘bd2. He sacrifices his queen on both of the next two moves.

12...♘xd5!! 13 cxd5

13 ♕xc5 allows 13...♘e3++, and now:

a) 14 ♔e2 ♗xc4+ 15 ♕xc4 ♘xc4+ 16 ♘e5 ♘4xe5 leaves Black a pawn ahead.

b) 14 ♔e1 ♘c2+ 15 ♔e2 ♗xc4#.

13...♗xd5! 14 ♕xc5 ♗b3++ 15 ♔c1 ♖d1# (0-1)

50)

B. Anderson – P. Garbett
New Zealand Ch, Auckland 1977

The combination starts innocently enough.

27 ♖xf6! ♗b5

The idea behind the exchange sacrifice is 27...gxf6 28 ♕h4 ♖g8 29 ♕xf6+ ♖g7 30 ♗h6 ♖g8 31 ♕h1! ♕xc2 32 ♖g1 ♕f2 33 ♗xg7+ ♖xg7 34 ♕xc6, when White wins with his extra piece because 34...♖xg2?? 35 ♕e8+ ♔g7 36 ♖xg2+ is curtains.

28 ♕h4!

White leaves both rooks *en prise*. Note that he must avoid 28 ♖b6 ♗xf1 29 f6 g6 30 ♗xf1 ♕xc2, when any advantage probably lies with Black.

28...♖g8

Forced, as after 28...♗xf1 White could play the silent rook sacrifice 29 ♖h6! gxh6 30 ♕f6+ ♔g8 31 ♗xh6 leading to mate. Now White leaves his f6-rook *en prise* for one more move.

29 ♖f3!! gxf6 30 ♕xh7+! ♔xh7 31 ♖h3+ 1-0

After 31...♔g7 White mates with 32 ♗h6+ and 33 ♗f8#.

The Unpinning Sacrifice

51)

Spielmann – Tartakower
Marienbad 1925

29 ♕h6!

The threat is mate in one. Black has no good defence to the mate and, despite being able to capture the rook with check, he has no way of pursuing the white king afterwards.

29...♕xe1+ 30 ♗f1 ♖e8 31 ♕g7# (1-0)

52)

Marić – Gligorić
Belgrade 1962

19...♖xc3!

Black pins his own rook against his queen because he has seen a decisive answer to White's forced reply.

20 ♖xf5 ♖b3!! 0-1

Black not only ignores the attack on his queen, but also unpins his rook by attacking the unprotected white queen and threatening mate on the back rank. White is obliged to give up either his queen or the f5-rook.

53)

Gargulak – Kogan
1909

White first draws the black queen onto an unprotected square by playing 1 ♖xe5!. After **1...♕xe5** he unpins his knight, attacking the unprotected queen with **2 ♘g6!!**. Black should now give up his queen by 2...hxg6, when he has drawing chances, but instead he allowed mate by **2...♕xh2? 3 ♘de7# (1-0)**. 2...♕xd5? also allows a pretty finish: 3 ♘e7+ ♔h8 4 ♕xh7+! ♔xh7 5 ♖h1+ ♕h5 6 ♖xh5#.

The Shunning Sacrifice

54)

Alekhine – Sämisch
Vienna 1922

After **14...♗xc3**, Alekhine's reply **15 ♗xf7!** threatens 16 ♘e6#. Not only has White won a pawn, but the black king is also distinctly uncomfortable. The game finished **15...♔c7 16 ♘e6+ ♔b8 17 bxc3 ♘de5 18 ♗f4 ♗xe6 19 ♗xe6 ♖f8 20 ♗g3 1-0**.

55)

Hennigan – Short
British League (4NCL) 2000/1

After **24 ♗xh8** Black refuses to capture the white rook, preferring instead to use the g2-pawn in his mating attack:

24...♕g3!

Exploiting the pin on the f-pawn to bring the queen into the attack. White has no defence to the mating threats.

25 ♗d4 ♕h3! 0-1

56)

Dely – Donner
Maroczy Memorial, Budapest 1961

19 ♘c6+! ♗xc6 20 ♖xa6!

White refuses to recapture the bishop because 20 ♖xc6 loses material to 20...♕xc6! 21 dxc6 ♗c5+ 22 ♖d4 ♖xd4 23 ♕f1 ♖d1+, etc. Leaving the bishop where it is allows him to gain time for the assault on the black king.

20...♗xd5

After 20...♗b7 21 ♖d6 ♕xd6 22 ♗f4 White wins the queen.

21 ♖b6+!

White could win by 21 ♖xd6 ♕xd6 22 ♗f4 or 21 ♗xd5, but he finds a quicker way.

21...♗b7 22 ♕xd6+! ♕xd6 23 ♖xb7+ ♔a8 24 ♖b4+ ♔a7 25 ♖a3+ ♔a6 26 ♖b7+ ♔a8 27 ♖xa6# (1-0)

Ambush!

57)

King – LeMoir
Hertfordshire vs Kent 1981

11...♕e8 equalizes comfortably, but Black has a stronger option.

11...♘d4!

If White goes ahead with 12 ♘f7+, then after 12...♖xf7 13 ♕xf7 ♗e6 the queen is ambushed in the truest sense – it is completely surrounded. Now the future grandmaster's pieces start to go backwards.

12 f3 ♗c8 13 ♗a4 c6 14 ♗b3

14 ♕a2 avoids the ruin of his pawn position, but puts his queen out of play.

14...d5! 15 ♕d3 h6 16 ♘h3 ♗xh3 17 gxh3 ♘xb3 18 cxb3

White's position is in tatters. I went on to win the game.

58)

Winter – E. Steiner
Olympiad, Hamburg 1930

After **13...♗f5 14 ♗xf5 ♖xe2**, White calculated that Black intended to reply to 15 dxc6 by homing in on his back rank. Still he went ahead:

15 dxc6! ♕xd4+ 16 ♔h1 ♕f2 17 ♖g1 ♖e1

Black's mating threats appear to be decisive.

18 ♗e3!!

White turns the tables by clearing his back rank with a gain of time.

18...♕xe3 19 ♖gxe1 ♗xe1 20 cxb7

Now White is on the attack.

20...♖e8 21 ♗e4 ♖f8 22 ♕b5 1-0

22...♖b8 loses at once to 23 ♕f5 followed by 24 ♕c8+.

59)

D. Shire – LeMoir
West of England Ch, Weston-super-Mare 1988

26...♗c3! 27 ♖d3

White declines the chance to protect the a-pawn with 27 ♖c1 followed by 28 ♖c2 since that allows 27...♖d8!, penetrating along the d-file.

27...b4! 28 a4

This is White's idea for safeguarding his a-pawn, as capturing *en passant* loses the black bishop. With this apparently clever idea, White has ridden into the ambush.

28...bxa3!! 29 ♖xc3 a2 30 ♖c1 ♖b8! 31 ♖a1 ♖xb3 32 ♖xa2

White realizes that he must either allow the pawn to promote after 32...♖b1+ or bow to the inevitable. He decides to bow.

32...♖b1# (0-1)

Chapter 11: Tail-Lights

The Quiet Follow-Up

60)
LeMoir – L. Retallick
Norfolk vs Cambridgeshire 2001

After **21 ♖xd6! cxd6 22 ♕xd6+ ♔e8**, I played **23 ♗g7!** threatening mate on f8, which can only be prevented by 23...♕d3, giving up the black queen. Therefore Black resigned. 23 ♗f6 is also decisive, since after 23...♕b7, 24 ♖d5 ends all resistance.

61)
King – Van der Wiel
Palma de Mallorca 1989

White gave up his rook by **34 ♘xe5! ♗xg4**. Now the black queen is attacked, but so is White's own queen. He solved his problem with the quiet move **35 ♕d4!!**.

White preserves his queen while threatening a discovered check by the knight, which cannot be prevented by 35...♗f6 because 36 ♕a7+ allows the knight to take the black queen next move.

White soon regained the exchange and won the endgame with his extra pawn.

35...♘e6 36 ♗xe6 ♕xe6 37 ♘xg4+ ♔h7 38 ♘gf6+ ♗xf6 39 ♘xf6+ ♔h6 40 ♘g4+ ♔h7 41 ♘f6+ ♔h6 42 ♘xe8 ♕e1+ 43 ♔h2 ♕xe8 44 c4 bxc4 45 ♕xc4 ♕f8 46 ♔g1 ♕f6

47 b5 ♕a1+ 48 ♕f1 ♕xa5 49 bxa6 g4 50 g3 g5 51 ♕c4 ♔h5 52 ♕f7+ ♔h6 53 ♕b7 1-0

The Sting in the Tail

62)
Anikaev – Seoev
Beltsy 1979

23 ♖c1! ♗xe1 24 ♕xb6!

Spectacular stuff. After the passive sacrifice of his e1-rook, White plays a queen sacrifice to remove the protection of Black's c8-rook.

24...♖e8

Both 24...axb6 and 24...♖xc1 allow mate on the move, but now White cannot recapture the bishop as his queen is still *en prise*.

25 f6!!

The sting in the tail, attacking the black queen. Now 25...exf6 allows the white queen to escape by 26 ♕d6+, and 25...♕xf6 allows the exchange of queens followed by the recapture of the bishop. Black's chosen defence doesn't stop the white queen escaping with check.

25...♕g5 26 fxe7+ ♕xe7 27 ♕h6+ ♔g8 28 ♖xe1 ♕e4+ 29 ♔h2 ♕e5+ 30 f4 ♕b2 31 ♖g1+ ♔h8 32 ♖g2 1-0

Quiet Stings

63)
Tal – Averbakh
USSR Team Ch semi-final, Riga 1961

From the second diagram, Tal played the quiet sting **26 ♗b3!**, not only threatening the f7-pawn, but also pinning the f-pawn so that he can continue to hound the king by capturing the g6-pawn.

26...♖b7 27 ♕xg6+ ♔f8 28 ♕h6+ ♔e8

28...♔g8 allows 29 ♖d6! with the deadly threat of 30 ♖g6#.

29 ♖d5 ♕b6 30 ♕h8+ ♔e7 31 ♕xc8 1-0

64)

Ivkov – Cirić
Yugoslav Ch, Zenica 1963

After the initial sacrifice, Black's moves are all forced:

28 ♖xg7+! ♔xg7 29 ♕g6+ ♔h8 30 ♕xh6+ ♔g8 31 ♕g6+ ♔h8 32 h6! ♖g8 33 ♗xf6+ ♘xf6 34 ♕xf6+ ♔h7

Now comes the quiet sting.

35 ♗f1!

The threat is 36 ♗d3+.

35...♗a6

35...e5 allows 36 ♗h3! ♗c8 37 d7, winning at once.

36 ♗xa6 ♕xb3 37 d7 ♖xg3+ 38 fxg3 ♕xg3+ 39 ♔f1 ♕h3+ 40 ♔e1 ♕g3+ 41 ♔d2 1-0

65)

Kovačević – Meštrović
Yugoslav Ch, Kraljevo 1967

27...♕h4! 28 ♖g4!!

This silent sacrifice diverts the queen from guarding the h6-square.

28...♕xg4 29 ♕h6+ ♔g8 30 ♕h7+ ♔f8 31 ♕h8+ ♔e7 32 ♕xe8+ ♔f6 33 ♕f7+ ♔g5

This is all forced, and now comes the quiet sting.

34 ♕g7!

White's threat of discovered check proves deadly.

34...♗xd5 35 ♗e4+(?)

White misses the immediate win 35 ♗e8+ ♔f5 (or 35...♔h4 36 ♕h6+) 36 ♗xd7+ and so slightly spoils the aesthetic effect of his fine combination.

35...♔h4 36 ♕xg4+ ♔xg4 37 ♗xd5

Black was able to play on until move 45 before resigning.

Chapter 12: Pawns Passed and Present

Passed Pawn Connections

66)

Csom – Yusupov
Olympiad, Lucerne 1982

41 ♖xd4! exd4 42 e5 ♕g7 43 e6 ♕f6

Black cannot save his rook, because after 43...♖f6, 44 e7+ wins the other rook and promotes at the same time. White will regain the rook and retain a dangerous passed pawn.

44 e7 d3 45 exd8♕+ ♕xd8 46 ♖d1 ♕e8 47 ♕xd3 ♕e5 48 ♖d2 ♗f8 49 ♖e2 ♕f4 50 ♖e4 ♕c1 51 d7 ♕b2+ 52 ♔f3 1-0

67)

Scherbakov – Hebden
Port Erin 2000

White is able to remove Black's a- and b-pawns.

28 ♖xa7! ♖xa7 29 ♗xb6 ♕b8 30 ♗xa7 ♕xa7 31 b6 ♕a8 32 a6 ♗c8 33 ♕b2 e4 34 b7! ♕b8 35 ♕b6 ♗f6 36 ♗g4!

White can also win prettily by 36 ♕xd6 ♕xd6 37 bxc8♕+.

1-0

Since 36...♗xg4 loses at once to 37 a7.

68)

Uhlmann – Bellon
Bucharest 1978

19 exd6! ♗xf1 20 ♗xf1!

The combination appears very effective since now after 20...cxd6, 21 ♗xd6 ♖fc8 22 ♗h3 regains the exchange for White with an extra (passed) pawn. However, Black can do better than that.

20...g5!

Black has in mind 21 ♗xg5 cxd6 22 ♗e7 ♖fd8, when his superior knight gives him permanent compensation for the pawn. Uhlmann has a radical solution.

21 dxc7!! gxf4 22 d6

White is a rook for two pawns down, but what pawns they are!

22...f3 23 ♖c1 ♘d7 24 ♗b5! ♘b6 25 d7 ♔g7 26 ♗c6 ♖ad8 27 cxd8♕ ♖xd8 28 ♖e1 ♖b8 29 h4 ♔f6 30 g4! 1-0

The Mating Habits of the Passed Pawn

69)

Anand – Izeta
Madrid 1993

24 ♗xh7!
This forces the rook to move, since the king is too exposed if the bishop is left alone.
24...♖xh7 25 f7+
This brings White's bishop into play.
25...♘g7 26 ♗xg7+ 1-0
After 26...♔xg7 27 ♘f5++, 27...♔h8 allows 28 ♖g8#, and any other move loses the rook, with mate to follow.

70)

Topalov – Speelman
PCA/Intel Grand Prix, Moscow 1995

20 dxe6! fxe5
20...♕xe5 21 exd7 ♖d8 22 ♗f4 wins the queen as 22...♕f5 23 ♗d6# is mate.
21 e7+! 1-0
White mates by 21...♔xe7 22 ♕xg7+ ♔d6 23 ♕f6+ ♔c5 24 ♗e3#.

The Pawn-Dash

71)

Tarjan – Webb
Hastings 1977/8

24 h5! f6 25 hxg6!! hxg6
White's idea was 25...fxe5 26 gxh7+ ♔xh7 (the dashing pawn dies, but in a good cause) 27 ♖h1+ ♔g6 28 ♕h6+ ♔f7 29 ♕h7+ ♔e8 30 ♕g6+ ♔d8 31 ♖h8+ ♔c7 32 ♕c6#.
26 ♕h6! fxe5 27 ♕xg6+ ♔f8 28 ♕f5+ ♔e8 29 ♕c8+ ♔f7 30 ♕e6+ ♔g7 31 ♕xe5+ ♔f7 32 ♕f5+ ♔g8 33 ♖h1 ♖b6 34 ♕h7+

♔f8 35 ♕h8+ ♔f7 36 ♖h7+ ♔g6 37 ♕g7+ ♔f5 38 ♖h5+ 1-0

72)

Forgacs – Duras
Hamburg 1910

37 hxg6!! dxe3?
Black should halt White's pawn-dash by 37...hxg6, although White can gain a fierce attack by 38 ♕h2!, with the threat of 39 ♕h8+ ♔e7 40 ♕f6#.
38 gxh7! ♔e7 39 ♖xe3!!
White could play simply 39 ♕xd5 ♗xd5 40 g6, but the flashy text-move intends to meet 39...♕xd2 with 40 ♗f6+ ♔f8 41 h8♕#.
39...♖f8 40 ♕xd5 ♗xd5 41 h8♕
41 g6 also wins.
41...♖xh8 42 ♗f6+ ♔f8 43 ♗xh8
White eventually won with his three extra pawns.

Chapter 13: Multiplication

Multiple Methods

73)

N. McDonald – D. McMahon
London 1994

19 ♗h6!! 1-0
The three main lines are:
a) 19...♗xh5 20 ♗xg7#.
b) 19...gxh6 20 ♕xh6 ♖f7 (or 20...♗g6 21 ♕g7#) 21 ♖xf7 ♗xf7 22 ♕xf6+ and mate in two more moves.
c) 19...♖g8 20 ♗xg7+! ♖xg7 21 ♕xe8+! ♖g8 (or 21...♖xe8 22 ♖xe8+ and mate next move) 22 ♕f7 mating.

74)

Mason – Janowski
Monte Carlo 1902

49 ♘d4!!

This is a passive sacrifice of the queen, a silent (deflection) sacrifice of the knight and an unpinning sacrifice of a rook all in one go.

49...♖xb2

Black has no choice. Capturing the knight loses the b8-rook, while after 49...♖xh8 50 ♖xb4 the black queen is unable to escape capture; e.g., 50...♕e8 51 ♖b7+ ♔d8 52 ♖b8+ ♔e7 53 ♖1b7+ ♔f8 54 ♖xe8+ ♔xe8 55 ♖b8+ winning the h8-rook.

50 ♕xb8! ♖xb8 51 ♖xb8 ♔c7 52 ♘xe6+ ♔xb8 53 ♘d4 ♔c7

Black is tied to the defence of the c-pawn and cannot resist White's kingside advance.

54 g4 h4 55 c3 ♔d7 56 ♔g1 ♔c7 57 ♔f2 ♔d7 58 f5 gxf5 59 gxf5 ♔c7 60 ♔e3 ♗g2 61 ♘f3 ♗xh3 62 ♘xh4 ♗g4 63 ♔f4 ♗e2 64 ♘f3 ♗xf3 65 ♔xf3 1-0

75)

Pein – Engqvist
Wrexham 1995

17 ♘f5!!

White exploits the a1-h8 diagonal with a silent knight sacrifice that also unguards the g2-bishop.

17...♔h8

This is the best try. Black can choose between five other feasible defences:

a) After 17...exf5 18 ♗xd5 White wins the exchange.

b) 17...♗xg2 18 ♘h6+! ♔h8 (18...gxh6 loses to 19 ♖xd7!) 19 ♖xd7! ♕xd7 and now the finish 20 ♕xf6! gxf6 21 ♗xf6# is one we have seen before, in Sikorski-Anon on page 74.

c) 17...♕xb3 18 ♘e7+ ♔h8 19 ♘xd5 removes the queen's guard and wins a piece.

d) 17...♖fe8 loses the exchange to 18 ♘d6.

e) 17...♖fd8 18 ♗xd5 exd5 19 ♖xd5 ♕xd5? 20 ♘e7+ and White wins the queen.

18 ♘xg7! ♔xg7

18...♗xg2 is better, but White wins by 19 ♘h5! ♗xf1 20 ♖xf1 e5! 21 ♘xf6 ♕c6! 22

♘xd7 ♕xd7 23 ♕xe5+ f6 24 ♕xc5, followed by the advance of the e-pawn.

19 e4! ♕xb3

19...♗c6 allows 20 ♖xd7 ♕xd7 21 ♕xf6+ ♔g8 22 ♕g7#.

20 ♕c1! 1-0

Pein gives the line 20...h6 21 exd5 e5 22 f4 ♖ae8 23 fxe5 ♘xe5 24 ♖xf6! ♗xf6 25 ♖e1 ♔g7 26 ♗xe5+ as an illustration of the hopelessness of Black's cause.

Chapter 14: Preparing to Sacrifice

76)

Alekhine – Flohr
Bled 1931

28 ♖c8 fails to 28...♕d6, protecting the rook, so Alekhine played **28 e5!** to cut out this defence. After 28...fxe5 29 ♕xe5, White has a positional advantage, but Flohr played **28...f5?** and resigned after **29 ♖c8!**.

77)

I. Zaitsev – Bonch-Osmolovsky
Moscow 1969

♘g5 would be mate if Black's king were on e6 and his h-pawn were missing. The sacrifice in order to sacrifice is an offer of the exchange to drag the king to e6.

1 ♗xe6+ ♗xe6 2 ♖xe6! ♔xe6

Now comes the main sacrifice to free up the g5-square.

3 ♕xh6!! 1-0

3...♖xh6 allows 4 ♘g5# and 3...f4 4 ♕g5 ♖hf8 5 ♕g4+ ♔f5 6 ♕xg6+ ♔e7 7 ♘g5 gives White decisive threats.

78)

Pachman – Bronstein
Moscow vs Prague 1946

20...♖xa1! 21 ♖xa1 ♗xd4 22 ♖xd4 ♘xb3 23 ♖xd6

Now the natural continuation 23...♘xa1 24 ♘d5 ♕xf2 25 ♘f6+ ♔h8 26 ♘xe8 hxg3+ 27 ♔h1 ♘c2 28 ♖d2 ♕e1+ 29 ♖xe1 ♘xe1 leads to the better endgame for White, whose rook is very powerful. Bronstein probably saw at the outset that he could, and should, now turn his attention to the white king. He starts with an unguarding sacrifice of the b3-knight.

23...♕xf2! 24 ♖a2

24 ♕xb3 loses to 24...hxg3+ 25 ♔h1 ♗xh3! 26 ♖g1 ♗g2+ 27 ♖xg2 ♕f1+ 28 ♖g1 ♕h3#.

24...♕xg3+ 25 ♔h1 ♕xc3 26 ♖a3

26 ♖d3 ♕c1! is a crucial resource that Bronstein needed to see in advance.

26...♗xh3 27 ♖xb3 ♗xg2+ 28 ♔xg2 ♕xc4 29 ♖d4 ♕e6 30 ♖xb7 ♖a8 31 ♕e2 h3+ 0-1

After 32 ♔g1 ♕e5 33 ♖d1 ♖a3 White is helpless.

Answers to Level 1 Test

1.1)
Réti – Duras
Opatija 1912

21 ♘g5!

A nice self-fork combining a silent and a passive sacrifice.

21...♘f8

Black defends h7. Neither piece can be captured, as 21...fxe5 22 ♕h7# and 21...fxg5 22 ♕f7+ ♔h8 23 ♕xg7# demonstrate.

22 ♕f7+ ♔h8 23 ♖f4! 1-0

There is no good defence to the threat of 24 ♖h4+ followed by mate.

1.2)
Makogonov – Reshevsky
Leningrad/Moscow 1939

35 ♖h8!

White's idea is 35...♔xh8 36 ♕xh6+ ♔g8 37 ♕h7+ ♔f8 38 ♕f7#, so Black must decline the sacrifice.

35...♕xg6 36 ♗f5 1-0

36...♕g5 allows 37 ♖h7+ winning the knight and after 36...♕d6 37 ♖h7+ ♔f8 38 ♖xh6 White mates or wins the queen.

1.3)
Portisch – Hort
Nikšić 1978

23 ♕xf6!

An unguarding sacrifice of the exchange.

23...♕xe2 24 ♗c1!

A deadly quiet move, saving the attacked bishop and simply threatening 25 ♗h6 with mate on g7. 24...♖e6 fails to push the white queen away as it leaves the f-pawn *en prise*. Black must give up his queen to make ...♖e6 possible.

24...♕xf1+ 25 ♕xf1 ♖xe4 26 ♗h6 1-0

After 26...♖e6 27 dxc5 bxc5 28 ♕b5, the black pawns start to fall.

1.4)
Leyton – P. McCabe
Hayes 1972

27 ♗f8! is a line-clearance and diversion sacrifice that threatens 28 ♖xh8+ ♔xh8 29 ♕h5+ followed by mate on f7 or h8. There is no good defence, and so Black resigned.

1.5)
Norwood – D. Collier
Isle of Man 1996

31 ♕d8!!

White forces promotion, since 31...♖xd8 allows 32 e7+, capturing the rook next move. Now 31...♕e1+ 32 ♔g2 ♔f8 33 ♕xd6+ ♔g8 34 ♕d7 is no good for Black, so he tries a desperate counter-sacrifice.

31...♕f3+!?

Black's idea is that he can now meet 32 ♗xf3 with 32...♖xd8 because 33 e7 is no longer check. White still wins very comfortably after 33...♖e8 34 ♘f5, but he prefers a pretty little shunning idea.

32 ♔g1! 1-0

White will escape from the checks without capturing the queen.

1.6)
Tartakower – Alekhine
Nottingham 1936

29...♘h2!

A surprisingly complex little move. It intends to decoy the queen to h2 and clear both the g4-square and the line to h4 for the rook to win it there: 30 ♕xh2 ♖g4+ 31 ♔h1 ♖h4. Meanwhile, the threat is 30...♖g4.

White gives up his queen another way but soon abandons the fight.

30 ♖e3 ♖f1+ 31 ♔xf1 ♘xf1 32 ♔xf1 ♕f7+ 33 ♔g2 ♕xc4 34 ♖e7 ♕d5+ 35 ♔h3 h5 0-1

1.7)
Alekhine – Bogoljubow
Dresden 1936

Black has played his rook to f6 so that he can reply to 40 ♖xa6 with 40...♗xd4 41 ♖xf6 ♗xf6, with an extra piece. Alekhine decides to fall into the trap, because his pawns will be unstoppable.

40 ♖xa6! ♗xd4 41 ♖xf6 ♗xf6 42 a5 ♗e5 43 b5 h4 44 a6 1-0

1.8)
Kotronias – King
New York 1990

After **26 ♕h6!** King resigned in view of 26...gxh6 27 ♘xh6#. The combination is identical to I.Rabinovich-Goglidze on page 82.

1.9)
Podgaets – Chekhelian
USSR 1979

After **30...♗xf3** White played **31 ♖d6!**, a shunning sacrifice combined with line clearance (the white queen's diagonal to g7) and diversion of the black queen. Black can only avoid mate or loss of his queen by 31...♕e7 (not 31...♕xd6 32 ♕g7#) 32 ♖xd8+ ♔f7 (32...♕xd8 allows 33 ♕g7#), but he would emerge a whole rook down after 33 ♕b3+ ♔f6 34 ♕xf3+. Black therefore resigned.

1.10)
Tukmakov – Kochiev
USSR Ch First League, Ashkhabad 1978

White avoids the obvious 25 ♖fd1?, since 25...♖xd1+ 26 ♖xd1 ♖a1! 27 ♕d3 (27 ♕xe6?? loses to 27...♖xd1+) 27...♖xd1+ 28 ♕xd1 ♕e7 equalizes for Black. Instead, he exploits the fact that his queen already attacks Black's a2-rook, reinforcing that attack with **25 ♗d5!**. Now Black can choose to be mated after 25...♖xd5 26 ♕c8+ or 25...♕xd5 26 ♕xd5 ♖xd5 27 ♖c8+, or alternatively to lose the a2-rook. He resigned instead.

1.11)
LeMoir – A.G. May
Gloucestershire vs Worcestershire 1966

26 ♘d6!!

This passive sacrifice of White's remaining rook blocks the black queen's defence of e5. Black is obliged to accept the sacrifice.

26...♖xd7 27 ♕xe5+ ½-½

Black agrees to the draw as he could fall into mate by 27...♔h6 28 ♕f4+ g5? (28...♔g7 29 ♕e5+ is perpetual check) 29 ♕f6+ ♔h5 30 h3 g4 31 hxg4+ ♔xg4 32 ♕h4+ ♔f3 33 ♕h5#. If he backs into the corner, it is still perpetual check: 27...♔g8 28 ♕xe6+ ♔h8 29 ♕f6+ ♖g7 30 ♘f7+ ♔g8 31 ♘h6+, etc.

1.12)
Martorelli – Pantaleoni
Turin 1987

22 ♕xf7+! ♔xf7 23 ♗c4+ ♔f6 24 ♗e7+ ♔f5 25 ♗d3+ ♔f4 26 h3!

This is the quiet follow-up that sets up the mating-net. Black can avoid the immediate mate by 26...♕xg2+ 27 ♔xg2, but the exchange disappears next, and his king remains over-exposed. He prefers a glorious death.

26...♗d4 27 g3+ ♔f3 28 ♗e2+ ♔e4 29 ♗f3++! ♔f5

29...♔xf3 allows 30 ♖d3+ ♗e3 31 ♖(either)xe3#.

30 ♗g4# (1-0)

Answers to Level 2 Test

2.1)
Ståhlberg – Najdorf
Buenos Aires 1947

31 ♗f7!

A multiple-method sacrifice combining unpinning with clearance of the d-file, potential diversion of the queen from guarding the d8-rook, and decoy of either the black king or queen into a pin on the f-file. If now 31...♖xd2 then 32 ♕xg6+ ♔f8 33 ♕g8+ ♔e7 34 ♕e8+ ♔d6 35 ♖xf6#. 31...♕xf7 allows 32 ♖xd8 winning the exchange. Black gives up the exchange another way.

31...♔xf7 32 ♖xd8 ♕xd8 33 ♕b7+ ♔g8 34 ♕xa6 e4 35 ♖e3 ♗d4 36 ♖xe4 1-0

2.2)
Spassky – Beliavsky
World Cup, Reykjavik 1988

25 ♘xg6! hxg6 26 ♕h6!

The threat is 27 ♕xg6+ ♔h8 28 ♕h6+ ♔g8 29 ♖d3. If Black blocks the action of White's light-squared bishop with 26...♗e6, he loses to 27 ♖d3!, when 27...♗xb3 is met by 28 ♖h3! and mate next move; he could instead play 27...♘e7, but White would reply as in the game.

2.3)
Goldin – Ambarian
Armenia 1955

18 ♕d5!! ♗xd5

Otherwise he cannot defend his f-pawn, as 18...♔e7 loses to 19 ♘f5+! gxf5 20 exf5+.

19 exd5 1-0

The sacrifice has opened the e-file (secondary line clearance) and eliminated the bishop that guards the c6-square. White is winning in all variations:

a) 19...♗g7 (or 19...♗h6) 20 ♘c6+ ♕xc6 (not 20...♔d7 21 ♖e7#) 21 dxc6 wins.

b) 19...♗e7 20 ♘c6+ ♕xc6 21 dxc6 ♗f8 22 ♖e8+! ♗xe8 23 c7+ ♔e7 24 ♖e1#.

c) 19...♕d7 20 ♗xd7 ♔xd7 21 ♘c6 ♔c8 22 ♖e8+ ♔b7 23 ♘a5+, winning the a8-rook.

2.4)
LeMoir – D. Jarrett
Bristol League 1966/7

19 ♘cd5!

At first sight this is simply a substitution sacrifice, to establish a knight on d5. But it also clears the c3-square, which is needed by the white queen so that it can simultaneously attack the c4-knight and the h8-rook.

26...♘e7

This defence of the g-pawn seems to hold the position as the c8-bishop is covering the h3-square, so that ♖d3-h3 is no threat. There is a quiet surprise waiting.

27 ♗c7!!

White intends 28 ♗xe5 followed by mate on g7 or h8, and Black has no good defence. He returns the piece but finds that he must also lose his bishop.

27...♘f5 28 exf5 ♗xf5 29 g4! ♗e4 30 ♖e1 ♗c1 31 ♕xc1 ♕c6 32 ♕e3 ♗h1 33 ♕h3 ♕xc7 34 ♔xh1 ♖e8 35 ♕h6 ♕c6+ 36 ♔g1 ♕f6 37 ♖d1 ♕c6 38 ♖d3 ♕e4 39 ♖h3 ♕b1+ 40 ♔g2 ♕e4+ 41 ♔g3 1-0

White gets a strong attack for the piece. The main variations, which you didn't need to calculate in great detail, follow 19...exd5 20 ♘xd5:

a) 20...♕d8 21 ♗xc4 ♘xc4 (or 21...♕b8 and White has a big positional advantage for nothing) 22 ♕c3 ♖f8 (or 22...♖h7 23 ♕xc4 ♗c6 24 ♘f6+! ♗xf6 25 ♕g8+, winning the exchange) 23 ♗xg5!! ♗xg5 24 ♖xf8+ ♔xf8 25 ♕h8+ ♔f7 26 ♕h7+ ♔f8 27 ♖f1+ leads to mate.

b) 20...♕c6 21 ♗xc4 ♘xc4 (or 21...♕xc4 22 ♖c1 and 23 ♘c7+) 22 ♕c3 ♖h7 (22...♖f8 23 ♘xe7 ♖xf1+ 24 ♖xf1 ♖xe7 25 ♗xg5+ ♔e6 26 ♕f6#) 23 ♘f6+! ♗xf6 24 ♕xf6 and Black must lose material in order to prevent mate.

In the game, Black collapsed without a fight.

19...♕d8? 20 ♗xc4 ♘xc4 21 ♕c3 ♖g8 22 ♕xc4 ♗b5 23 ♘c7+ ♔d7 24 ♘xb5 ♖c8 25 ♕d3 axb5 26 ♕xb5+ 1-0

2.5)
Murey – Grinberg
Ramat Gan 1980

22 ♗b7!!
A double diversion of the rook (22...♖xb7 23 ♗xc5+ ♗e7 24 ♕h8#) and the queen (22...♕xb7 23 ♖xd7! ♖xd7 24 ♗xc5+ ♗e7 25 ♕h8#) from guarding the c5-square. Black preferred to lose a piece.

22...♗f5 23 ♕h8+ ♗e7 24 ♗xc8 ♖xh8 25 ♗xf5 cxb4 26 c5 ♖b8 27 ♖d6 a5 28 ♖a6 ♖b5 29 ♖d1 g6 30 ♗c2 1-0

2.6)
Broer – Laurentius
Holland vs Estonia 1935

1 ♖d7!! interferes with the black queen's defence of the f-pawn. After **1...♗xd7** White mated by **2 ♗xh7+! ♘xh7 3 ♕xf7+ ♔h8 4 ♘g6# (1-0)**.

2.7)
Donnelly – Kroon
South African Ch 1971

Black is able to defend against mate, but not by 1...♗xd8? 2 ♕f8+ ♔g5 3 ♘e4+ ♔h4 4 hxg3#.

1...♖f3!!
The rook gains time by hitting the white queen, and 2 gxf3 allows 2...♗xf3+ (line-grabbing) 3 ♔g1 ♕g4+ 4 ♔f1 ♕g2+ 5 ♔e1 ♗h4#.

2 ♕xb7 ♘xd8
Black overlooks an immediate win by 2...♗f4!, but the move played leads to a prettier finish. One idea is that now 3 ♕b5 is met by 3...♕h4 4 ♘d5 ♖f2 5 ♕b4 ♖xg2! with a mating attack. Another idea occurs in the game.

3 ♕xa7 ♗f4 4 ♕g1 ♖h3! 0-1
It is mate by 5 gxh3 ♗f3+ 6 ♕g2 ♕xh3 7 ♕xf3 ♕xh2#.

2.8)
J. Walton – LeMoir
British Clubs Ch, London 1973

21...♖e8!
Now the c-pawn must promote.

22 ♕f6+
After 22 ♖f1 ♗d3! 23 ♕f6+ ♔d7 24 f3 ♕xg2+! 25 ♔xg2 ♗xf1+ Black promotes next move with a winning material advantage, while 22 ♖c1 allows a neat mate by 22...♕d1+! 23 ♘xd1 (or 23 ♖xd1 cxd1♕+ 24 ♘xd1 ♖e1#) 23...♖e1#.

22...♔c5 23 ♘a4+ ♔xa4 24 ♕c3+ ♔c4!
It is still possible to go wrong by 24...♔b5? as after 25 ♖xe8 the c1-square is covered by the white queen.

25 ♕a5+ ♔d6 26 ♕a3+ ♔d7 0-1

2.9)
Chandler – Vaganian
Olympiad, Dubai 1986

24 ♘d5!

24 ♕e5 is probably enough for a big advantage, but this combination of passive and silent sacrificial methods is decisive. The queen cannot be captured (24...♖xc5 25 ♘xf6+ ♔f8 26 axb5 with an extra piece for White) and the two ways of capturing the knight both lose (24...exd5 25 ♕xc8#, or 24...♘xd5 25 ♕xc8+ ♔e7 26 ♕b7+ ♗d7 27 ♕xd5 and White is a rook up).

24...♕g7 is the only move left. However, it loses another pawn to 25 ♘c7+ ♔d8 26 ♘xe6+! fxe6 27 ♕b6+ ♖c7 28 axb5 and also leaves his king stranded in the firing line. So... **1-0**.

2.10)

Pietzsch – Meštrović
Sarajevo 1967

36...h3! 37 cxb6 c6!

The immediate 37...♕d1+ forces the h-pawn's promotion but after 38 ♕xd1 ♖xd1 39 bxc7+ ♔c8 40 ♔xd1 h2 White has fighting chances thanks to his queenside passed pawns. The text-move seeks an improved version.

38 ♕c2

38 ♖xc6 allows 38...h2, promoting. Now White intends to get a major piece back to the first rank to stop the h-pawn.

38...♕d1+!! 0-1

White's plan is foiled. After 39 ♕xd1 ♖xd1 40 ♔xd1 h2, the white king is in the way and the rook is unable to prevent the promotion of the pawn. Incidentally, 38...♕xc2+ 39 ♖xc2 ♖d1! is equally effective, but presumably Meštrović's beauty compulsion made him go for the most aesthetically pleasing option.

2.11)

Kotov – Kholmov
USSR 1971

Kotov sets up an apparently simple pin by an exchange sacrifice.

26 ♖xc5! ♖xc5 27 ♖c2 ♖fc8 28 ♕b5!!

In fact, it is a double pin. This double deflection wins material as after 28...♖xb5 29 ♖xc8+ ♔f7 30 ♗xa7 White is a piece ahead.

28...♖xc2 29 ♗xa7 ♖xa2 30 ♗c5! h6 31 h4 ♔h7 32 h5 1-0

There is no good defence to White's plan of ♗d4 followed by ♕d7.

2.12)

Rossetto – Aguilar
Argentine Ch 1945

1 ♗xc6!!

White intends to mate on a7. The first point of this unpinning sacrifice is 1...♗xd1 2 dxe5, when the mate is unstoppable. Black's forced reply keeps a7 covered, but White is not to be denied. He keeps the mate in his sights with a mini pawn-dash.

1...♘xc6 2 d5!! exd5

After 2...♗xd1 3 dxc6 the mate at a7 still stands.

3 cxd5 ♕e7 4 dxc6!

This second unpinning sacrifice obliges Black to give up his queen to prevent the mate, but he emerges a rook down.

4...♖xd1+ 5 ♘xd1 ♕xe3 6 ♘xe3 1-0

Answers to Level 3 Test

3.1)

Hennings – Möhring
East German Ch, Colditz 1967

The two silent sacrifices that White did not play were:

a) 16 ♕h6! ♘xb3+ 17 axb3 e5 18 ♘d5 gxh6 19 gxh6+ ♔h8 20 ♘xc7 ♖b8 21 ♘d5 ♗d8 22 ♗e3 with a pawn advantage.

b) 16 ♘d5! ♘xb3+ 17 axb3 exd5 18 ♕h6 f6 19 gxf6 ♗xf6 20 ♗xf6 ♖xf6 (20...♖f7 21 ♖xd5 ♖a7 22 ♖dg5 wins for White) 21 ♕xf6 dxe4 22 ♖xd6 with a rook for a bishop.

16 ♗f6!!

It will be mate after both 16...gxf6 17 gxf6+ ♔h8 18 ♖g7 and 16...bxc3 17 ♕h6!!.

16...♖e8

Black hopes for 17 ♕h6? ♗f8, but White is patient.

17 ♖g3! bxc3 18 ♖h3 cxb2+ 19 ♔b1 ♗xf6

19...h6 allows 20 ♕xh6! gxh6 21 ♖xh6 ♗xf6 22 gxf6, mating.

20 gxf6 ♔f8

Here 20...gxf6 allows 21 ♕h6! ♘xe4 22 ♖g1+ ♘g5 23 ♕xf6! with a decisive attack.

21 e5!

White could also win with 21 fxg7+, but the text-move wins more quickly by ensuring that the black king will not be allowed to escape. White will keep control of the f6-square or get an open d-file.

21...♘e4 22 fxg7+ ♔e7 23 ♕h4+ f6 24 ♕xe4 d5 25 g8♕! ♖xg8 26 ♕xh7+ 1-0

3.2)

Rizhkov – Chepukaitis
USSR 1971

34 ♘g5!!

This complex silent sacrifice clears the f-file, and deflects the f-pawn in the variation 34...fxg5 35 ♖xe4! ♕g7 (not 35...♕xe4 36 ♖f8+ ♖xf8 37 ♕xf8#) 36 ♕xg7+ ♘xg7 37 ♖xg4. White wins at least the g-pawn because 37...gxh4? loses to 38 ♖f7 ♖g8 (or 38...♘h5 39 ♖xh4 ♘g7 40 ♖g4 ♘h5 41 ♖g5, winning the knight) 39 ♗xd6, winning the exchange thanks to the pin on the seventh rank.

Black's reply appears to keep his defence solid.

34...f5 35 ♖xe4!

White will open the f-file by hook or by crook.

35...fxe4 36 ♖f7 ♕xf7 37 ♘xf7+ ♔g8 38 ♘xd6 ♗xd6 39 ♗xd6 ♖e8 40 ♗xc5

With a material advantage and the attack, White won eight moves later.

3.3)

P. Shrank – Leyton
British Clubs Ch 1976

18...e4!?

Black starts a pawn-dash.

19 ♗xf8

If White declines with 19 ♘d2 then Black can secure an edge by 19...♗xc3; e.g., 20 ♗xf8 ♖xf8 21 h4 ♗d4 22 ♕f4 e3 23 fxe3 ♗xe3 24 ♕xe3 ♖e8 25 ♕xe8+ ♗xe8, when the queen and bishop are slightly stronger than White's two rooks and knight.

19...exf3 20 ♗xg7 fxg2 21 ♖g1 ♔xg7!

White was willing to give up his queen with 21...♖e8 22 ♗f6 ♖xe3+ 23 fxe3, when Black is only slightly better. Instead, Black quietly recaptures the bishop, shunning the immediate win of the queen as it cannot escape.

22 ♔d2

22 ♕f3 ♖e8+ 23 ♔d2 ♖e2+ 24 ♕xe2 ♗xe2 25 ♔xe2 allows Black to win several pawns starting with 25...♕xc3. White believes that he has found a way to save his queen, only to find that he has walked into an ambush.

22...♖e8 23 ♖a1 ♕xa1! 24 ♖xa1 ♖xe3 25 ♔xe3 ♗f1! 0-1

White cannot prevent the pawn-dash from ending with the pawn's promotion.

3.4)

Tolush – Bronstein
USSR Ch, Moscow 1948

Black plays to expose the white king.

23...♘c3!! 24 ♗xc3

24 ♗xe6 allows 24...♘e2#.

24...♗xc4 25 ♗xa5 ♕xa5 26 ♕xc4 ♕xa3+ 27 ♔d2 ♖b2+ 28 ♔e1 ♕f3 29 ♖h2 e3 30 ♕d3

Black's attack is very strong, and now comes the quiet sting in the tail of his combination that brings the game to a quick end.

30...♖e8!

Suddenly the threat is 31...exf2++ 32 ♔f1 ♖e1+ 33 ♖xe1 ♕xd3+ 34 ♔g2 f1♕#. White returns the piece, but fails to prevent mate.

31 ♘f4 exf2++ 32 ♔f1 ♕xf4 33 ♖h3 ♖e1+! 34 ♖xe1 fxe1♕++ 35 ♔xe1 ♕f2+ 36 ♔d1 ♕g1+ 0-1

3.5)
Sämisch – Ahues
Hamburg 1946

White wants to mate on g7, but 1 f6 allows the exchange of queens by 1...♕c5+. Instead, he finds a beautiful double interference.

1 ♖e5!!

The rook sacrifices itself at the intersection of the long diagonal and the fifth rank. Black resigned in view of the following lines:

a) 1...dxe5 blocks the long diagonal, allowing 2 ♕g7#.

b) 1...♗xe5 blocks the fifth rank so that 2 f6 ♕c5+ doesn't exchange queens, and it is mate by 3 ♔h1 ♖g8 4 ♗g7+ ♖xg7 5 ♕xg7#.

c) 1...♖g8 allows 2 ♕xg8+ ♔xg8 3 ♖e8#.

d) 1...f6 allows a neat finish by 2 ♕xf6+ ♔g8 3 ♕g5+ ♔h8 (or 3...♔f7 4 ♕g7#) 4 ♖e7 ♕c5+ 5 ♔h1 ♖g8 6 f6! ♖xg5 7 ♖e8+ ♖g8 8 ♗g7#.

3.6)
Rohde – Seirawan
USA Ch, Cambridge Springs 1988

White can turn his pawn deficit into a pawn advantage by 25 ♘xf7 ♘xc4 (not 25...♖xf7? 26 ♗d8!) 26 ♘d6 ♘f6 27 ♕xc4+ ♔h7 28 ♕xb4. Not satisfied with that, he plays for higher stakes.

25 ♗xf7+! ♖xf7 26 ♗d8!!

The bishop diverts the queen from the protection of the rook and decoys it to a square where it proves to be vulnerable.

26...♕xd8

26...♕d7 27 ♗xb6 wins the exchange.

27 ♕xf7+

27 ♘xf7 is very good for White, but his chosen way is not only very effective but also prettier.

27...♔h8 28 ♕b3!

This is the best queen retreat (threatening 29 ♘f7+ winning the queen).

28...♘g5

Black's queen is lost anyway after 28...♕f8 29 ♘f7+ ♔g8 30 ♘xh6++ ♔h8 31 ♘f7+ ♔g8 32 ♖d8, so Black gives it up at once.

29 ♘f7+ ♘xf7 30 ♖xd8+ ♘xd8 31 ♕xb4

White is bound to win an extra piece thanks to 31...♘c8 32 ♕b8 and 31...♘d7 32 ♕d6. Black eventually resigned on move 41.

3.7)
Tseshkovsky – Marjanović
Minsk 1982

White must watch out for mate on g2, and 27 ♗xb4+ d6 28 ♕e4 ♕xe4 29 ♖xe4 ♖xb4 30 ♖xd4 d5 leads to no great advantage for him.

27 ♗g5+ f6 28 fxe6!

28 ♕xd4 ♖xg5 29 ♖f3 ♖h8 gives Black counterplay.

28...♖xg5

After 28...dxe6 29 ♕xd4 fxg5 30 ♕f6+ the black king is battered to death. White is remorseless.

29 exd7+ ♗e5 30 ♖xe5+! ♖xe5 31 ♕g7+ ♔d8 32 ♖d1!

Here 32 ♕f8+ ♔xd7 33 ♕xb8 ♖g5 34 ♖d1+ ♔e6 35 ♖d2 still leaves Black fighting.

32...♕a8

32...♖e1+ 33 ♖xe1 ♕xd7 loses the black queen to 34 ♕xf6+ ♔c8 35 ♖e7, but Black's attempted defence is no better.

33 ♕xf6+ ♖e7 34 ♕f8+ 1-0

34...♔c7 35 d8♕+ ♖xd8 36 ♕xe7+ ♔c6 37 ♖xd8 is curtains.

3.8)
Honfi – Tal
Sukhumi 1972

27...♕a7 appears to be very strong, but White can survive by 28 bxc4 ♕a1+ 29 ♔c2 ♖xc4+ 30 ♔d3 ♖xc1 31 ♖xc1 ♕xc1 32 ♕c2. Black needs both a- and c-files completely open.

27...♗e2!!

This complex silent sacrifice clears the c-file and intends either to divert the rook from being able to move to the c3-square (28 ♖xe2 ♕a5 and mate next move) or, as White plays, to decoy the queen to a square where it will eventually be captured. The bishop cannot be left alone as Black's main threat is 28...♕a5 29 ♖c3 ♖xc3 30 bxc3 ♕a2#, when the bishop blocks the queen's defence of the second rank (partial interference).

28 ♕xe2 ♕a5 29 ♖c3 ♕a2+ 30 ♔c2 ♖xc3+ 31 ♔xc3 ♗b4+! 32 ♔xb4

32 ♔d3 allows 32...♕xb3#.

32...♕a5+ 33 ♔c4 ♕a6+ 0-1

The queen is lost on e2.

3.9)

Burgess – S. Bjerke
Troll Masters, Gausdal 2002

White would like to play 25 ♗h5, but the idea fails after 25...♕xh5 26 ♘xg7 ♖xf1+ 27 ♖xf1 ♕g6 28 ♕xe5 ♘bd7 29 ♕e7 ♖a8. Some preparation is needed.

25 ♗e3!

The bishop eyes several targets on the g1-a7 diagonal and is now one move closer to the d4-square.

25...♘ba4

Protecting the knight by 25...♕c8 simply loses the e-pawn which opens lines for White's attack. After the move played, all is ready.

26 ♗h5!!

This silent sacrifice combines line clearance (the f-file), diversion of the queen from protecting the f8-rook, and the decoy of the queen to a square which allows the follow-up knight sacrifice to gain a tempo by attacking it.

26...♕xh5

Black may as well accept the sacrifice as 26...g6 loses to 27 ♘d6 ♖xf1+ 28 ♖xf1 ♕e7 29 ♘f7+ ♔g8 30 ♗xg6, while 26...♕b8 27 ♘h6! gives Black no satisfactory defence:

a) 27...gxh6 28 ♖xf8+ ♕xf8 29 ♕xe5+ ♖g7 (29...♕g7 allows 30 ♕e8+ ♕g8 31 ♗d4+ ♖g7 32 ♗xg7+ ♔xg7 33 ♕e5+ ♔f8 34 ♕f6+ ♕f7 35 ♕xf7#) 30 ♖f1 ♕g8 31 ♗d4 will soon mate.

b) 27...♖xf1+ 28 ♖xf1 gxh6 29 ♗xh6 ♘d3 30 ♖f8+ ♕xf8 31 ♗xf8 ♘xc3 32 ♕f3 leaves Black helpless against the queen and bishops.

c) 27...♖f4 28 ♗xf4 exf4 29 ♖xf4 gxh6 30 ♖bf1 ♘d7 31 ♖f8+ ♕xf8 32 ♖xf8+ ♘xf8 33 ♕b8 forks f8 and a7.

d) 27...♘xc3 allows White to exploit the weakness of Black's back rank by 28 ♖xf8+ ♕xf8 29 ♖f1 ♕c8 (29...♕e7 30 ♕xe5!) 30 ♕xe5 ♘3xe4 31 ♗e8!, etc.

27 ♘xg7! ♖xf1+

27...♕g6 is likewise best answered by 28 ♕xe5.

28 ♖xf1 ♕g6

28...♖xg7 allows mate in two.

29 ♕xe5 ♘d7

Again, the g7-knight is immune due to ♖f8#.

30 ♕e7!

The quiet sting in the tail. In contrast with the position after the immediate 25 ♗h5, the black rook is attacked by the e3-bishop, and the d7-knight is not defended by its colleague. Moreover, ♗d4(+) ideas make a decisive difference in many lines, and mate by ♖f8+ is threatened.

30...♖a8

30...♕xg7 allows 31 ♕d8+ ♕g8 32 ♗d4+, etc. The text-move leaves the knight *en prise*, but there was no good alternative.

31 ♕xd7

White, who was now short of time, reclaims his piece while retaining a winning attack. However, 31 ♗d4! is a little neater.

31...♘xc3 32 ♘f5 ♘xe4

32...♘e2+ 33 ♔f2 does not help Black, since the knight will perish on e2, as it cannot move without allowing White to play ♗d4+.

33 ♗d4+ ♘f6 34 ♘h4 ♕h6 35 ♗xf6+ ♔g8 36 ♕e6+ 1-0

3.10)
M. Gurevich – Kholmov
TV game, Moscow 1987

White plays to the TV gallery.
28 ♘e6! fxe6 29 ♕g4 ♔h7 30 f7! d4
Black decides to close the long diagonal. There are two main alternatives:

a) 30...e5 fails to 31 f8♕ ♘xf8 32 ♗xe5, when Black must return the piece as 32...♕e7 33 ♗xd6 ♕xd6 allows 34 ♖f7+, mating.

b) 30...♕g5 31 ♕xe6 and now Black cannot play 31...♘xb5 thanks to 32 f8♘+ ♗xf8 33 ♖f7+ ♔g8 34 ♖d7+, mating. He can, however, play 31...d4 32 ♗c1 ♕h5!, hoping for 33 ♕xd6? ♗xg2 34 ♔xg2 ♖a2+ with good counterplay. Instead, White can retain a big advantage with 33 ♗c6!, as the d6-knight is going nowhere.

31 ♗c1!
After this quiet move, Black finds that he is unable to defend his h-pawn and g6-knight without allowing the white f-pawn to promote.

31...♗c8 32 ♕h5 ♕f8 33 ♖f6 ♕g7 34 ♖xg6 1-0
34 ♗xh6! is a prettier way to win, but the text-move is good enough to force resignation.

3.11)
Karlsson – H. Olafsson
Lucerne 1979

24 ♕b3
Now Black decides to allow White's intended combination, having seen an ambush starting with his 26th move.

24...♖b8 25 f4 exf4! 26 ♖xe6 f3! 27 ♖d6

27 ♗xf3 loses to 27...♕xg3+ 28 ♗g2 ♖xe6, while 27 ♖xc6 ♕xg3! 28 ♕c2 ♖e2 is an immediate win for Black.

27...♘d4! 28 cxd4 ♗xd4+ 29 ♔h2 ♖e2! 30 ♘c2 ♖xg2+ 31 ♔h1 ♕e7!
The threat is 32...♖h2+! 33 ♔xh2 ♕e2+, mating.

32 ♘xd4
After 32 ♖e1 ♕xe1+! 33 ♘xe1 ♖g1+ 34 ♔h2 f2 the pawn will promote.

32...cxd4 33 ♘e5
33 ♘e3 loses nicely to 33...dxe3 34 ♕xd5 e2! 35 ♕xf3 ♖f2!.

33...♕xe5 34 ♗f4 ♘xf4 35 ♖d7+ ♔h8 36 gxf4 ♖h2+! 37 ♔g1 ♕e3+ 0-1
After 38 ♔xh2 the axe falls with 38...♕f2+ 39 ♔h1 ♕g2#.

3.12)
Nunn – Murshed
Commonwealth Ch, London 1985

It is clear that there could be mating opportunities for White on g8 or g7.
37 ♗e5!!
This is a complex silent sacrifice, combining diversion (37...♕xe5 38 ♖g8#) with substitution (brought about, after 37...♗xe5, by the surprising 38 ♖g8+! ♕xg8 39 ♕xe5+, when the queen replaces the bishop to force mate). Black must decline the sacrifice.

37...♖xf2 38 ♖e4
Nunn later admitted that 38 ♗xf6+ ♖xf6 39 ♖e4! ♕f8 40 ♖e8! is one move quicker, "but when you've found one forced win, there is little point in looking for another one". Who needs a quicker finish when you can play one as nice as that played by Nunn in the game?

38...♗xe5 39 ♕g7+! 1-0
After 39...♗xg7 we suddenly have a completely new mating pattern in 40 ♖xe8+ ♗f8 41 ♖xf8#.

That seems to me to be a suitably spectacular way to sign off.

Index of Games

Numbers refer to pages. When a player's name appears in **bold**, that player had White; otherwise the first-named player had White. When a page number appears in *italic*, this signifies an exercise.